Endorsements

"Though it sometimes reads like a thriller, fast-paced, filled with fascinating characters, betrayal, and bad behavior, Tainted Glory is really the best insider's examination of a corrupt system I have ever read - and I wrote about Marshall in Ridpath's time. His ringing call for higher education to reclaim universities from college sports is a powerful and important message."

—Robert Lipsyte, former New York Times columnist and author of "An Accidental Sportswriter."

"Ridpath takes us past the hoopla and huddles into the hallways of athletics where ethics are fuzzy and fleeting. Yet he's not a cynic. He's in love with college sports — like so many of us — and that's what makes his story so vivid and compelling."

—Rus Bradburd, author of "Forty Minutes of Hell"

"Having been involved in pointing out problems and trying to devise solutions regarding college sport for more than 30 years, I feel I have a good grasp of the issues. Tainted Glory does a great job in presenting all those issues. It calls out for the righting of the wrongs that still persist in college sport. The work of David Ridpath will be very important for a very long time."

—Richard Lapchick, Director for The Institute for Diversity and Ethics in Sport, University of Central Florida

``This is one of the most important books ever written about sports. Tainted Glory is certainly the most compelling sports book this year. David Ridpath has taken a sledge hammer and smashed a hole right through the heart of a corrupt system. Tainted Glory should be must reading by anyone who cares about the cesspool better known as college athletics and who still believes it is worth saving."

—Paul Finebaum, Host of the Paul Finebaum Show, Named one of the Top 10 sports talk shows in the country by Sports Illustrated

"If you care, truly care, about sports and academics—you have to read this book"

—Sonny Vaccaro, Noted Basketball Entrepreneur

TAINTED GLORY

Marshall University, the NCAA, and One Man's Fight for Justice

B. DAVID RIDPATH

iUniverse, Inc.
Bloomington

iUniverse books may be ordered through booksellers or by contacting:

iUniverse
1663 Liberty Drive
Bloomington, IN 47403
www.iuniverse.com
1-800-Authors (1-800-288-4677)

ISBN: 978-1-4697-9087-9 (sc)
ISBN: 978-1-4697-9088-6 (hc)
ISBN: 978-1-4697-9089-3 (e)

Library of Congress Control Number: 2012903751

Printed in the United States of America

iUniverse rev. date: 8/29/2012

Special thanks to the Center for College Affordability and Productivity and Director Dr. Richard Vedder for their generous support to enable publishing of this book.

The Center for College Affordability and Productivity

Founded in 2006, The Center for College Affordability and Productivity (CCAP) is dedicated to researching the rising costs and stagnant efficiency in higher education, with special emphasis on the United States. CCAP seeks to facilitate a broader dialogue on the issues and problems facing the institutions of higher education with the public, policy makers, and the higher education community.

www.centerforcollegeaffordability.org

Contents

…one day you and I are gonna wake up suddenly we're gonna be like every other team, in every other sport, where winning is everything, and nothing else matters.

Matthew McConaughey as Marshall University head football coach Jack Lengyel in the 2007 Warner Brothers Motion Picture, *"We are Marshall"*

Acknowledgments

It is difficult for me to take time to thank all of the people who have been an influence to me and assisted me on the long road to publishing this book.. There are so many that it would almost take the entire text of this book to do so and so many people had an influence on me completing this project. I know I will miss many but I want to thank several people in no particular order, including my attorneys and members of 'Team Ridpath' Jason Huber, J.D. Hartung, Roger Forman, Jon Matthews, Jerry Crawford, Jeremy Schulman, Bob and John Tscholl and Kathy Noble, along with others at the law firms of Forman & Huber and Hartung & Schroeder who assisted me in the past. My Drake Group colleagues and friends in the fight for NCAA reform Jon Ericson, Linda Bensel- Meyers, Allen Sack, Ellen Staurowsky, Jason Lanter, Kadie Otto, Amanda Paule, John Gerdy, Joel Cormier, Frank Splitt and Sally Dear and all of the other members of TDG and the greater Higher Education community continuing to do the right things and keep education paramount. Other prominent colleagues and friends were invaluable like Richard and Deborah Southall, Terry Holland, Gerry Gurney, John Kiger, Groundwalker, Sonny Vaccaro, Robert Lipsyte, Mark Nagel Richard Lapchick, and members of the media who often made my fight their own. In particular, I want to thank Paul Finebaum, Dennis Dodd, Alex Wolff, and Don Yaeger for their encouragement and advice over the years. The other endorsers of the book such as the talented Rus Bradburd and Dale Brown are so appreciated for taking interest in this work. Of my former colleagues in intercollegiate athletics and higher education who have remained friends and supporters, special thanks go to Steve Rackley, Michelle Duncan, Chad Gerrety, Kevin Klotz, Sam Goines and friends and former co-workers at Ohio University, Weber State University, and Marshall University.

Tony Moss, a Senior Editor for CBSSports.com did yeoman's work in reviewing, editing and enhancing the manuscript simply because he believes in the story. A huge amount of gratitude goes to my colleagues at the Center for College Affordability and Productivity (CCAP) Matt Denhart and Dr. Richard Vedder for their assistance —financial and editorial — in making this book a reality. I would be remiss if I did not mention my colleagues and all of my past and present students at Mississippi State University and at Ohio University, the College of Business, and the Department of Sports Administration specifically Hugh Sherman, Robert Zullo, Greg Letter, Ming Li, Teresa Tedrow, Jim Kahler, Heather Lawrence, Andy Kreutzer, Charles "Doc" Higgins, Michael Pfahl, Rebecca Thacker, Athena Yiamouyiannis, Aaron Wright, and Packy Moran who have been staunch supporters of me in spite of many times having differing views from my own-a true academy.

My church, Grace Christian Center in The Plains, Ohio and my pastor and dear friend Leon Forte were always there providing moral support and help whenever I needed it. Still the most thanks goes to my family including my brother Brett, who shared the ups and downs of this interesting journey and without all of them, I would not be where I am today. Mostly I want to say what I said to my beautiful wife Jacqueline and my children Chiara and Bradley II when I successfully defended my doctoral dissertation in 2002 at West Virginia University, and it still rings true today: I just want to make you as proud of me as I am of you. It is an honor to be a husband to a wife, and a father to two wonderful children, who have stood by me through many highs and many lows.

This book is dedicated to Jacqueline, Chiara and Bradley

Foreword By Dale Brown

Former Head Men's Basketball Coach, Louisiana State University

I first met Dr. David Ridpath at a Drake Group meeting in San Antonio in 2003. The group was started in 1999 by college educators that wanted to reform big-time college sports and to ensure a quality education for athletes.

It was clear to me from that very first meeting that he was a man of great integrity and had a passion for college athletics and a deep concern for the welfare of the college athlete. He also had the tenacity of a wolverine in exposing the truth of the NCAA, its investigative tactics, and its use of innocent people as scapegoats. The only people who can truly understand the abuse of the NCAA's brand of "justice" are those who have gone through it, like he has. This is a system that has failed in its mission, and Dr. Ridpath is determined to expose the truth and bring about a change in NCAA tactics.

He told the truth and was punished for it, yet he has never wavered in seeking justice. Robert F. Kennedy said, "Moral courage is a rarer commodity than bravery in battle or great intelligence, yet it is the essential vital quality for those who seek to change a world that yields most painfully to change."

Walter Byers, former NCAA Executive Director for 36 years, was candid and honest after he retired when he strongly stated, "Time and circumstances have passed the entire system of intercollegiate athletics by. Reform will not come from within. The beneficiaries of the current monopoly will not give up a good thing."

Dr. Ridpath experienced this truth, as well as the reality underlined by what Brent Clark, a former NCAA investigator, said in front of a congressional hearing, "I believe the NCAA enforcement machinery allows NCAA personnel to inflict selective punishment. Unfortunately, the many fine services the NCAA renders have been overshadowed by manipulative and corrupt enforcement."

The secret of life is not what happens to you, but what you do with what happens to you. David, whose mission was to educate athletes and improve their way of life decided to do something about what happened to him and wrote this marvelous book. There is no bitterness or embellishment in his words but only a transparent look at unfair practices that can destroy lives and reputations. The consequences of doing nothing and remaining silent can take away our very freedom. Martin Luther King said, "The hope of the secure and livable world lies with disciplined, non-conformists who are dedicated to justice."

It is not easy or pleasant to stand up for what you know is right against a Goliath opponent like the NCAA or any giant system. We so desperately need strong and committed people who will courageously do battle for the truth and are dedicated to see justice reign. David happens to be one of those David's who is not afraid of Goliath. His aim is not to be a cynic but a bearer of the truth.

Foreword By Dr. Richard Vedder

Professor Emeritus, Ohio University and Executive Director of the Center for College Affordability and Productivity

Dr. B. David Ridpath' s compelling story of his experiences in intercollegiate athletics is all the more relevant in light of increased national attention to the problems confronting college sports. The Penn State incident was so shocking that it captured the national consciousness, aided by a number of other smaller scandals involving iconic schools in intercollegiate athletics, such as Ohio State, and the universities of Miami and Southern California. Cheating, lying, and even more heinous forms of immoral conduct appear widespread. The Ridpath story is a case study –and an exciting page-turner at that – that demonstrates the ubiquitous nature of the problem –extending to schools beyond those in the top tier of football powers.

Americans' passion for the drama and excitement of competitive sports provides much joy in our lives, but it also the necessary prerequisite for this problem to occur. The commercialization of college sports and the high stakes involved make scandals all but inevitable. Winning is of utmost importance, and coaches are held to a brutally high standard. This is true of professional sports as well. But the scandals that have enveloped college sports largely arise from the suppression of a free labor market and the use of a cartel (the NCAA) to enforce the substantial and growing economic exploitation of college athletes.

From 2006 to 2009, Tim Tebow played football exceptionally well for the University of Florida. He guided the Gators to two national championships, and in the process became one of the few underclassmen to ever win the Heisman trophy. Florida reaped millions from its football success, raking in more than $68 million from its football program alone during Tebow's senior year. Yet Tebow received perhaps less than $20,000 a year in compensation in the form of a football scholarship. By contrast, several months later, he was selected in the first round of the NFL draft and signed by the Denver Broncos to a five year contract reportedly worth $11.25 million. The most commercially valuable college players receive compensation equal to, at best, one or two percent of the value they add to the team.

The monies that in a normal market would go to the Tebows of the world, instead are directed to coaches (who are valuable for being able to recruit such financially lucrative talent), other personnel, sometimes athletes in minor sports, and, rarely, into university revenues. Where millions of exploitive profits exist, as in Tebow's case, the temptation to cheat is enormous. Indeed, coaches and athletic directors often wield more power than the university president. Fueled by the very strong incentive to win at any cost, athletic departments too often ignore rules of campus conduct, and even the conduct expected under the law. Sadly, this system creates an environment ripe for tragedies such as seen at Penn State and outlined, albeit in a different context, at Marshall University where David Ridpath strove to obey the rules and maintain academic integrity.

Cheating in sports is nothing new. But the mixing of highly commercialized sports with institutions of higher education is uniquely American. Yet, some great American institutions–the University of Chicago and the California Institute of Technology come readily to mind–have only nominal athletic departments, staying completely away from big time sports —and have flourished in spite of their bucking the prevailing American custom. The same is true, albeit to a slightly lesser degree, at our nation's most prestigious liberal arts colleges, schools like Amherst, Williams and Swarthmore Colleges. Harvard, Yale and Princeton, with crummy football teams, are light years ahead academically of, say, the University of Alabama, the University of Oklahoma, or Boise State —all of which could wipe out those Ivy League teams on most given Saturdays.

Yet, despite their problems, college sports are likely not going away anytime soon. Indeed, there are many admirable qualities associated with intercollegiate athletics. Sports, for example, teach student athletes leadership and teamwork skills while often binding university communities together. However, as Ridpath outlines in this book, the commercialization of big time sports has led universities to compromise their academic and moral integrity. The time for reform is now.

Introduction

I have been asked many times why I felt the need to write this book and tell this story, especially since the school depicted in it is no longer celebrating the type of football glory it experienced, nor likely ever will again, when I worked there. While it is a truism that Marshall University as an athletic department and football team have fallen off the front pages since dominating the headlines over a decade ago, the small school near the coal fields and abandoned steel mills of Appalachia and its fledgling football program were one of the hottest sports stories in America during the late 90's and early 2000's. The university and its football team became media darlings in the wake of their success, with attention paid by the likes of 60 Minutes and Time Magazine.

Marshall University had the most successful mid-major football team in America during the 1990s. In essence, Marshall University football was Boise State before Boise had the success on the gridiron that more recently enabled it to challenge the "big boys." Unfortunately for Marshall, its success happened before mid-major schools could compete in major Bowl Championship Series (BCS) bowl games. The University's football successes included recovering from a devastating plane crash in 1970 and several NCAA 1-AA football playoff appearances that culminated in national championships in 1991 and 1996. After making the jump back to NCAA Division I-A, the success continued and even grew, including five straight Mid-American Conference (MAC) championships, five bowl game victories in six bowl appearances, and three legitimate Heisman Trophy candidates in Randy Moss, Chad Pennington, and Byron Leftwich, a number still unmatched by any mid-major program in college football history. The story of a team rising from the ashes of a plane crash and achieving remarkable success on the field is the stuff of feature films and national headlines. The unspeakable tragedy of the plane crash and ensuing success eventually did lead to a major Hollywood motion picture in 2007, *"We are Marshall,"* starring Matthew McConaughey and Matthew Fox, along with many other books and documentaries that discussed the tragedy and ensuing years of the football program.

Though the success of Marshall University football was long ago, this book serves not just as a history lesson or back story, but also as a cautionary tale to those who desire to follow in the footsteps of Marshall University and attempt to pursue athletic fame and riches by any means necessary, ostensibly to assist in marketing and promoting the university as a whole. Marshall University also happens to be my former employer and many of its employees had a major hand in essentially ending my career in college athletics. While I remain personally troubled by what I view as several instances of personal and professional betrayal, I am beyond being bitter or vindictive about my personal experiences, but my experiences do speak loudly to larger problems in the business of intercollegiate athletics. This is a story that must be told, as it can serve as a catalyst for positive change in an industry that desperately needs it.

I absolutely loved much of my time working in intercollegiate athletics as a coach and as an administrator. I believe there are three types of people that want to work in college sports. Some, like me, are former competitors and coaches who want to continue in a career that inspires passion. This group works hard, but it is typically not intent on doing anything to change the system to make it better.

Another type of college administrator is often referred to by the derogatory term "jock sniffer." These folks love their school and college sports so much that they are clouded into believing all is well within the system. If there is anything negative going on, it is vastly outweighed by the benefits and likely not going on at "their school." People in this category are the ones who speak up when it is discovered that an athlete never attended class but somehow managed to remain eligible for athletic competition by rationalizing it-almost becoming an apologist for an incompatible system. Worse yet, those in this group become enablers to the system and even rationalize things like NCAA violations or even covering up revolting issues like the ongoing sexual abuse scandal at Penn State in an effort to protect the brand of an individual(s), an athletic program, and institution.

The third group is where I fall and where I believe most intercollegiate athletic administrators fall (even if we are only a slight majority). We pursued a career in college sports because, while we share some characteristics with the previous two groups, we simply believe very strongly in the stated purpose and ideals of intercollegiate competition, and we buy into them. Being passionate is one thing, but believing and enforcing integrity against a backdrop of amateurism rules all even if it damages the brand.

Despite the title of this book, this is more than a story about the NCAA, Marshall University, or even me. It is a story about the state of the business of intercollegiate athletics told by someone on the inside who lived it —the good and the bad. While parts of this story are sordid and disturbing, it is not just Marshall University that sold its integrity and institutional reputation at the altar of intercollegiate athletics and the perceived benefits that are promised but rarely delivered.

Sadly, many schools could be plugged into this story. The names and locations are all that distinguishes them from what went on at Marshall during my tenure. Instead of Marshall, it could be about Penn State, Ohio State, St. Bonaventure, North Carolina Southern California, Auburn, Michigan, Alabama, Minnesota, Baylor, or even small, nondescript schools like Texas A&M-Corpus Christi, to name a few that have been embroiled in scandal during the past decade. The reality is this list barely scratches the surface, and the most frightening part is what we don't know and what has not been publicized —yet.

This book is broken down into three parts. Part I discusses how I became involved in intercollegiate athletics along with my naïve passion for a vocation that would become my life. It is this that often drives rational people to behave irrationally. Part II focuses on my experiences both positive and negative in an incompatible system within higher education at Marshall University while serving as Assistant Athletic Director of Compliance, as well as my legal fight against the system of big-time college sports and the effort to save my reputation. Part III focuses on what can be done to change a culture of problems and corruption in college sports, to save something that many are passionate about before it kills itself.

Marshall University is a broad lens to address problems in college athletics at other institutions, and considering recent stories like Penn State, North Carolina and Syracuse, the problems and culture of protectionism are more significant today than at any other time in the 100-plus-year history of college sports. Many people of integrity are getting pushed out by those who neither want nor care to do the right things. The intercollegiate athletic system so many people know and love is getting worse by the day, and it is through this book that I hope to make it better.

PART I

PROLOGUE

I RECEIVED THE CALL on Monday morning, October 1, 2001.

Something wasn't feeling right, as it was a rare occurrence for a Senior Vice President to call a lower-level staff member like me. This was Monday, October 1, 2001, and Dr. Ed Grose, the Vice President for Operations at Marshall University, was summoning me to his office. Grose had direct oversight of Marshall athletics. On the short walk across campus to Old Main, the uneasy feeling I'd had since July sat in my gut again like a block of ice. For the past two years, I had been mired in an NCAA investigation into improprieties within our football program. As Assistant Athletic Director of Compliance, I was at the center of a storm that seemed intent on destroying everything in its path. I had tried to send out warnings for months, warnings that were ignored by my bosses. Now, inevitably, the storm was upon us, and I was standing directly in its violent path. Before I hung up I had asked Grose, half-jokingly, whether I was in trouble. He assured me that I was not, but to hurry over. Though the signs were ominous, I knew that I was a part of Marshall's solution, not its problem, and I believed the power brokers within the administration and athletic department understood the same.

I had arrived at Marshall in 1997 with a vision of implementing a first-class athletic compliance program at an institution with a previous history of scandal. The university had developed a mostly deserved reputation of playing fast and loose with NCAA rules, thanks in no small part to two major NCAA infraction cases, coupled with the fact that the school was once kicked out of the Mid-American Conference for recruiting violations in the late 1960's.[1] My hiring at Marshall four years prior was supposed to be the university's attempt

3

to break from its checkered past, though I had subsequently found out the hard way that the institution's interests lay mainly in conducting business as usual.

It was while investigating an allegation of academic fraud, in which a professor had improperly distributed advance copies of an exam to a group of football players, that I discovered a wide-ranging and lucrative "no-show" employment scam, also involving members of the football team, in concert with a prominent booster. It seemed that the more I dug into these cases, the more I found, until I was dirty by association.[2] My attempts at addressing the problems in an above-board manner were met with equal measures of ambivalence, hostility and back-room underhandedness intent on protecting those deemed valuable to the university.

Academic fraud and impermissible extra benefits for athletes. These were two of the worst things to be associated with for an NCAA member institution. Now we were right in the middle of not one major allegation, but two. Academic integrity, perceived or otherwise, might be lacking at times in college sports, but many institutions and individuals try to do it right and manage the system as an educational entity. Yet, many will try to push the system and bend or outright break rules to maintain a competitive advantage believing that the reward of winning far outweighs any risk of potential NCAA violations. This is exactly what happened at Marshall University. A professor with close ties to the football team, allegedly with encouragement from the coaching staff, provided copies of a final exam to selected football athletes who were facing possible eligibility consequences should they not pass the class. The other violation consisted of an improper and unreported employment scheme designed by a major booster to give specific athletes pocket money, to the tune of $25 per hour, for doing little or no work.

In the 100 plus years of intercollegiate athletics, there are many constants, and academic improprieties and under the table payments have literally existed since the early 1900's and before that. Marshall was and is no different from schools like Oklahoma, Southern Methodist, the University of Minnesota, and Ohio State University that have faced similar situations over the years. The larger question is why? Why will people associated with a university, whether a coach, booster, or administrator risk employment, a secure future, and other penalties just to win a few more games? Does the reward outweigh any risk? These are questions that have plagued the industry for years, but the scandals keep on happening and there is no end in sight.

I still harbored some naïve hope that my efforts were valued by the university, that even if things weren't happening as quickly as I might have liked, change was still possible. My superiors both inside and outside the athletic department repeatedly told me that I was a crucial member of the team, and it was easy to believe them. Grose had just said to me less than a week before in front of the Athletic Director, Lance West and the Senior Women's Administrator, Beatrice Crane, "We need you, Dave." He said this in response to a difficult time I was having with Beatrice, including the fact that I felt she was someone who wanted to blame me for the violations so as to distance herself from her own culpability. Admittedly, I did not handle the issues with my co-worker professionally and the stress of the investigation and the worries about my job and career were occupying my every thought and I could feel my world was unraveling. It was nice that Grose gave me that vote of confidence, but why would he call me back now, less than a week later?

Grose's office door was closed. I knocked several times before he answered. He let me in and instructed me to sit at a conference table at one end of his spacious office .There was a newspaper there, and I nervously thumbed through it as he went back to his desk to continue a phone conversation. He did not say much to the other person on the line except cryptic one-word answers like "yes" "no" and "maybe," but I was certain he was talking about me. When Grose hung up the phone, I said as cheerfully as I could, "Well, you have me curious Dr. Grose." He didn't hesitate and he just simply said, "Dave, we have decided to make a change."

That statement would change the course of both my life and that of the university.

CHAPTER 1:

KICKOFF

It was November 15, 1997, and in my mind I had arrived. I was making the cross-country drive from my former home in Ogden, Utah to my new one in Huntington, West Virginia, and it was probably the most pleasant drive of my life.

It was a dreary day - gray, cold, and rainy - as, along with my very pregnant wife, Jacqueline, I approached Huntington on Ohio Highway 52 after two long days of driving. "Not exactly the scenic West Virginia I was picturing," she said, patting her belly. She was due in two months with our first child. We passed through the blue-collar towns of Portsmouth and Ironton, Ohio and Ashland, Kentucky, a journey that gives a motorist a good view of dilapidated steel mills, boarded-up shops, and the occasional smokestack with huge flames shooting out. "This is not as pretty as Utah," she said. She was right, it did look awful on this day but I was beginning to tire of her lack of faith in our new home. I knew it would get better. "Everything is going to work out fine," I assured her.

Huntington itself is situated on the banks of the Ohio and Big Sandy Rivers, smack-dab in the middle (as many West Virginians would say) of the Rust Belt, visible to the south and east of those towns in Ohio and Kentucky. While it is a large city by West Virginia standards, it is a small U.S. city whose population dwindled precipitously with the decline of the American industrial complex, specifically the decline of the steel and coal industries.

When I arrived in late 1997, Huntington was a city of slightly over

50,000 people, and the population was once twice that. It is a city of hard-working, outwardly religious, politically conservative, and mostly poor people. Huntington has taken its shots and survived the boarded-up windows downtown, and the hundreds of jobless citizens, with Marshall University - notably its much-beloved football program - at the forefront of the city's sense of community. Many of the boarded up windows had football scheduling posters hung on the plywood and the fire hydrants were even painted green and white—the colors of the beloved Thundering Herd.

"The town really perks up on a sunny day," I said.

"I sure hope so," she said.

My cheerfulness had much less to do with the physical journey we were undertaking, and more with the metaphorical road I had traveled to get to Marshall. Just a few years earlier in 1993, I was working in Augusta, Georgia, not in the golf industry, but managing a Taco Bell on Washington Road about a mile away from the storied Augusta National Golf Club. Even though I was physically close to the cathedral of golf, stuffing tacos and burritos every day was about as far away from my career dreams as one could be, but I was as determined as ever to one day make an impact in sports. I spent whatever spare time I had volunteering in the sports information department at nearby Augusta College to gain experience. Jacqueline had moved with me from her native Germany and was working as an au pair for a military family that was stationed at nearby Fort Gordon.

Prior to working at Taco Bell, you could have found me in the ball-bearing factory town of Schweinfurt, Germany, finishing up a four-year tour as a Field Artillery Officer for the 3rd Infantry Division of the United States Army, and dreaming of a life in sports. I had joined the Army as a 17-year-old kid in 1982, in a quest to find a job, a sense of direction, and a way out of a dysfunctional home life in Manitou Springs, Colorado. I was also a certifiable sports nut, though my athletic ability was not enough to carry me to college. The Army offered me a chance to get a great start in life and an outlet to continue participating in athletics. I traveled the world as a member of the Army's wrestling program. I had remained in the Army in some capacity for over 11 years, even during my four years as an undergraduate student at Colorado State University, where I participated in Army ROTC and was a member of the Colorado Army National Guard.

All the while, sports were the number one source of was good in my life, and even when I returned to active duty upon graduation from CSU in 1990, I knew that athletics were the place I wished to be. The Army was a great life, but it was no longer what I wanted to do. My professional goals were to be in the sports industry. I knew I wanted to do something else, but was not sure exactly what, nor how to get there.

It was shortly after beginning my Field Artillery Officer Basic Course at Fort Sill, Oklahoma in the Fall of 1990 that I had an epiphany. One of those moments that you wonder if it didn't happen where would you be? I had just stepped out of the shower and was preparing to head out for a long Saturday of watching college football at a Lawton, Oklahoma Sports Bar called Champs. The television was tuned to ESPN (as usual) and at the beginning of one of my favorite shows, This Week in Baseball, there was a tease about a university that trained future administrators in the sports industry.

Intrigued and still dripping wet, I sat on the edge of my bed and waited for the segment that would tell me more about this university. I listened as commentator Warner Fusselle described the Sport Administration and Facility Management Graduate Program at Ohio University. He talked about graduates like then-Oakland A's general manager Andy Dolich, and Rick Sund, then GM of the Dallas Mavericks, among others who worked in college athletics, NASCAR, and the World Wrestling Federation.

As much as I thought I knew about sports, I never knew there were programs like this where someone could actually get a master's degree and go on to work in the industry. I knew immediately that this was exactly what I wanted to do, and I wished that I did not have four more years to serve in the Army as a result of being commissioned as a Regular Army Officer in 1990. Still, my desire had been rekindled, and now there was an exact plan of what to do and where to go to start my sports career.

When my second tour in Germany finally ended in 1993, along with my time in the Army, I was no less determined to find my way to Ohio University Unfortunately; I was woefully unprepared for the process of gaining admission. The university would typically admit only 25-30 people per year to the Sports Administration Program, out of hundreds of applicants worldwide, and the interview process was arduous and geared toward someone who already had experience in the sports industry.[3] I simply did not have the credentials and my application was justifiably rejected, but I persisted throughout the next year, soliciting advice from students who had been on the interview committee and also with Dr. Charles "Doc" Higgins, who was the director of the program at the time. My second interview at Ohio went almost perfectly. I was better prepared; more relaxed, and was accepted in the summer of 1994 to start graduate school. It was not too hard to quit Taco Bell and pack up a U-Haul and move to Athens, Ohio and Ohio University.

My experience at Ohio University during graduate school was probably one the best of my life. In addition to getting married my second day in town (Jacqueline's student visa was running out, though I kept my promise and eventually took her back to Germany for a formal wedding two years later), I had an opportunity to be part of a top-notch graduate program, network with movers and shakers in the industry, learn from the best in the business, and be associated with classmates who to this day are some of my best friends, many of whom have gone on to great careers in the sports industry.

In addition to my formal studies, I was given the opportunity to serve as the graduate assistant coach of the wrestling team, learning from collegiate wrestling legend Harry Houska[4] and gaining an insider's perspective that would be critical in my future dealings with coaches and within the realm of NCAA compliance. Harry was struggling with a longtime congenital heart ailment, and many times I was thrust into important responsibilities in the areas of coaching and management. I was attending staff meetings, meeting with the senior athletic staff, coordinating recruiting visits, dealing with budget and financial aid issues, and even serving as acting head coach when the other assistants were on the road recruiting. This was a bit of a baptism by fire for someone who was making tacos with a bunch of high school-aged employees a few months before, but the experience was invaluable.

One of the requirements of the graduate program at Ohio, after serving a year-plus in residence, was securing a one-year internship in the sports world. All internships for members of the Sports Administration program had to be paid, and all students had to be treated as employees with real responsibility. I was initially focused - perhaps a little too focused - on working in college athletics at a big-time school. I interviewed with the likes of Florida, Georgia, and Auburn, and felt I was close to a marketing internship at the University of Nebraska, but none of these positions panned out. It turned out to be a longer road for me than the rest of my classmates, but it was understandable, as most of my peers had much more experience and a better-established network. In fact, I was one of the final members in my class of 30 to get an internship or job after leaving the residency component.

One big opportunity for me to find a job or internship would be at the capstone event of my academic year-in-residence at Ohio, the annual Ohio University Sports Administration Symposium, which functions as an alumni reunion and professional development seminar. I interviewed for several internship positions that weekend, including some with "big-time" schools, one with the Mid-Continent Conference, and another - just for the experience - with Weber State University. I had visions of getting a position at Florida or Auburn. I was even offered a media relations spot at the Mid-Continent Conference, but turned it down in the hopes that I would get one of the bigger jobs that I coveted. In the end, the Auburn and Florida positions went to other, more deserving, classmates of mine. While I did not completely regret turning down the Mid-Con, I was kind of kicking myself for doing so as it would have at least been a place to start my career. My plan at the time was to continue working with the wrestling program at Ohio University, while hoping that something would break.

Initially, I had no desire to work at Weber State. Selfishly and naively, I wanted the big time and I thought my career progression would stagnate if I started at a "small school." Weber State was not a complete unknown to me, since their men's basketball team had an incredible Cinderella run in the 1995 NCAA tournament, beating Michigan State and nearly toppling Georgetown before losing on a last-second shot, but I could not shake the small-time image from my head. Yet here was Weber State, and then-Associate Athletic Director, Steve Rackley, pursuing me for a marketing internship. Rackley, a fellow alumnus of the Ohio University Sports Administration program, offered me a chance to come out for an in-person interview. I went to Ogden, Utah for the interview with no real idea if I would take the internship, or even if the staff would like me. There was a part of me still waiting for that call from the "big time" school, but it turned out that the Weber State offer was a pretty good one, at least on the surface. The pay would be $1250 per month with full benefits, almost unheard-of compensation in the low-paid world of internships in athletic administration. . I was thirty, newly married, and money mattered. I wasn't in a position to turn this down.

Rackley did a great job selling Weber State as a great place to start my career. "Smaller schools give you the opportunity to do more and you will be treated as a full time employee," he continually said. "You won't just be making coffee; you will be doing tangible things that will make you more marketable for the next job."

It made sense. I accepted the internship at Weber, and lucky for me I wouldn't be an intern for very long.

Chapter 2:

Building a Winner

Working as a marketing intern at a place like Weber State was a great experience, though a bit humbling at the same time. I was older than many of the people to whom I was reporting, but knew I wasn't entitled to expect any different given my career change.

While I was a marketing intern at WSU, my duties were pretty diverse, which was exactly what I needed at this early stage in my career. I developed promotional and marketing plans for all sports in the department, secured sponsorship and trade deals, and solicited ticket sales, group sales and promotions. On game days, I received a terrific crash-course in game management, game promotions and marketing, and of course there were the dreaded "other duties as assigned." In all, it was a most valuable education, one I certainly could not have received sitting in a classroom somewhere.

My first direct boss was a young man by the name of Chad Gerrety, who was in his early 20's when he became the Director of Marketing at WSU and, by his own admission, resembled Opie from the old Andy Griffith show. We were certainly Mutt and Jeff because we could not have been more different in age and experience, but Chad was experienced beyond his years and worked hard to get to where he was in the profession. Chad was egoless, an excellent person from whom to learn, and also had no problem leading and giving direction. Like a good soldier, I did what I was told and learned what I could. Chad and I developed a good working relationship and a friendship. After spending not even a full year working under Chad, and just before my year in

Ogden was due to be completed, Weber State received notice that our highest-profile program - the men's basketball team - was under investigation by the NCAA.

Steve Rackley pulled me aside shortly after the notice came, and wanted to gauge my interest for a full-time job as the university's NCAA Compliance Coordinator. One of the problems that the NCAA investigators were beginning to hone in on was that there had not been anyone devoted to compliance on a full-time basis at WSU, and Steve thought that it might be a good pre-emptive move for us to get this position approved and get someone immediately working on improving the culture of rules compliance in the Weber State athletic department.

I was bowled over, and it took me very little time to say yes. Though my only experience with compliance had come in a limited capacity while I was a graduate assistant for the wrestling program at Ohio University, when weighed against the fact that my salary was being doubled, I was getting my own office, and being afforded the opportunity to serve in a vital, permanent position in a Division I athletic department, there wasn't much need for deliberation.

My career had been jump-started, and everything seemed to be going as planned. Of course, I had no real idea what I was getting myself into. Andy Dolich, the Ohio University Graduate School product and then-Oakland A's general manager who I had seen on that mind-blowing This Week in Baseball segment all those years ago, once told me that to make your mark in athletics, you had to attach yourself to a disaster.

Luckily, and unluckily, Weber State was a compliance disaster. To be fair, most schools had not really caught on to the new trend of employing full-time professionals to handle NCAA compliance, and Weber was no exception. All too often, institutions would short-change compliance as a way to save money, making the program an ancillary duty for a staff member or coach, or a primary responsibility for an administrative assistant or green graduate assistant.

At Weber State, prior to my appointment, compliance was an additional duty for Steve Rackley, and as Associate AD he simply had too much on his plate to oversee a compliance program effectively.

Even though I was initially unprepared to take on such a daunting task, I jumped into it as thoroughly as possible. I relished the opportunity and challenge, so I began to cram and get up to speed on what it took to be an effective compliance coordinator and get a better grasp on the ever-growing rules and regulations of the NCAA. Even with my coaching experience and involvement in recruiting, eligibility, academics, and financial aid, there was much more to learn and many things to do at Weber State.

First and foremost, I was determined that we would play by the rules. Part of that insistence was innate, and part of my military background, but I felt we had to do what was written. I came from a decidedly black-and-white kind of experience, and NCAA rules can be gray, but I felt the rules could be followed and the envelope should not have to push to the level of violations and investigations. Some NCAA rules are silly when actually executed, and some seem impractical or nonsensical, but it was the game we signed on to play, and it was my job to ensure that everyone at Weber State knew the playbook.

There was some resistance at first to my firm approach from coaches and members of the athletic department, who had long flown under the radar of such intense regulation, but the seriousness of an NCAA investigation, and the fear that it wrought, allowed me the ability to enforce change. Weber State was finally taking compliance seriously, and using that fact as leverage to mitigate potential NCAA sanctions. Thus, it fell to me to create a program, literally from scratch. While it was frustrating at times, I was able to rally people and begin to put an effective program in place.

As I grew in the job, I began to institute more and more standards that were hallmarks of an effective compliance program but had not really existed in any coherent form prior to my position being established. Recruiting phone logs, stricter eligibility monitoring, practice hours and greater oversight on recruiting visits were just some of these.

Later in my tenure, as the initial grace period of acceptance wore off, some coaches and staff members began to resent the ever-restrictive (albeit strong) compliance program. Even our men's basketball program, under NCAA probation, disliked the new routine of self-reporting violations, rules education meetings, and the compliance culture in general. It was basically considered a nuisance, something that kept coaches away from doing what they "had to do to win." Former Weber State head football coach Dave Arslanian[5] once told me, "Every hour I waste with you is an hour that I lose to (The University of) Montana and getting this program better." Even within a department on probation, compliance with NCAA rules can be a very tough sell with competing interests - namely winning and revenue generation - trumping the reasons to do the right thing.

This started some of the coaches to turn to the athletic director, Gordon "Dutch" Belnap[6], to have me loosen the reins. Belnap had a sympathetic ear for coaches, since he had carved out his legacy as head basketball coach at Utah State University during the 1970's before becoming vice-president of a bank and eventually ending up at Weber State. While Belnap had many years of experience in coaching and athletic administration, the gap of years while he was in the private sector was a time of sea change in college sports. Simply put, he came from an era when compliance did not exist at schools, and other matters like gender equity were not high on his priority list either.

Publicly, Dutch supported me, but he was at his core a consummate "coaches AD," and behind the scenes saw me as more of a distraction than anything else. This is typical of most athletic directors in today's intercollegiate athletic environment. They always seem to preach compliance and integrity, but most want to find any loophole they can to gain success and will support their coaches in that endeavor to include attempting to overrule the compliance office and force bending if not tolerating outright breaking the rules for an advantage. Many coaches and administrators will lament not being able to do something that another school is allegedly doing, to which I often responded, "just because they are doing it, doesn't make it right."

Dutch, like most Athletic Director's, didn't want coaches to feel like they were restricted from doing things - within NCAA rules or otherwise - that would make them less competitive. Predictably, we began to clash over some of the guidelines I was implementing, but I dug my heels in because I knew my position was strong and my cause was just. Since my hiring and the establishment of my position were ways to mitigate NCAA sanctions, it would look bad for the school to push me out the door for doing my job. So I maintained authority, even against my boss, and would not acquiesce.

I still had solid support from Steve Rackley, but he was also exploring moving on in his career due to his own conflicts with Dutch. Part of the issue was that Steve felt it was understood that the Weber State AD job would be his after Dutch retired. It was not to be, as Dutch handpicked then-Eastern Washington University Athletic Director John Johnson to be his replacement in 1996. Johnson served as AD in waiting until officially being given control of the department in 1998.

Steve was devastated by this development. I was personally saddened when Steve made the move to Marshall in 1996 to become Associate Athletic Director, though I was happy he had landed on his feet with what seemed like a pretty good step for his career.

I pressed on at Weber, helping to usher the athletic department through an NCAA investigation centering on the participation of the men's basketball program in a scheme to procure bogus junior-college credits for recruits from a poorly administered, but well intentioned correspondence course program at a Bible school in Florida.[7] Everyone at Weber State breathed a sigh of relief when the NCAA handed down a punishment that did not include any postseason or additional scholarship penalties. A crisis mostly averted, though it still stung to be publically embarrassed and sanctioned by the NCAA, and it became an experience that would be pivotal to my career down the road.

But all was not well for me, as my ability to continue improving the compliance program was being somewhat limited by Belnap and many of the coaches. I was beginning to get frustrated at their resistance, and sensing that I had done all that I could in an environment where my compliance and governance efforts weren't going to be fully supported, it was time to seriously think about moving on to the next phase in my career.

I was ready to leave, but just like my experience in trying to secure an internship roughly three years earlier, getting jobs was competitive and tough. It seemed at times that everyone in the world wanted to work in college athletics. I held out hope that my networking and connections would someday land me a job at a bigger school, and that I could continue on my quest to be a Division I athletic director.

My hopes and patience paid off when my old friend Steve Rackley - the very same man who had given me two tremendous boosts with an internship followed by a full-time position - gave me a call to talk about a potential job opening.

The call came from the 304 area code ... and the state of West Virginia.

CHAPTER 3:

MEETING THE PLAYERS

LIKE MANY STRATA OF business, college athletics is the type of environment in which a job applicant sending out a blind resume, without having any established contacts at the place doing the hiring, is already eliminated from contention. When filling their most important and highest-paying positions, most athletic departments have a very good idea of their two-to-three top candidates even before the job is advertised, even though there are state laws that must be followed in hiring at public institutions. These rules are rarely followed in intercollegiate athletics and exceptions are continually made - especially in the coaching ranks - to facilitate quick hires that often break human resource policies and procedures.

By the fall of 1997, even as a relative newcomer to college athletics, I had already dealt with the negative end of this reality several times over by sending out reams of resumes. But now, having cultivated a network in the profession, and having experienced some real, measurable success at a Division I institution, I found myself atop the wish list of a university with a position to fill, something that anyone with a desire to work in the profession hopes for.

Rackley did not hesitate when he called my office on that autumn afternoon. He asked immediately if I would be interested in the Assistant Athletic Director for Compliance job at Marshall, to which I replied, "Is a school bus yellow?"

I was thrilled - gratified that my hard work appeared to be paying off, pleased that I would have an opportunity to leave a situation at Weber that was growing more tense by the day, and excited about the prospective challenge of joining the team at Marshall, an up-and-coming university that was beginning a transition to the high-profile world of I-A football. I was not really thinking that the same problems that I experienced at Weber likely exist everywhere. Even if I had, a fresh start can still be a good thing.

Marshall had been a dominant member of I-AA football during the 90's, winning national titles in 1992 and 1996, and was beginning its first year as a member of the I-A Mid-American Conference. I knew the MAC well from my days at Ohio University and it was a conference I always wanted to return to.

Inside the athletic department at Marshall, I was already somewhat well-known by the strength of the Ohio University network. In addition to Steve, I was acquainted with the university's Senior Women's Administrator - Beatrice Crane - who was a fellow alumnus of the Ohio University Sports Administration program. Our paths had previously crossed at alumni events, as well as at the NCAA offices the previous year. At that time, Beatrice was the compliance coordinator at Louisville, and since Louisville and Weber State were in the midst of hearings related to infractions within the athletic department, she and I compared notes.

When Steve was seeking a Senior Women's Administrator during his early days at Marshall, I recommended her to Rackley as someone who would make a great SWA. Though she was only in her mid-20's, I felt that Beatrice was a rising star in athletics, and thought she was someone who could be a credit to a university like Marshall.

While I did not know Beatrice well, she was someone I was very impressed with. As an Ohio Sports Administration graduate herself, we certainly had a bond that all alums of the program shared, plus she had accomplished much in her young career. I specifically remembered Beatrice when I came to interview in 1993. She stood out in a crowd as an attractive young woman who exuded confidence and was well spoken. Given that many Senior Women Administrators, to be kind, simply do not look nor carry themselves like Beatrice, these unique features made her popular in the male-dominated world of college athletics. Beatrice was someone who could work her charm, flash a smile, and bat her eyelashes in order to get things done.

Crane, on the heels of my glowing recommendation to Rackley, came to Marshall from the University of Louisville where she had served as Senior Women's Administrator and Assistant Athletic Director for Compliance. She also spent three years at North Carolina State, her alma mater, as the Coordinator for Compliance and Athletic Programs, and had worked previously as Operations Assistant at the PGA Championship and on the T.C. Jordan Golf Tour.

I had run into Beatrice at the 1997 National Association of Collegiate

Directors of Athletics (NACDA) conference in Las Vegas and encouraged her to take a serious look at Marshall, but she was having her doubts. We sat down to have a couple drinks at the Bally's Hotel and Casino, where the convention was being held, and had a long discussion about her future. She told me that she had to leave Louisville as quickly as she could, calling it an "evil place" that did not care about following NCAA rules. She was also despondent at the treatment of then-Louisville head football coach Ron Cooper, who was likely going to be terminated soon. I wasn't sure why she felt so strongly about Cooper - who had an abysmal record at the school - until she admitted to having a "very close" relationship with Cooper, and hating to see him suffer. I wasn't sure exactly what that meant, but I believed that Beatrice and I were from the same program, and should watch out for each other.

At the end of our pleasant conversation, knowing I had a friend who was in need I told her, "Just take a look at the Marshall job, at worst you can just stay there for a couple years and move on." She did have some other possibilities but she assured me that she would at least go and take a look. The rest was history, as she soon after arrived on the Marshall campus. Fortuitously, or so it seemed, she was now among those trying to persuade me to make the move.

Apparently I had left a positive impression on Beatrice, since Steve was now telling me that she had pretty much convinced the Marshall athletic director, Lance West, to interview me. I appreciated her going out of her way to assist me, as I was always told the Ohio University network would. Also banging the drum for me in a positive way was David Steele, the school's Assistant Athletic Director for Business Operations and another Ohio alum. I did not even know David, but it was gratifying to know that he was pulling for me. This was truly a case of why networking and "who you know" matters. Keep in mind that no job announcement or advertisement had even been initiated and here I was already pretty much negotiating for the position. The system was working for me, and I was in no position to protest.

The man I would still have to convince that I was the right person for the job was West, the university's youthful athletic director. I immediately began to do some research on the man who might become my boss. I had met West once before at the 1995 NCAA convention in Dallas, Texas. It was an accidental meeting but we ended up having coffee and chatting about the Big Sky Conference. He had overheard me talking to my old boss, former Ohio University athletic director Harold McElhaney, about Weber State while we were having breakfast. At the time West was running the Big Green Scholarship Foundation at Marshall and had just arrived in Huntington. We had a nice conversation and I remember being impressed with him at least initially.

West was just 33 years old in 1997, but had already climbed to the top of a Division I athletic department thanks in large part to his success as a fundraiser and marketer at his alma mater, The University of Idaho, where he had served as Associate Athletic Director for External Operations.

With the millions of dollars it now required to run Division I collegiate athletic departments, fundraising had evolved into the chief concern of athletic directors from coast to coast. The ability to relate to and direct staff, to deal with coaches and student-athletes, to handle crises big and small regarding players and coaches, and concerning oneself with NCAA rules and regulations, all had become secondary to the issue of generating capital.

Since Weber State was in the Big Sky along with Idaho during the 1990's (U of I subsequently moved to the Sun Belt Conference and later ended up in the Western Athletic Conference where they remain as of 2012), I had the opportunity to ask many people about Lance West and his abilities. Overall, the Big Sky folks I talked to did not give West a stellar endorsement, and many expressed outright shock that he was already an AD at a Division I school, but consistently said he was an expert fundraiser, versed in external operations, and a quality person.

At this stage, I saw what I wanted to see, which was a rising star in college athletics that was at the pinnacle I wanted to reach one day, and who was just a year older than me. In a case of not quite seeing the forest for the trees, I did not take any of the negatives I heard about Lance West to heart. On the contrary, West's presence at the head of the athletic department only brightened the stars in my eyes.

My impression was that this was an athletic director going places, this was a person from the western U.S. that would one day be considered for AD jobs at the giant universities of the Pac-10 and Mountain West, and to whose wagon I could hitch my own star. I was dreaming big. I wanted to go to Marshall not only because I wanted to move up a notch in the profession, but because I wanted to latch on to a young AD and become part of his team, become a person he just could not do without. This was fairly standard in the business, as those in charge liked to hire "their own people" that they were comfortable with. I felt that Lance would not die at Marshall, and would be in position to take a big-time job in a part of the country I wanted to be. I felt Lance West was my kind of guy, and I was excited to confirm it for myself.

Steve and Beatrice both encouraged me to send in my resume as quickly as possible so Lance could look it over. I hurriedly polished up my vitae and faxed it over that evening. The great thing for me, (but not for others who applied) about interviewing for the Marshall position was that it was more of a courtesy than a formal interview that would affect my candidacy. I had essentially been given the job before I left for Huntington on that day in October of 1997, so once I arrived on campus I could pretty much relax.

What I found when I arrived in Huntington was exciting. That weekend, the Herd football team was traveling to Oxford, Ohio to face the always-tough Miami University Redskins. Marshall was 5-1 in its first season in I-A, with the only loss a 42-31 thriller to the mighty West Virginia University Mountaineers in what was arguably the most-anticipated college game in the history of the state. There was a buzz, and it was all because of the football team, now a part of the big time and led by future NFL first-round draft picks Chad Pennington and Randy Moss.

I had the night prior to my interview free, and I walked around the town to get a feel for it. I had been to Huntington a few times before, but since I knew this could be my new home, I wanted to really check it out. It did not take long for me to become convinced, this was a Marshall town through and through. Everywhere I looked was the green and white of the Marshall Thundering Herd, right down to the green and white fire hydrants. This type of excitement is what I desired, and what my passion was. I was already a member of the Thundering Herd in my mind.

But there was the little matter of the interview, and in a reversal of the way these things usually worked, I had some leverage.

Before I left for my interview in Huntington, I had been invited by the NCAA national office to interview for a position on its membership services staff. Job searches in college athletics are feast of famine, and I was finally getting the feast. The final member of his grad school class to get an internship was now receiving job offers left and right (or at least it felt like it to me), and the dual interviews represented a little trump card that I could play with either Marshall or the NCAA to ensure that I would get the job I wanted at the right price. I made sure the folks at Marshall knew that I was interviewing at the NCAA two days later.

Everyone who I met at the institution bent over backwards to make me feel welcomed, and encouraged me to take the Marshall job. Crane especially made an effort. She used our previously-established friendship to gently and humorously cajole me into "possibly not going on the interview at the NCAA." I really appreciated the concern, and told Beatrice that I wanted to hear what the NCAA had to say, but my heart was in being on a campus. Before I left Huntington, Beatrice gave me a note that said, "…have fun at the NCAA, but not too much. Enjoy the limo ride." The NCAA typically sent a limousine to pick up prospective employees at the Kansas City Airport upon their arrival for interviews.

West drove me to the airport, and we had a great exchange. He did his best selling job on Marshall University and the athletic department during our drive. He did not officially offer the job, but did let me know that he was concerned about the NCAA interview and felt that Marshall was the place for me and my family. Although my view of his personality would change, Lance had and still has an incredible, outgoing demeanor, to the point of almost presenting himself as a fake. Yet, to a person who did not really know him, it was reassuring and comforting to speak with him, as he could say what a person wanted to hear even if he had no intention of following up. This particular lengthy conversation convinced me even more that he was dynamic, effective, and taking Marshall places far beyond where it was in college sports. I was excited that I could actually be a part of it and I was convinced I would be back soon as a member of the Thundering Herd athletic department.

I felt much more important than I was two days later when I went back to the Salt Lake City airport to journey to Kansas City and my interview with the NCAA. Between Huntington and Kansas City, I received about a half dozen calls from Marshall people telling me how much they enjoyed meeting me, with West stressing that he was waiting for university approval to offer the job to the "top candidate." This was all a huge boost to my self-esteem after years of struggling to break into the profession..

When I stepped into that limousine at Kansas City International, waiting there was a box of chocolate chip cookies and a note from the NCAA welcoming me to KC along with a reminder to be ready at 7:00 a.m. sharp for the start of the interview the next day. This was big-time. Working in the NCAA national office would really put me in a position to move up the athletic ladder and the connections I could make would be unbelievable. Speaking of unbelievable, the hotel I stayed in near the Overland Park headquarters of the NCAA was palatial. I treated myself to a big steak dinner on the invitation of the NCAA, and retired to my room for the night.

NCAA interviews are very structured and formal. The interview included me giving a formal oral presentation and a written practical exercise on NCAA rules and rule interpretations. I enjoyed the entire exercise immensely and I felt I made a good impression on the staff. All of the feedback with the NCAA and people that I knew at the national office was positive, and it appeared I was a person they wanted.

The benefits of the job were also immense ... free health club membership, Final Four tickets, great medical and dental, the list went on and on. I thought to myself that I had made it, I was in the club, and now I would have my choice of two great jobs. The one negative of the NCAA job was that the national office would be pulling up stakes to move the operation to Indianapolis in less than a year. Since my wife was pregnant with our first child, such a move was a concern.

I was back at work in Ogden the next day at 7:30 a.m., knowing that no matter what I decided, my time at Weber State was growing short. It was only a few minutes later that my phone rang. It was Lance West officially offering me the Marshall job. He said that he did not want to lose me to the NCAA. He offered $40,000, plus moving expenses. I was pumped. 40K was a lot less than what I made in the Army, but it was almost double what I was making at WSU, and a little bit more than the NCAA would offer, although they had better benefits. Market forces dictate pretty low pay in college sports administration, but if one works their way through the ranks the rewards can be worthwhile.

I told Lance that I wanted to discuss it with my wife, and asked if he could give me 48 hours. He agreed, but pressed me to make a decision soon because there were several others interested in the Marshall position. It is never good to look a gift horse in the mouth, but I wanted to be sure this was the best move for me and my soon-to-be-larger family. After hanging up with West, I immediately called John Leavens, then Director of Membership Services at the NCAA, to tell him about the Marshall offer and also my predicament. I was no longer absolutely sure which job I wanted the most.

John was sympathetic but told me that a bureaucracy like the NCAA had to follow specific procedures in hiring, and it could not make the type of quick decision on hiring that I was asking for. Still, he asked me to hold off for a couple of hours while he conversed with his colleagues on my potential hire. He called back a few hours later to say that the NCAA could not offer the job to me for at least a few days, if not weeks, if at all considering there were others to interview and they needed to finish that process to be fair to all applicants. After talking it over with Jacqueline, we agreed this was a sign that I was destined to be on campus and at Marshall University. I called Lance back with the words he wanted to hear - I was going to become a member of the Marshall Thundering Herd.

Everyone has their "path not taken" stories in life, and self-reflective questions about whether the decision they made at a fork in the road was the correct one. As it turned out given my future dealings with the NCAA, my "path not taken" story would grow ever more interesting, and substantially ironic.

CHAPTER 4:

ASHES TO GLORY

SOMETIME AFTER 7:30 PM on November 14, 1970, Southern Airways Flight 932, bound from Kingston, NC to Ceredo, WV, began its descent into Tri-State Airport with 71 passengers and four crew members aboard. In an apparent haze of rain and fog, the chartered DC-9's crew may have descended the aircraft lower than the FAA-mandated minimum for descent altitude during adverse operating circumstances, possibly due in part to altimeter readings skewed by moisture, and crashed nose-first into a hillside one mile short of the airport's runway No. 11.

The exact cause of the crash has never been determined.

According to the official report by the National Transportation and Safety Board (NTSB), the fiery accident was "unsurvivable." All 75 aboard were killed, including 37 members of the Marshall University Thundering Herd football team, eight members of the coaching staff, and 25 boosters and community leaders who had watched the team's 17-14 loss at East Carolina University earlier that day.

In a moment, the community in and around Marshall University had its collective heart torn out. Thousands of lives were directly affected throughout the tight-knit town of Huntington. Seventy children lost at least one parent in the crash, including 26 who were left orphaned. In addition to the 37 young football players, head coach Rick Tolley and his entire staff, four of the city's six physicians, a city councilman, and a state legislator was aboard the flight.

The notion of Marshall University again fielding a football team was regarded as a trivial matter, and rightly so. The program was nearly discontinued altogether, and the first head coach hired to replace Tolley, Georgia Tech assistant Dick Bestwick, left after just two days on the job.

But the then-unknown head coach of tiny Wooster College, Jack Lengyel, accepted the position and, as dramatically portrayed in the 2006 hit film "We Are Marshall," galvanized the community. Prior to the allowance of freshman eligibility in athletics, Lengyel successfully petitioned the NCAA to allow freshmen to play in order to field a team for the 1971 season, and in the squad's first home game since the crash, defeated Xavier, 15-13, on a last-second touchdown pass.

It is this series of events that has, for better or for worse, helped to shape the identity of Marshall University in the ensuing 35-plus years. Despite the subsequent founding of a School of Medicine, a professional school and doctoral programs in many fields over the past few decades, among many other achievements, it is the football program's quite literal rise from the ashes that continues to serve, right or wrong, as bullet point number one in Huntington's image of the university.

Though Marshall is dwarfed in nearly every meaningful respect by its not-so-friendly rival to the north, West Virginia University, the junior university's profile has been expanded exponentially over the past half-century, and there is no underestimating the effect of athletics, specifically the resurrection and later success of the football program, on that evolution. The importance of football has been both an integral part of Marshall's development and at times an albatross around the neck of a university that has sought to ensure that its marquee program succeeded by any means necessary.

Despite the feel-good portrayal in the film, the football program at Marshall was not off and running with that win over Xavier. Lengyel was 9-33-1 in his four years at Marshall, as a program still haunted by the specter of the tragedy, and unable to gain much recruiting traction without a conference affiliation, struggled to compete.

After unsuccessfully bidding to be reinstated to the Mid-American Conference, which had kicked Marshall out for recruiting violations in 1969, the university joined the Southern Conference in time for the 1977 campaign. Progress was slow in the Southern Conference as well, as coaches Frank Ellwood and later Sonny Randle led the team to a conference record of 5-35-1 over the team's first seven seasons in the league (1977-1983).

Things began to change in 1984, when new head coach Stan Parrish led the program to a 6-5 record, its first winning mark since 1964. The next season saw the Thundering Herd improve to 7-3-1, and though Parrish left to accept the head job at Kansas State, the relative success of the Marshall program prompted state funding for a new stadium in 1990. While plans were developed for the new facility that would eventually open in time for the 1991 season, new head coach George Chaump rode the wave and molded Marshall into a I-AA powerhouse.

The Herd made their first-ever playoff appearance in 1987, advancing all the way to the I-AA title game in Pocatello, Idaho before losing to Louisiana-Monroe, 43-42. When Chaump left for Navy after the 1989 season, it was successor Jim Donnan, formerly the offensive coordinator under Barry Switzer at the University of Oklahoma, who took the program into the stratosphere. Donnan went 64-21 with five playoff appearances in his six years in Huntington, including four national championship appearances and a I-AA title in 1992.

Donnan was hired at the University of Georgia in 1996, after Kansas head coach Glen Mason accepted the job and then abruptly changed his mind.[8] Marshall was then on the hunt for a new head man, and alumnus, former assistant coach under Randle, and Beckley, WV native Bobby Pruett began to actively lobby for the job. It appeared that Pruett's job as defensive coordinator for the University of Florida was about to come to an end, after the Gators turned in an abysmal defensive performance in getting thrashed by Lawrence Phillips and Nebraska, 62-17, in the 1995 Fiesta Bowl. Then-Florida head coach Steve Spurrier was known to dispense with coaches quickly who caused him embarrassment, which meant the clock was ticking on Pruett. Pruett was not initially considered the top candidate at Marshall, but had reason to lobby hard for the job considering he was looking at a demotion or outright firing at the hands of Spurrier, and many of his influential friends in the area were pushing hard for him as well. Pruett was able to convince then-Marshall athletic director Lee Moon that he was the best choice and was eventually hired. Initially it appeared to be a stroke of genius, as Pruett guided Marshall, and its newest transfer Randy Moss, to a 15-0 season and its second national title with a resounding 49-29 defeat of defending champion Montana, the same team that defeated the Herd in the previous year's championship game. The thumping of UM would mark the program's final game at the I-AA level.

The Mid-American Conference, a member of I-A since the NCAA re-classification in the late 70's, suddenly embraced the program it had once jettisoned, then spurned for re-admission, once its football program had achieved a pattern of success. Now, Marshall University football would become a very big fish in a small pond and not just be immediately competitive, but even dominant in the lower tier of Division I-A football. The school would immediately possess the best football facilities in the conference, a 24-station radio network and a television package that saw nearly all of its games accessible to Marshall fans across the country. In reality, even in its first year in I-A, Marshall was far and away ahead of other MAC schools when it came to football infrastructure.

The then-coach at Toledo, and current Missouri head man Gary Pinkel, said the inclusion of Marshall into the MAC forced others to "raise the bar" to compete with the Herd. A statement like that was unheard of in discussing the prospects of a I-AA moving up, but in this case it was accurate. Marshall University football became the biggest thing in the MAC since future NBA players Gary Trent and Ron Harper played hoops in the league.

The excitement surrounding the Marshall football team was at an all-time high when I arrived on campus in the fall of 1997, and for good reason. The difference in atmosphere between my final game at Weber State on Nov. 8th, when about 4,000 fans showed up for a meaningless blowout of Sacramento State in a duel of Big Sky also-rans (though Weber was quarterbacked that day by eventual Oklahoma star and Heisman finalist Josh Heupel, who would transfer to Snow Junior College and on to the Sooners), and my first game at Marshall on Nov. 15th, was pretty striking. The Thundering Herd, now 8-2, would host my old employer, Ohio University, with the right to advance to the inaugural MAC Championship game at stake. The MAC title game with Toledo would be played in Huntington on Dec. 5th, no matter who won the Marshall/Ohio contest.

I wanted to be in Huntington for the upcoming game because it would be a great time to see old friends from Ohio University, mingle with new co-workers, and catch what figured to be an exciting contest. It was a watershed day for both teams. Ohio, after years of football futility, had begun to show some life under head coach Jim Grobe, who himself was a Huntington native and a former assistant coach at Marshall on the staff of Sonny Randle, along with Bobby Pruett.[9]

If the powerbrokers at Marshall, or anyone else for that matter, had harbored any doubts about whether the university was equipped for the I-A level of football, they were cured of them on that day. An overflow crowd of 32,012 - the third-largest attendance in school history at the time, only behind only the stadium inauguration in 1991 and the I-AA title game against Montana in 1995 - watched as Chad Pennington, Randy Moss, and the Thundering Herd pummeled the Bobcats, 27-0, before a delirious audience.[10]

In a figurative sense, Marshall had arrived. In a literal one, so had I. My first weeks on the job at Marshall were memorable, and not only due to the hoopla surrounding the football team's upcoming appearance in the nationally-televised MAC Championship.

It was apparent from the start that I had inherited one of the worst, if not the worst compliance program in the country.

PART II

CHAPTER 5:

BABY STEPS

BEFORE MY ARRIVAL AT Marshall in November of 1997, the university's athletic programs had been hit with two major infractions cases since the NCAA began its enforcement and infractions program in 1952. In 1969, it was discovered that the football coaching staff led by head coach Perry Moss, in concert with a group of boosters looking to super-charge the struggling program, had taken the liberty of auditioning 135 athletes from around the country for 35 available scholarships. This egregious breach of NCAA rules led to 144 NCAA violations and expulsion from the Mid-American Conference.

In 1991, the then-successful men's basketball program was placed on two years' probation and banned from postseason play after the NCAA discovered a series of improprieties within head coach Rick Huckabay's program. Again, the presence of powerful boosters was noted. Marshall reported to the NCAA that a basketball player was given a $2,000 loan which boosters repaid for him, while other players were impermissibly given clothing, jewelry, small amounts of cash, places to stay and transportation to public appearances by coaches and program supporters. Huckabay, who resigned after the school reported the violations in 1989, would never coach in the college ranks again before dying of cancer in 2006.[11]

Though those cases were ancient history by the time I took over the compliance program at Marshall, the university still seemed saddled with a reputation in college athletic circles as an institution that played fast and loose with NCAA regulations. I initially felt that was largely just hyperbole based on the past, rather than anything factual, and was also no indication of where the program could be in the future.

Still, it was this history and reputation that made me a bit apprehensive about taking the job, while conversely making me excited about accepting it. I really felt that I could fix whatever leaks remained in the ship, and reasoned that things could not have been as bad as they were in the early 90's.

In addition, I knew that the presence of two prior major infractions cases was not earth-shattering in and of itself, as many institutions have run afoul of the NCAA and its many rules through the years, including some that have done so on multiple occasions.

I also knew firsthand from my experience at Weber that sometimes violations happened unintentionally due to lack of compliance education among administrators, staff, and coaches, and I felt that a little organizing and educating on my part could go a long way.

Even with my experience and preparation, what I found during my first days and weeks at Marshall was a major shock to the system. In short, despite the presence of some good administrators including Beatrice Crane and Steve Rackley, both of whom had background in compliance, there really was not a compliance program to speak of at Marshall. It was worse than I could ever have imagined. This doesn't totally reflect on my predecessors at the university, nor Crane and Rackley, because they were fighting a losing battle against a renegade culture that had existed for years.

It became apparent to me, very early on, that as rumored Marshall University simply did not follow the rules, did not have good, strong leadership to ensure an ethical program, and did not place playing by the rules above winning games, in particular on the football field. I knew we had a problem as soon as I began cataloging the school's self-reports of secondary violations to the NCAA over the past year.

As opposed to a major infraction, such as those that had previously landed Marshall in hot water, a secondary violation is defined as one that is isolated, inadvertent, and results in a minimal or non-existent competitive advantage.

Due to the size and scope of the NCAA rule book and the many constantly moving parts within collegiate athletic departments, all institutions commit secondary violations. It is virtually impossible to avoid. Though it might seem a contradiction, an institution not reporting secondary violations can be looked upon unfavorably by the NCAA, and send up red flags that the school is not self-policing its program. In a strange catch-22, you almost want secondary infractions, so it demonstrates that the institution has a strong compliance program. At Weber State, I was told emphatically by members of the NCAA Committee on Infractions and members of the enforcement staff that a history of self-reporting and self-correcting secondary violations shows an engaged compliance program and an athletic department committed to following the rules in the spirit of fair play.

While the inevitability of secondary violations does not preclude you from trying to eliminate them, and they still have to be treated seriously given the intense media scrutiny that will likely follow, such violations are reasonably routine. While at Weber State, I routinely reported 4-6 secondary infractions per month, and was complimented on my approach by both the NCAA and the Big Sky Conference. I actually liked this process because it assisted me in identifying weak areas, fixing them, and improving the overall program - which is what the process is designed to do. However it does present a bit of a conundrum in that those secondary violations can come back to haunt you if there are too many. There is no set amount of "too many" but it certainly might encourage people not to report to much, something Beatrice Crane alleged happened at Louisville routinely.

Anyway, my look back at Marshall's self-reports over the preceding months didn't take long ... there were none. The university had not reported a secondary violation for almost a year prior to my arrival and this was a huge red flag. It was clear that I had some work to do.

I immediately scheduled a meeting with the coaches and athletics administration in order to indoctrinate the entire athletic program into the new culture of rules compliance. I was firm, but realistic. I told the group that there was nothing that could not be fixed, but that I could not do it alone. I had the entire staff raise its hands to take a pledge, telling them, "We are all compliance officers, and we all will have specific and general responsibilities to ensure the process runs smoothly."

I started to build the rules compliance program in the best way I knew how ... assess, plan, correct, execute, and revise. The point was to conduct what we referred to in marketing as a SWOT analysis: Identify the strengths, weaknesses, opportunities, threats, and build your mission, goals, and objectives from that analysis. This was a layered approach that gave me overall responsibility for the program, but relied on input from all coaches and staff members in order to run effectively. The NCAA is emphatic that rules compliance is everyone's responsibility and having a participatory program and process insures broad-based involvement and buy-in. I too strongly believed in this philosophy, given that I did not have the resources to do it all on my own.

For example, if a basketball athlete wanted to play in a summer league, or work at a camp, he or she had to first seek approval from the coach, then the coach would forward a form to me along with the athlete. I would approve or disapprove, copy the player and coach on the relevant paperwork, and maintain that information in the player's file. If all hands are on deck in this regard, the process can run extremely well and it is crucial to keep the coaches involved so they cannot claim ignorance later -something that happened all too often in the world of NCAA compliance.

Even though I already knew we had problems, I told everyone that they needed to continue what they were doing with regard to recruiting, eligibility, financial aid, and other areas. I reminded them about keeping up with the basics, including phone logs, recruiting visit records, scholarship offers, etc. I would then meet with every member of each coaching staff and each athlete to review their procedures, and make a plan to standardize all compliance operations. This was really the only way to keep business running, and also build a program.

Since little to no importance was placed on compliance prior to my arrival and there was very little support for the compliance office on the administrative end, each team and entity was doing their own thing in respect to following the rules, which in some cases meant they weren't doing anything.

My job was to get everyone on the same page, standardize, organize, educate, and continually improve the program. This was a very tall order considering that I had to effectively build the program from scratch, but initially it seemed that I had support from the athletic director, Lance West, and the president, Dr. J. Wade Gilley.[12] I took advantage of this support and started to build the program step by step, and in the same model that I built the program at Weber State.

Meanwhile, the football team marched on. In the ESPN-broadcast MAC title game, which was played in a driving snowstorm, Marshall recovered from a 7-3 halftime deficit, with two Chad Pennington-to-Randy Moss touchdown passes in a span of three minutes helping to turn the tide in favor of the home team during the third-quarter. The Thundering Herd would prevail, 34-14, winning the conference title in their inaugural year in the league and earning a berth to the Motor City Bowl against Ole Miss, to be played in Detroit the day after Christmas.

Things were good, unless you were the guy in charge of managing the extra NCAA paperwork that came along with the bowl game.

In this case, the document in question was the NCAA agent affidavit form, a form that all student-athletes participating in NCAA postseason competition must fill out, which verifies that he/she has not signed with, or received benefits from, an agent. I scheduled a meeting with the football team and coaching staff in order to explain, and have the players sign, the document. I was not really nervous about the meeting, since as an ex-Army officer I had spent much of my adult life in large groups filled predominantly with men, and I certainly was not going to let a few college football players intimidate me, though I was a little taken aback when I walked through the door in this case.

I was always used to coaches cracking the whip when a guest was coming, to make sure everyone was on their best behavior, and was also something I ensured occurred when I was a coach. As I walked into the football staff room, however, it was chaos, and coach Pruett was either unwilling or unable to stop it. So I helped him out. As I moved to the front of the room, I shouted, "Knock it off, and listen up!"

You could have heard a pin drop, initially. Then some grumbling started, along the lines of, "Who in the hell is this guy, etc." Finally, Coach Pruett, in his pronounced southern West Virginia drawl, spoke up.

"OK guys, let's pay attention here to Dave Ree-pass (not the last time he failed to get my name right), as he tells us about rules and stuff."

As I started to discuss the agent affidavit form, I could not help but be distracted by Pruett and a player talking at the back of the room, making no real effort to listen to what I had to say. The player was none other than Marshall's most famous "student-athlete" of the moment … Randy Moss. Pruett was having Moss sign footballs, and they appeared to be having a merry old time chatting. My military background would not allow me to let this go, and I figured it was a moment that I had better seize, lest I have no respect amongst the football program.

I calmly said, "Coach, let's hold off on what you are doing for now, this is important, especially for Randy." Now you could really hear a pin drop. The notion of someone challenging the almighty Bob Pruett and Randy Moss was unthinkable around these parts. The collective shock around the room was palpable and I had the rapt attention of Pruett, Moss, and the rest of the coaches and players for the remainder of my presentation. I had accomplished my mission … almost.

After the meeting, as the room was clearing out, I asked Pruett to stay behind. Without mincing words, I said, "Coach, don't ever embarrass me like that again. When I am speaking, I expect the coaches and players to pay attention and be quiet."

Pruett was stunned. He now knew that he had an administrator that would not back down to him and grant his every wish. It was an eye-opening day for both of us, but I think Pruett at this moment began to rue the day I was hired. Most coaches, at least the ones I had encountered, viewed compliance as an irritation and it was clear to me that Pruett, like many other coaches, had never been challenged by a lower-level administrator before, especially one in compliance.

I would soon learn that he had a very good reason to regret my hiring, since he had a great deal to hide and was terrified there might now be someone at Marshall who was diligent enough to find it.

CHAPTER 6:

TROUBLE IN PARADISE

SHORTLY AFTER MY AWKWARD meeting with the team, I discovered my first violation at Marshall. Not surprisingly, it was within the football program. As if I needed another one, this violation was a wake-up call as to how rules compliance had been handled at the institution and within the athletic department prior to my arrival.

Following the team's 35-28 loss to Ole Miss in the Motor City Bowl, I did a comparison of the travel list submitted by the football office for the game along with the players who signed the agent affidavit forms, and the NCAA squad list form and MAC eligibility report. The accuracy of these reports is crucial to running a proactive compliance program. What I discovered was a whopping 22 players who were listed by the program as having made the trip to Detroit, but did not appear on the official NCAA or MAC paperwork. In fact, there were no existing records within the department that these 22 guys were even on the team. It is important to note that I did not attend the bowl game that year as we had a previously planned trip to Germany for the holidays. I did approve a bowl travel list before I left, but I was never told about "extra" players who would be traveling. These players were going along for the ride and would not play, though no one ever bothered to tell me about it. The lack of information flow would be a continual problem within the athletic department. Frankly, they had no real reason to even make the trip, and did not need an all-expenses paid, week-long trip to Detroit given the financial position of the athletic department. More importantly, this was a clear violation, and one that showed utter disregard for even the most basic of rule-monitoring procedures. Not even having the correct people on the squad list was a bad omen for how much work I truly had to do to fix what was quickly becoming an overwhelming mess.

I was livid, and would only become more incensed when I confronted Coach Pruett, who seemed to be suffering from a serious bout of amnesia. And though Chad Pennington had the best arm on the team, Pruett could have shown him a thing or two about buck-passing.

The entire football staff was trying to deflect blame on the roster snafu, though Coach Pruett was the most active in trying to distance himself from any violation, claiming that the players in question were walk-ons and that he "did not know who they were." Mind you, these guys had uniforms, lockers, and received academic assistance, but the head coach did not know who they were. I would have to talk to the assistants, Pruett told me.

The shell game continued, as most of the assistant coaches claimed that other assistants, or Coach Pruett himself, directed certain people to be added to the roster, many times over the objections of the assistants, specifically associate head coach Mark Gale.

Gale had come with Jim Donnan from the University of Oklahoma in 1990,[13] rising from tight ends coach under Donnan to Pruett's top lieutenant during Marshall's rise to football prominence during the 90's. Mark was a stand-up guy and immediately became one of the few trustworthy people I found in Pruett's employ, at least initially.

Gale informed me privately that there were no checks and balances in place with regard to roster management, nor any procedures to ensure that everyone on the staff actually knew who was on the team. Gale added that coaches would bring players onto the team "when they feel like it, usually at the behest of Coach Pruett."

I confronted Coach Pruett on this issue in the best way I knew how, face to face and man to man. Pruett's amnesia disappeared when I told him the assistants claimed that they added players only at his direction. He said that he kind of remembered that, but roster management was up to Coach Gale and he should have reported any changes to the compliance office.

After throwing his top assistant under the bus, Pruett proceeded to partially blame then-president J. Wade Gilley for the situation, telling me that Gilley had enacted a policy of forcing the football team to accept all walk-ons since Marshall accepted Randy Moss.

Moss had been accepted at Marshall despite a criminal charge of assault and battery prior to what was supposed to be his first year at Notre Dame, followed by a positive marijuana test that got him kicked off the team at Florida State.[14] Though Moss was a local hero from Rand, West Virginia, his acceptance at Marshall did not sit well with some on campus, and what

Pruett was telling me was that walk-ons were now being accepted, no questions asked, in order to enhance student relations. Pruett's defense was that he had no choice.

Later, Gilley would tell me that he made no such statement to Pruett, astutely noting that allowing such an open-door policy would cause Title IX concerns for the university. After listening to Pruett's efforts at shifting blame and self-preservation, I was nauseous.

I spent over 11 years in the Army, so the fact that the most prominent "leader of men" at Marshall - the closest thing the university had to a general – was looking out for his own interests above that of his charges galled me. True leaders do not operate that way, but it was apparent to me from this moment that Pruett was about number one - himself - not his players, staff, and certainly not the university.

One of the most clear and basic NCAA bylaws instructs institutions to self-report every violation and to take corrective measures to ensure that they don't re-occur. But Pruett was adamant that we should not self-report this to the NCAA. When I insisted that we would be reporting the violation, he grew angry. He had often requested that we not self-report "piddly stuff," but I was adamant that we were going to follow NCAA rules to the letter.

"Well, I'm going to President Gilley, because I am not getting in trouble for this," he screamed.

The threat to go to the president was a tactic he used often to try to intimidate those in the athletic department, something many high profile coaches would and still pull as a way to get what they want. No one wanted to be on the bad side of BOTH of those most powerful people on campus, and those who Pruett threatened generally knuckled under. But I wasn't falling for it, and I had already beaten him to the punch. I informed him that I had already discussed the situation with the president, and that Dr. Gilley had given me the green light to self-report.

Meanwhile, the Mid-American Conference had directed us to write a letter of reprimand to the responsible individual. I determined that person was Pruett, but he would not go down without a fight on this point either. He went ballistic on Lance West, stating that he was not going to accept a letter of reprimand under any circumstances.

Not for the first or last time, West acquiesced to the ravings of his head coach. The blame was placed on my predecessor, Joyce Howse, who had nothing to do with the football program's lack of roster management but had the disadvantage of not being present to defend herself. Joyce had taken a non-athletics position at Radford University in Virginia. I was sick over this. I could not believe how weak Lance West was and how he bowed to the whims of Pruett, at the expense of an innocent person.

And though I hated the way Pruett handled the situation, when the smoke had cleared I decided to give him the benefit of the doubt for the good of the department, something I did too many times and came to regret. Still, in his defense, there had been a half-dozen different people in charge of compliance in the past 10 years, and no consistent voice to give him a hand in following the proper procedures. He was a new head coach, there was a new athletic director, and almost the entire athletics staff had turned over in the past two years.

In some ways, Pruett's reaction was understandable, albeit wrong. He had been around college athletics long enough to know the one thing, other than losing, that gets people who work at NCAA member institutions fired, many times without any severance or remainder of contract paid, is being associated with NCAA violations. Even the most minor of violations - even isolated and inadvertent ones - can come back to haunt a person and can be the reason they are fired, scapegoated, or not hired for a future position.

While it is mandated that a school self-detects, self-reports, and self-corrects secondary and major problems, when backed into a corner, institutions will put themselves in the best possible light to mitigate and minimize any appearance of impropriety, which means offering up a sacrificial lamb or two to the NCAA in the name of "corrective actions."

Rick Huckabay[15] experienced this when he was forced to resign under pressure in the late 80's, although generally it is politically expendable, and often completely innocent, people like Joyce Howse who are offered up to help save and protect people in positions like Bobby Pruett.

NCAA history is littered with assistant coaches, secondary staff members, and others who were blamed for "breakdowns in the system," in order to protect higher-ups. Most will not fight back, some because they don't want to further damage their own opportunities of future employment in the seductive world of college sports, and others because they are unwilling or unable to fight against the powerful, deep-pocketed institutions or the NCAA.

Thus the blame game and dirty little secrets start amongst personnel at NCAA institutions to ensure that no one is blamed or only expendable people are blamed. Therein lays one of the biggest problems with the NCAA enforcement and infractions process. But at this point, I still took the approach that tomorrow was a new day, and that I would soon have everyone on campus buying into the compliance program and understanding the value of self-reporting and self-correcting.

Even though it repulsed me that Pruett did not at least get a letter of reprimand, I naively wrote this off as a one-time incident, and decided to pick my battles and focus on other critical areas that needed immediate attention. I rationalized that with my hard work and dedication, Pruett, his staff, and the rest of the department would come around. They just had to.

And though we had lost to Ole Miss in the Motor City Bowl, all was not lost for me as I knew Randy Moss was leaving Marshall for the riches of a pro career, and gone would be the potential baggage and problems of having a mega-star athlete on campus. Unfortunately, any and all potential corrupting influences in Huntington did not fade way when Moss became the property of the Minnesota Vikings.

CHAPTER 7:

THE TOOLS OF POWER

AFTER THE MOTOR CITY Bowl, I was even more determined to focus on critical areas that needed immediate attention, while reviewing past procedures, revising current ones, and all the while running an active compliance program to serve the current student-athletes and coaches.

My goal was to have all new policies and procedures in place before the new 1998-99 academic year. This included not just the daily rules compliance processes, but also meant developing a comprehensive departmental compliance manual, setting up university-wide committees, developing a student-athlete handbook, interpretations procedures, and a rules education program.

My focus was on improving the program and working within the system that all of us in the industry had signed on to uphold. Regardless of the often legitimate complaints about that system, it is what it is, and everyone needs to follow the rules. It was my job to coordinate that. I was constantly self-reporting NCAA violations, including a couple inadvertent secondary violations on myself. Not that I was proud of it, but I was always clear that I made mistakes in this job and I will never shy away from that, nor would I shift blame to someone else. The two that stood out were approving a signed men's basketball recruit to sit on the bench , and allowing a baseball player to impermissibly be counted as a student assistant coach based upon some incomplete records I was given. In both of these cases I could have been more thorough. I did not ask all of the questions needed, and was justifiably reprimanded. I actually reported myself to the conference office, something that was not uncommon among those of us who sat in that chair. I never had a problem self-reporting if an oversight on my part had caused an NCAA violation, which is somewhat routine when you're a compliance coordinator dealing with many issues and details on a daily basis, especially when understaffed and under supported. It was simply the right thing to do, and I knew that not reporting myself could have negative ramifications down the line. The point was that if I am going to admonish others who make mistakes, I cannot expect any different when I make them. Still, it was critical that I do everything I could and have systems in place to minimize any exposure that could cause further violations - by me or anyone else.

It was a very tough mountain to climb, especially since I was virtually doing it all on my own, but at this point I felt that I could accomplish it all. In defense of Marshall and the many people that I would come to criticize later, I was very much supported when I started at the university. I encountered little if any resistance to my reforms from the athletics or university administration. The little resistance I did get was from the coaching staff, specifically within the football program. Still, other than the first football self-report, there was nothing terribly out of the ordinary, nor anything I felt I could not

handle. My goal was to work very hard and develop a workable program that everyone could buy into, then the cooperation would take care of itself.

But as the days dragged on and I began encountering crisis upon crisis, it was becoming increasingly difficult, if not impossible, to create a new program and procedures while still trying to manage the current program. Since I was not getting any help, other than some part-time help from my inexperienced assistant, Dave Reed, there was a powder keg of mistakes, made by everyone including myself, seemingly waiting to blow. It was even getting tough to get a good night's sleep because of the stress and worry I was now under. Despite my efforts, my continual pleas for help fell on deaf ears. This was not atypical in compliance at many institutions as it is an area that often gets low priority when the choice is paying coaches more, or adding bricks and mortar.

The first major crisis I had to face following the Motor City Bowl issue was the dismissal of our head baseball coach, Craig Antush, a decent man who was caught in a hopeless and terrible situation.

Craig was a part-time coach of a struggling baseball program that he clearly felt didn't need to be struggling. Marshall's baseball facilities were sub-standard, right down to the fact that the team didn't have its own field, and fell short in relation to most of its competition in regard to both facilities and scholarships. Meanwhile, in true small college fashion, one of the highest-profile coaches on campus was also in charge of all athletic facilities and event operations, an almost unheard-of circumstance at a school with a I-A football program. The time he was forced to spend concentrating on matters not related to coaching his own team was certainly not conducive to running a sound baseball program devoid of NCAA rule violations.

Craig was not afraid to voice his displeasure about this setup, and did most of his complaining publicly to the (mostly) local baseball booster group, The Dugout Club. Several people in Marshall's administration did not appreciate this public criticism, most notably President J. Wade Gilley, Senior Vice President for Operations Ed Grose, and General Counsel Layton Cottrill. This trio had set their sights on Antush's dismissal for what they determined to be gross insubordination. Unfortunately, I unwittingly gave them a major assist in pushing him out the door for different reasons altogether.

The stated reason why Craig Antush was fired in the middle of the 1998 baseball season was because he was playing four kids that were not certified as eligible for competition through the proper eligibility certification process. I had recently overhauled the eligibility certification process, since the process I inherited had too many people involved, namely the football and baseball academic advisor, Laurie Fox, while keeping coaches out of the loop. Fox had married into one of the richest families in West Virginia, a family that were major donors to both the department and university. Inasmuch, she was basically untouchable, and it was clear from the beginning of my tenure that she didn't feel she needed to listen to me.

In this case, Fox had told Craig that the four players in question were eligible, which would have been correct-except that I had no record of those players as would have occurred if proper procedures were followed. Because I had not been notified, the players in question had in turn not been certified by the Faculty Athletics Representative (FAR), Robert Sawrey. NCAA rules are clear that no one may compete unless their competitive eligibility has been certified by the FAR.

As per policy, I reported this information to the athletic director West, Grose, and Cottrill. Sensing an opening, Grose approached the president and both decided that Antush would be terminated immediately because of his lack of attention to what they decided was a very important detail. Tellingly, Laurie Fox had been at just as much fault as Craig but didn't receive as much as a written reprimand.

I felt physically ill knowing a man's career and life's love was for all practical purposes over, though at the time, I couldn't disagree with the decision. Craig had been lax on some things before this, he really should have confirmed that these players were eligible, and I knew his firing would send a clear message that got the attention of the rest of the coaches. I did believe that the immediate firing was overly harsh, as there was only about a month to go in the season, but at the time, I felt it had to be done.

When the decision was made, Beatrice Crane broke down, even though she agreed that Craig should go. When Crane, Lance West and I summoned Antush from the baseball field to West's office to inform him of his termination, I looked at Craig and it hit me that this was not a simple act but involved someone's life.

Whatever had happened, this guy was a person, with a family, who did work hard. I also considered Craig a friend and here I had a major hand in his dismissal. I thought to myself, "Could I have done more? Should I have spoken up and argued that in reality this was more out of his hands than most people realized?" I did nothing and I went along as the administration assured me we were doing the right thing. It remains a major regret that I did not do more.

I just hoped that some good would come of this, that this move would give me a more solid base to stand on and announce, loud and clear, that I meant business and that this was going to be an athletic department of integrity that did everything by the book.

Once Craig was dismissed, assistant coach and lifelong Huntington resident Dave Piepenbrink was given the job on an interim basis, eventually being given the job full-time. When the coaching situation was stabilized, I was asked by Cottrill to do a full investigation of the baseball program to see if there was anything else nefarious there. Much to my dismay, there was.

I discovered several more violations of NCAA rules including impermissible summer baseball arrangements (no more than five from any team can play on any one summer team and Marshall was fielding an entire squad of Marshall players), private fundraising that was not being run through the normal university and athletic fundraising process, and the employment of too many baseball coaches.

The last one was the most disconcerting, because I had given approval for the size of the coaching staff. College baseball teams are allowed three paid coaches and one volunteer coach who cannot receive any monies that could be considered compensation for their efforts. There is another little-used exception for student assistant coaches, who are allowed on the staff if they have not graduated and still have eligibility on the five-year eligibility clock. NCAA student-athletes have five years to complete four seasons worth of eligibility, with their "clock" beginning the day they enroll in their first college class.

Antush had a student named Matt Spade who had begun his career at Clemson, and according to the squad list I had on file, still had requisite eligibility to serve as a student assistant coach. I told Craig to go ahead and use Spade in a coaching capacity.

What the existing paperwork didn't tell me is that Matt Spade had played three years in the minor league organization of the Pittsburgh Pirates before he ended up on Craig Antush's staff. The day he had signed his professional contract, his collegiate eligibility was forfeited, and thus he didn't fit the exemption providing for student coaches. This was just one example of how baseball, like most of the department, was a God-awful mess, and I exacerbated it by making the crucial mistake of trusting the information I had been presented and not digging deeper. I accepted responsibility, and received my first letter of reprimand from Lance West.

Unfortunately I would receive more, but I started to assert myself and make it clear to West and Cottrill that if I did not get the help I needed, more mistakes would happen, not only by others, but also by me. I turned out to be a prophet.

CHAPTER 8:

FRIENDS WITHOUT BENEFITS

My first few months at Marshall yielded eight self-reports of NCAA violations across the spectrum of the university's teams, including the one on me related to the student-assistant issue in baseball. Despite the problems, I felt good that we were reporting and fixing mistakes, especially since the NCAA enforcement and infractions arm lauds institutions that self-report and correct.

At the same time, two people in the athletic department were growing overly sensitive about the self-reports. One, not surprisingly, was Bobby Pruett. The size of the football team meant Pruett's program would naturally be subject to the most potential violations, and he had to know that the combination of his ambivalence toward rules, my insistence on following them, and the disorganization of his program in general was bound to have a toxic effect.

I wasn't surprised when Pruett told me he thought we reported too much, though I was a little taken aback when I found that one of his allies was one of the people I had expected to serve as one of my most loyal supporters … Beatrice Crane. Beatrice had been one of the biggest champions of my hiring at Marshall, and when I took the job, I was sure that in addition to being able to count on her friendship and collegiality, she would support my effort to strengthen the compliance program. Beatrice knew the ins, outs, and trials and tribulations of compliance, because she had worked in the field at three different schools, and I had always respected her efforts.

What I hadn't properly gauged, among other elements of her character, was her ambition. Beatrice was so protective of her place on the food chain at Marshall that when I failed, or when someone powerful within the university disagreed with me on an issue either great or small, she always allied herself with the power. Whether her compliance training told her my point of view was right or not, she would rarely even give me the benefit of the doubt.

While the hunger for power was disconcerting from someone I had considered a friend, what became more worrisome to me was that a person with growing influence within the university appeared to me to be personally unstable. Beatrice had a fragile ego and terrible insecurity, traits that were revealed to me during an ugly episode with a colleague of mine, Rick Thompson.

At the time, Rick was serving as Marshall's Associate Vice President for Athletic Development and Director of the Big Green Scholarship Foundation, and Beatrice had fallen for him hard. In Thompson's case, it was another matter altogether. Simply put, Beatrice was a convenient and willing partner, and both broke the cardinal rule of getting romantically involved with a co-worker. Beatrice wanted more, and Thompson wanted nothing that resembled a serious relationship. As he felt Beatrice closing and tried to pull away, Thompson found out the real meaning of the old chestnut, "Hell hath no fury like a woman scorned."

It was soon after their breakup that I began hearing stories from Thompson and his then-assistant and roommate, Dan O'Dowd, that Beatrice was stalking Rick, making threats, and showing up at their apartment at all hours of the night. I just could not bring myself to believe that all of this information about Beatrice was accurate, despite my recent experiences with her. But by now, her sometimes-violent outbursts and threats toward Rick were affecting the entire athletic department. She was making me nervous, and though I should have known better and stayed out of it, I decided to confront her.

I went to Beatrice's office and told her I thought she needed professional help. I had already encouraged Rick to get a restraining order, I told her. But she was far from contrite, telling me, "I swear I will get him back." The Fatal Attraction-style scenario continued, and the stories would grow even more unsettling. There was a rumor in the gossip-rich, close-knit bureaucracy of the university that Beatrice was intervening in job searches at other institutions in order to blackball Thompson, from whom she was determined to get her pound of flesh.

I went back to her office, literally begging her to stop and telling her that she was single-handedly bringing the athletic department down over what was nothing more than a sexual relationship. She was livid.

"I can't believe you're siding with that bastard," she screamed.

To which I replied, "I am only trying to keep you from destroying your life, his life, and this department." With that, she broke down and fell to her knees sobbing, pounding the ground, moaning, "I am going to make him love me … why does he not love me … why?"

This was getting surreal. No matter what tension was brewing between us in athletic department and university circles, at this moment I felt nothing but sympathy and pity for this broken-hearted young woman, not even out of her 20's. I helped Beatrice from the ground, gave her a hug, and helped her clean up her runny mascara. I told her how sorry I was, but that she needed to let him go.

She gruffly thanked me for my concern but said she would do what she had to do. Thompson would eventually escape Beatrice's wrath and land a position at Texas Christian University and continue on with a very successful career at several institutions including Oregon State and Kentucky. I would not be so lucky, as my well-intentioned intervention would only drive the wedge between Beatrice and I in deeper. Her talons were sharpened, and she was ready to attack when the opportunity arose. In the summer of 1998, she was afforded just such an opportunity.

CHAPTER 9:

UNDER THE GUN

IN CONCERT WITH THE major powerbroker Pruett, Crane was arguing that the compliance program was self-reporting too much, and both received some vindication when the MAC infractions committee went after Marshall with a vengeance at a quarterly conference meeting in the spring of 1998.

The infractions committee was comprised of a selection of MAC athletic directors, including Marshall AD Lance West, and faculty athletic representatives from around the conference.[16] At the meeting, held at Northern Illinois University, the committee expressed collective disgust with Marshall in general.

Reacting to the somewhat misleading fact that there were eight NCAA self-reports during 1998-99, when there had been zero the year before, the committee fried us. They were adamant that the increase of eight self-reports was unacceptable, and expressed serious overall concerns from a historical perspective about Marshall. This was a complete miscarriage of responsibility by the MAC and went against the very self-policing processes we were supposed to promote. The university had a tainted history with violations in their past dealings with both the MAC and NCAA, and many league institutions had been reluctant to admit Marshall back to the conference based on this history.

Now, with the football team having stampeded through the league just one year after arriving from I-AA, those prejudices and jealousies were manifesting themselves in this forum. Members of the committee revealed that they were debating calling the NCAA enforcement staff to initiate an investigation of Marshall University athletics, something that was disingenuous and almost unheard of among fellow conference institutions. Hearing all of this, Lance West simply sat and let the committee hammer him. He didn't stand up for the university, for what I was trying to do, nor did he explain that self-reporting actually showed we were doing our job.

It would have been clear to anyone who paid attention that we had laid down the gauntlet in the past year, and were taking rules compliance seriously. The self-reports, the termination of Antush, even my hiring proved that. Yet instead of taking a stand and appealing to the committee that there was a new day at Marshall, a new person in charge of compliance, and a new attitude for the newest/old member of the conference, West put his tail between his legs and let the conference whip us.

West made apologies and attempted to explain, but as I had come to find out, when he did that, he made everything worse. Instead of being praised for improving compliance, which by all rights we should have been, we were annihilated by this committee for violations that had not even made it to the NCAA for review yet.

I was steaming when I heard about it, and could not believe our conference would do something like that when I had been working night and day to try and do things right. I knew first-hand that other compliance programs in the conference were not even touching areas that we did, such as total athletic department control of learning disabled services for student-athletes, yet the league was sending out a message that we were inept at best, renegades at worst.

I demanded that we fight back, at the very least expressing our collective displeasure with the treatment by the MAC infractions committee and their threat of initiating an NCAA investigation. Everyone in power at Marshall told me to calm down and said that as the new kid on the block, we needed to take our lumps. With apparent glee, Pruett and Crane reminded everyone who would listen that we needed to be more cautious in self-reporting, to the extent of "not reporting everything." My blood boiled. I knew if I capitulated here, I would lose control of the program and Marshall would end up right back where I found it, as the worst compliance program in the country. Self-reporting and self-detecting violations was the national standard to demonstrate you had institutional control, and now we were getting punished for it?

I kept the pressure on the committee through Rob Fournier, then-Associate Commissioner for Compliance at the MAC,[17] by insisting that we were not treated fairly and reminding him that self-reporting and self-correcting were actually supposed to be good things. I implored him to convey to the committee that it was a new day at Marshall, and that we needed to give the historical considerations a rest. Surprisingly, Fournier somewhat agreed, and brokered a deal with Infractions Committee chair Dave Jameison, then the FAR at The University of Akron. Fournier would make a site visit to Marshall and report back to the committee on Marshall's progress and my compliance plan, implementation and revision. Fournier also encouraged me to continue self-reporting.

We had bought some time, and dodged a bit of a bullet.

Fournier visited late in the spring of 1998, and the visit went better than I could have imagined.

In spite of three minor misinterpretations on my part during my first two years, Fournier was glowing with praise with regard to my efforts and the efforts of members of the compliance team. In his final report, Fournier wrote, "The work of Dave Ridpath has effectively coordinated many diverse functions within the university that must be directed with a compliance oversight. His organizational skills and personal style has greatly aided the Compliance responsibilities of Marshall University."

To me, his visit confirmed what I was trying to do. I felt that I had really solidified and affirmed my position despite the bumpy road and mistakes along the way, and it appeared that everyone, including football at least temporarily, since they were a bit scared by the MAC infractions committee, was buying in to my program. I truly felt we were turning the corner and becoming a program and institution of integrity.

We still had a few self-reports, but things seemed to stabilize. I wasn't sure if it was because of the collective fear of reporting on the part of the coaches, or if things were actually getting better. Again, I continued to turn myself in for a couple more inadvertent rules misinterpretations. Nothing earth-shattering, but I wanted everyone both inside and outside the university to know that I made mistakes like everyone else, and I would underline this point by sending memos to the entire department with copies to the president, Grose, and Cottrill. I stepped up to the plate and was willing to take whatever punishment I deserved. As the Army taught me, you lead by example.

I was also able to make a change in our Faculty Representative Position. The previous FAR, history professor Robert Sawrey, was too close to the old athletics regime, specifically former AD Lee Moon, and the fact that he despised West and Gilley was unhealthy in my opinion, even if somewhat justified. In addition, it appeared to me that Sawrey was more interested in traveling to games and participating in fun activities like golf tournaments than being an active, engaged FAR that assisted the compliance department. Sadly, many FAR's across the country fit into the former description rather than the latter. I liked Bob as a person and I still do, but I felt to move the program forward, we needed a new person in his position. I pressed Gilley and the university's general counsel, Layton Cottrill, for a change.

President Gilley appointed Linda Wilkinson, the Assistant Provost at the Marshall Community and Technical College, as the new FAR. I respected Linda and was happy with the move, for the time.

Fournier also applauded that move, as well as giving the overall compliance program, and my efforts, a very favorable rating. He had one-on-one meetings with the admissions office, the registrar, Grose, Cottrill, West, Wilkinson and others. The administration, athletic staff, and coaches at Marshall could not say enough good things about me. Everything I did was praised, especially from the administrative offices, which had prior to my arrival grown weary of some of the underhandedness present in the athletic department.

As 1999 continued in the intervening months following the MAC infractions hearing, I had been able to continue developing the program, finishing up a comprehensive compliance manual, initiating monthly rules education sessions for coaches and staff, shoring up athlete employment issues, and tightening up all other areas I could think of. Along with my assistant Dave Reed and other support staff on campus we were continuing to improve the compliance program and climate daily. The various compliance committees in eligibility, financial aid, institutional compliance, and the professional sports council were up and running. The compliance manual had now been in effect for a year along with other policies and procedures. I felt better and better about the program and the direction we were going. We still had secondary violations, though not as many as when I first arrived in 1997.

Still, every time you felt good about yourself, something would slap you in the face. The not-so-funny joke in compliance nationwide is that you are only one phone call away from chaos. How true that statement is.

In early 1999, the biggest crisis was a ticket caravan/football promotion tour gone bad. NCAA rules allowed for coaches and players to barnstorm through the state, or in our case states, to promote the program to would-be ticket-buyers. These meet-and-greet events could be held at commercial locations, but it could not be advertised that players, by name, were going to be at the location. The danger of using a commercial establishment is that they may take additional marketing license to increase foot traffic at their locations. In spite of the immense revenue that college athletes generate at many institutions, the only marketing they can do is for the institution itself.

One of the locations was a West Virginia bank, City National, which made the big mistake of putting the picture of starting quarterback Chad Pennington and other players on the advertisement for their particular event. The ad was not cleared by me, nor would it have been. Exacerbating the problem was how I found out about the violation. I was contacted by Charleston Gazette sports reporter Mitch Vingle, who told me about the advertisement, that he had already called the NCAA to confirm it was a violation, and he wanted my comment. I walked right into this ambush, and should have deferred comment until I confirmed the facts. I didn't know the content of the ad and spoke way too soon without verifying information, a lesson I learned the hard way.

I initially balked at what Vingle said, telling him on the record that we were certainly able to do a ticket caravan, with players and pre-advertisement.[18] While technically correct, such are the nuances of NCAA rules that because the bank had produced the ad, my assertion was wrong, and I had egg on my face. I regretted challenging Vingle because it turned out that he was absolutely right, the advertisement was indeed a violation. The marketing staff had missed it and I could have done more to prevent it, but the fact that I was still woefully understaffed and overworked had contributed greatly to a bad situation.

At this point, though, I had to own up to my mistake. I handled all calls with the media and appeared on a few local radio shows about the incident. It was amazing the coverage that a minor secondary violation created. I was surprised at the uproar, but I felt it better that we handle it head-on and not hide anything. Transparency is best in situations like this, and deep down, I hoped the very public incident would encourage the administration to give me the support I needed to field a compliance program that could better help us handle these situations.

But Crane and West, who teamed up to give me a tongue-lashing, had me exactly where they wanted me. These were two people desperate to protect themselves, so keeping the focus on me and my errors helped to keep them out of the spotlight. Seeing them turn on me for doing the job the way I was supposed to was particularly grating. I stressed that we could implement preventative measures for these types of incidents by increasing the compliance staff, but the constant refrain was "no money," this despite continual raises for members of the football coaching staff and select others. Maybe they thought strengthening the compliance program would result in the discovery of more dirt, which in turn meant more of those dreaded self-reports they didn't think were necessary.

I was quickly losing any respect I had previously held for West, whose biggest sin was a refusal to lead. He was milquetoast all the way, allowing both his superiors and subordinates to drive his thinking, lest he might actually have to make a decision and offend someone. That said, I never felt like Lance was acting, or not acting, out of a sense of intentional malice. He was just clueless, and reacted at times like a child trying to deny he broke a window. Unlike Lance, Beatrice continued to take delight in my struggles for some warped, narcissistic reason, even when she had helped cause some of the problems herself.

This tete a tete with Crane was building toward an eruption and was destabilizing the department. Whatever friendship or professional respect we had for each other had ended with the Thompson incident. Something would happen and she would either want to minimize it or blow it out of proportion, depending on which approach cast her in a more favorable light. This latest issue was a great example, as the person who was arguing that we self-reported too many secondary violations was screaming from the rooftops about our commission of a secondary violation.

At the same time, she would downplay potential major violations and sticky issues involving her close friend and academic advisor Laurie Fox, the one from Marshall's biggest family of benefactors. It was mind-boggling to watch her at work, and she certainly knew how to play the game. Her above-average looks and the female charm she flaunted within the decidedly male-dominated environment of the university didn't hurt. Clearly, I wasn't going to be able compete with that, and it was a losing battle from the start.

Still, on many occasions I would try to take the high road and we would patch things up for the good of the department, even though I knew it would be just a matter of days or weeks before she was at it again. She was once my biggest supporter, but by doing a good job in the eyes of those at the university and the conference, as illustrated in Rob Fournier's report, I had stolen some of her thunder and was apparently a threat to her power base.

In addition to the all-encompassing compliance crap-storm I was dealing with on a daily basis at this university, I now had a full-fledged feud on my hands, and it was growing daily. It turned out that Beatrice Crane would be a tough adversary indeed.

Chapter 10:

Red-Zone Violation

In the world of college athletics, the month on the calendar that inherently includes the most down time is July. Though my office remained relatively busy due to eligibility issues and the daily grind during the month, most of the coaches were out enjoying some final vacation time before the start of the dog days of August, when everything starts back up at a fairly rapid clip.

On this particular Friday afternoon in July of 1999, I was outside scraping my backyard gas grill and getting ready to cook up some burgers to kick off an extended, four-day 4th of July weekend. My cell phone rang. On the line was a colleague and friend, Michelle Duncan, the Director of the Buck Harless Student Athlete Program (BHSAP) at Marshall. The BHSAP was the academic support service that fell under the athletic department umbrella. It was not unusual for Michelle to call - we talked several times a day - though in this case I detected some tension in her voice.

Michelle informed me that she had just had an uncomfortable meeting with Bruce McAllister, who at the time was a faculty member in the Exercise, Sport Science, and Recreation Department (ESSR) at Marshall. McAllister was also assisting with the football program, ostensibly under the direction of the Sports Medicine division, and I was more than familiar with him because as Assistant Athletic Director, one of my ancillary duties was direct supervision of the Sports Medicine department.

Prior to adding his responsibilities within athletics, McAllister was a tenure track professor who was not going to achieve tenure because he had not yet completed the requirements for his terminal degree. Bruce's wife had passed away from cancer the year before, and though he had been given an extension to finish his doctorate due to his wife's illness, he had still not done enough research and grant activity, nor completed his degree, to be awarded tenure. It became apparent that Bruce was not going to be retained as a faculty member, so members of his department began searching for a way for him to remain at Marshall. His direct supervisor and the chair of the ESSR department, Robert Barnett, was a longtime friend of Bobby Pruett. Barnett reached out to Pruett to see if there was anything that McAllister could do within the football program.

In a show of sympathy for the widower's plight, Barnett and Pruett came up with the idea of creating the position of flexibility coach for McAllister, someone who could aid in the stretching and flexibility of all student-athletes, not just the football players. The position was a kind of catharsis and new beginning for Bruce, and he began to get out of his funk. He became a regular fixture in the athletic department. It was like he was not even a professor anymore, as the bulk of his time was spent in the athletic department with the athletes.

But there was resentment and confusion over McAllister's role among our extremely hard-working, underpaid and under-funded athletic training staff. Our head athletic physician, a wonderful and talented man named Dr. Jose Ricard,[19] found out about McAllister's appointment just like most of us in the athletic department … in the newspaper. Even our media relations director didn't know about the arrangement. This was another major disconnect in our dysfunctional department. I found out more stuff that was going on in my department out in the street than I did as an employee.

Problems with Bruce began almost from the start, as he began to assert himself while often usurping the authority of Ricard and the athletic training staff by recommending alternative treatments for injuries. Most famous was a confrontation that the two got into on the sidelines of the 1998 MAC Championship game against Toledo. In the third quarter of that contest, with Toledo clinging to a 7-6 lead, star quarterback Chad Pennington went down with a groin injury that caused a large, bulging contusion. It was so bad that Pennington could barely walk. In came true freshman Byron Leftwich, who proved he wasn't quite ready for primetime by throwing an interception on his first pass attempt of the night.

It was looking bleak for the Thundering Herd, and it appeared that if they were to win this game, Pennington would have to return. McAllister, who some felt had an unhealthy obsession with Pennington in the first place, began to apply direct pressure to the groin contusion as I looked on from a few feet away. According to Ricard, this was the wrong thing to do, and the two argued until

Pennington left the two to their bickering, limped off the bench and forced his way back into the game despite his obvious and continued discomfort. Moments later, the QB threw a 19-yard touchdown pass to wideout Nate Poole, and the Herd were off and running to an eventual 23-17 victory that gave them a second straight MAC championship and another berth in the Motor City Bowl.

In the wake of the victory, McAllister began loudly heralding his own efforts to get Pennington back on the field. And Pruett, who was still looking to ensure that McAllister could become a full-time, salaried member of the support staff, fostered the myth by going into the post-game press conference and referring to McAllister as the "real MVP" of the MAC Championship game. Local media picked up on the angle, and though it was really Chad's toughness and desire to win that saved the team, and McAllister's treatment had in fact been the wrong one, Bruce was becoming a bit of folk hero around Huntington. Ricard and the athletic training staff were furious, as this had not been the only allegation of out-of-line behavior by McAllister.

I had been hearing unsubstantiated, but disturbing rumors that Bruce would perform full body massages on many of the male athletes for no apparent reason. One male soccer player told me he had a bum ankle, yet McAllister asked him to "strip naked" so he could massage other points that were connected to the ankle. I'm no expert in kinesiology, but these stories made me a bit squeamish and worried for the athletes' safety. Although I did not know if the stories were true, something needed to change.

Ricard demanded, and I joined in his demand as athletic department liaison, that Lance West dictate and define what role McAllister would have, if any, with the athletic trainers. Ricard made it clear that McAllister did not have the training nor expertise to overrule the treatment recommendations of him or his staff, and that the well-being of student-athletes was being placed in peril.

The solution offered up by West and Pruett was that McAllister's role would be solely flexibility (as it was supposed to be when he was hired), and that he would now report to head strength coach Mike Jenkins. The fear of alienating a respected physician like Ricard, who perhaps more importantly to West and Pruett was a longtime department benefactor, forced them to mandate that McAllister not be permitted to overrule the doctors or trainers again.

Though this clarification calmed things down, McAllister was nonetheless enjoying his new-found position. He traveled with the team, was given access to every perk, and Pruett made it clear that he was to be treated as a coach. Bruce wore the same coaching apparel as Pruett and his position coaches, and began to spend more and more time in the athletic department. I predicted that despite West's constant mantra about our department's money woes, McAllister would be hired full-time. I was right, as Pruett announced to anyone who would listen in the early summer of 1999 that Bruce would be hired full-time.

That said, though McAllister was viewed by many as a clown who was taking up space within the walls of the athletic department, I didn't worry about his teaching, nor was it my role to monitor academic integrity. But my antennae should have been up over the fact that, after McAllister had gained his volunteer position in athletics, more and more athletes were being steered toward his classes. One summer, his class was all athletes, predominantly football players, except for one female non-athlete named Andrea. That would be Andrea Pennington … Chad's little sister.

My job was not to monitor who was registering for classes and why. That was an academic issue and one I should not be concerned with, unless the athletic department had been actively involved in getting a special benefit for athletes not afforded the rest of the student body. The phenomenon of pushing athletes to certain majors for ease of eligibility was a practice that existed at Marshall then, and still exists on college campuses today, known as "academic clustering." Often friendly faculty will be wined and dined as a go-to professor to assist academically-troubled athletes. Many people see nothing wrong with this, as it is a way to keep athletes eligible to compete, and many times they are a group that needs extra assistance. However, there is something very wrong with the practice, as evidenced by recent scandals at Auburn and Michigan which consisted of athletes taking an inordinate amount of independent study hours, completely out of step with what other students were allowed to do, to maintain enrollment and eligibility numbers. Other notable clustering scandals included schools like Ohio State using multiple elective hours in physical education, sometimes upwards of 40, to keep players eligible. The clustering phenomenon was exacerbated even more by the famous HBO Real Sports interview of former Texas A&M basketball star Antoine Wright.[20] Wright was interviewed on the subject of more than 70% of A&M football and men's basketball players majoring in "Poultry Science." No disrespect to the completely credible major of Poultry Science, but this major had basically been singled out by football and basketball coaches as an easier path to eligibility. Wright made it clear that he was forced into the major, even being told that he would not play if he went into the major of his choice. As Wright memorably put it to interviewer Bryant Gumbel, "I didn't want to know nothing about those chickens."

As basically a defender of the status quo when I worked in the business, I accepted the practice of clustering as a necessary evil. I was buying into the same bill of goods as many college football fans out there, the one that said these kids were getting a legitimate education. In many cases, far too many, that was not nearly the case, and it took my involvement in a scandal to realize how pervasive and wrong this long-accepted practice is. Yet when I worked at Marshall, and since I was not directly involved in academics — ignorance was bliss when it came to McAllister in the classroom. My concern was what he was doing in the athletic department, what he did academically was not my job to supervise, it was Robert Barnett's. Barnett failed miserably in oversight of his faculty, but few faculty want to get in the crosshairs of athletics, lest their own job might be in jeopardy.

Any suspicions I might have harbored about Bruce in the classroom were not fully aroused until I got the phone call from Michelle Duncan on that fateful July day. Michelle began by mentioning that she was worried that McAllister was currying favor to the football players. I asked her why she thought that, and she said in almost a frightened whisper, "He just left my office, but when he came in he put a class roster on my desk, with certain football players' names checked, and he asked me, 'What grades do these guys need to get in my summer class to be eligible in the fall?'"

Michelle said she put on a poker face, told McAllister, "Let me get back to you," and then called me. I knew we had a bit of a problem, if for nothing else than the fact that it was a violation for McAllister to be discussing the eligibility of football athletes with Duncan which absolutely fell under my purview, though what she would say next nearly knocked me off my feet.

She told me that McAllister had been bothering her lately due to a situation with a final exam for a spring semester course he taught called PE 201, Scientific Methods. Duncan went on to say that Bruce had passed out copies of the final exam to certain football players via the weight room, so that these players would be able to pass the final and maintain eligibility.

I couldn't muster the strength to speak, but I do remember grabbing a lawn chair and sitting down, because by this point my knees were literally beginning to shake. I tried to mumble something, but Michelle kept going with her story. It seemed like it was only days ago that I finished up the Weber State case which concerned academic fraud, and here I was again staring a major violations case right in the face.

Duncan said that any potential violation had been nipped in the bud because the night before the test, Missy Frost, an assistant softball coach and also a graduate teaching assistant for McAllister, had fortunately noticed a copy of the final exam in the hands of a women's soccer player by the name of Arica Houvouras. Frost was at the home of her boyfriend, Marshall baseball player Ryan Roush, and Arica happened to be there studying for the PE 201 exam with Ryan's brother Jason. Panicked, Frost asked Houvouras where she got the test, and Houvouras matter-of-factly told her that she got it from men's soccer player Matt Romenello, who had himself received it from an unidentified member of the football team. Romenello had told Houvouras that all the football players in the class had copies of it.

Houvouras believed that the test was a study guide, though Frost was working for McAllister and knew it to be the exact exam. Prior to the test being distributed the next day, Frost hastily made changes to ensure that it wouldn't be identical to the "study guide," but remained extremely uncomfortable with the situation. As a former NCAA athlete and current assistant softball coach, Frost knew this situation could be radioactive, and tried her best to rectify it before it got out of hand. After the exam, Frost approached then-Marshall head softball coach Louie Berndt[21] and asked for advice, because she was afraid she may have been complicit in a case of academic fraud, even though she tried to change the test.

Berndt, who should have immediately sent Frost to me, instead told her to go see ESSR department chair Robert Barnett, McAllister's faculty boss but also the buddy who had, along with Pruett, arranged the flexibility job. Barnett also happened to be the former wrestling coach at Marshall, so he knew a compliance powder keg when he saw one.

Barnett praised Frost for making changes, and said he would talk to McAllister. Barnett later told NCAA investigators that Bruce claimed to not know how the players got the test, or even if they did, because he had simply given out a comprehensive study guide to the players. When Barnett reminded him that every member of the class had to be given the study guide, not just the players, McAllister backtracked and said that everyone had access to it. If someone had the test, McAllister said, then it was probably stolen. In turn, Barnett - who obviously wanted this incident to go away – determined that there was not any way to ascertain if or how the test was leaked. This may have been true, though Barnett's recommendation on the matter was astonishing. Since there was doubt over whether everyone had received the same benefit, i.e. access to the "study guide," Barnett had determined that everyone in the class should receive the same grade on the exam … an A.

At this stage of Duncan's story, I was practically hyperventilating.

Not understanding the magnitude of what had occurred, Michelle said, "Wasn't that great what Missy did? She is a smart cookie and she did the right thing by going to Barnett." Michelle figured that the situation had been expedited within academic channels, and thought the silver lining was that McAllister would be scared into compliance. The test issue wasn't even the reason she was calling, it was his coming to her office and asking for sensitive information that could benefit the competitive eligibility of an athlete that prompted her to call me.

What I said next upset my friend Michelle Duncan greatly.

I took a deep breath and said, "Michelle, we have some big problems, very big problems. I will first address that he cannot speak to you about academic eligibility of football athletes, but the other thing, with the test, is the biggest problem. We are going to have to investigate and report this to the MAC and the NCAA." Michelle shot back and said, "No, Dave, I wasn't even supposed to tell you, and it was already handled by academics."

I replied, "Yes, in theory it was, but there are many other things at play here, like we still have a person working in the athletic department, teaching kids, and potentially giving them benefits that constitute academic fraud, and now he is asking you things like this. Sorry Michelle, but I have to get involved, and you know you should have told me earlier."

She was certainly saddened, terrified of the ramifications of any investigation, but also knew I was right. In an effort to calm her down, I told her that I would say nothing until Tuesday, and we could all just try to enjoy the weekend because there was nothing we could do now, with most of the athletic department gone for the weekend and coaches on vacation during July. She understood, and when I hung up the phone, I let out a pretty hearty "God damn it to hell!", so loud my wife came running outside.

At this stage I had no idea whether McAllister was working alone, or whether he was acting on orders from the coaching staff on either the exam or grade-query issues. Because he had found a new purpose in life, I knew he would do just about anything Pruett and his coaches asked. I also knew that getting straight and truthful answers out of Bruce McAllister and Bobby Pruett was going to be exceedingly difficult.

And I knew that whatever the truth of the matter, all hell was going to break loose when I arrived at work on Tuesday.

CHAPTER 11:

PRIVATE INVESTIGATION

July 6th arrived and I knew it was go-time. While I harbored some faint hopes that I might receive information that would prevent this from becoming a compliance issue, I feared the worst.

My first call was to Linda Wilkinson, who had the year before been appointed Marshall's new Faculty Athletic Representative. Linda was doing a great job in her role, and was someone I knew I could count on at this point in our relationship. I left a message for Linda to call me as soon as she got in the office, and to clear her calendar for the day. She called back a few minutes later and simply asked, "What's up?"

I calmly told Linda the story, and made it clear that we had a very large problem beyond Bruce McAllister pressuring Michelle Duncan for the grade information of football players. If he was indeed advancing copies of the final exam to football athletes via the weight room, there was a possibility that the coaching staff was either directly involved or had prior knowledge this was going on.

Linda quickly realized the gravity of the situation, and said that we should immediately request a meeting with Layton Cottrill, the university's general counsel. I called Layton, who seemed to be in no mood to discuss athletic issues after the long holiday weekend. I told him about the incident, and he instructed Linda and I to come over to his office at Old Main. Before he hung up the phone, Cottrill told me he would "fire that fucking professor today" if these allegations were true. Like the rest of us, Layton was disturbed that no one - not

Robert Barnett, nor Louie Berndt, nor Michelle Duncan, at least immediately - had alerted us to the situation earlier. He shared our worry that the football coaching staff knew about the exam, or had some level of involvement.

At our meeting at Old Main, which in addition to me and Linda included Lance West and Dr. Ed Grose, the university's senior vice President for operations, Linda and I were instructed to investigate. My approach was to start with Pruett, since we had a better chance of getting straight answers from him at the beginning of the investigation than after he had learned of the potential scandal and had a chance to formulate a self-serving exit strategy.

Pruett was in town, and West called him and told him to report to Old Main as quickly as he could. In less than five minutes, Pruett walked into Grose's expansive office and looked stunned to see all of us sitting around a conference table. This was not a look I had seen from Pruett before, he was truly worried. He looked at me and said, "Dave, what is going on?"

I told him to sit down because we had an issue to get to the bottom of. As I went through the scenario, Pruett had a defeated look on his face. When I finished I asked him directly if he knew anything about this. Surprisingly, Pruett admitted that he did.

"I had heard a rumor when I was out recruiting that Danny Derricott (a defensive back on the team) was bragging that he passed a final and had a copy of the test. I asked Mark Gale to check it out, and Gale called me and said that it was a false alarm and it was a study guide … not a copy of the test."

I pressed Pruett, asking him why no one contacted me about the issue, to which he replied that he didn't think there was an issue because it was a study guide, not a final. I moved on to ask Pruett questions about McAllister, his role, and if there had been any pressure on McAllister to assist players academically so they could remain eligible.

Pruett was beginning to get frustrated by this line of questioning and said, curtly, "Hell Dave, I wouldn't know who was in his class or not. He helps us with flexibility and he does a great job." I knew by now that Bob was aware of exactly who was in what class, when they went to class, and what they were doing at literally all times, but after the Motor City Bowl issue I knew I wasn't going to get him to cop to anything, so I moved on to the reality.

"Bob, it is July and even if this is remotely true, we are looking at this class grade being vacated, and that will likely have huge eligibility consequences for many of these players. Clearly, if true, McAllister will be gone."

I also told him about the incident a few days prior with Michelle Duncan. He seemed surprised, but denied that he or any member of his staff prompted McAllister's questioning about grades. He stated his belief that Bruce just wanted to be part of the team, to help in any way he could, and that he likely decided to cross the line on his own. I was not convinced this was true, but it was certainly plausible given the joy Bruce was clearly feeling being affiliated with the football program.

But Pruett was less concerned about McAllister than the issues that could threaten the football eligibility of some of his players, and this became the focus of the meeting. He was getting more and more agitated, because the opening of fall camp was just around the corner and the prospect of losing key players was beginning to sink in.

He couldn't understand why the players would be punished if they had been misled by McAllister into thinking the actual test was a study guide. I spoke up and confirmed that yes, it was possible we would find that McAllister acted alone, preserving the eligibility of the athletes in question, but that we were not yet prepared to make that call. Pruett became more and more animated as reality became clear. Thinking fast on his feet, he asked if all of the players in question could enroll for an additional class during the upcoming five-week summer session, known as D Session, which was set to begin the following week. If the PE 201 grade was indeed invalidated, the players would be able to replace those credits with these new ones.

Although it was clear that he was desperate, it was not a bad idea, given the distinct possibility that the players had been duped by McAllister, who was trying to do them a misguided favor. The NCAA might frown upon the appearance of this pre-emptive measure if they were to get involved, but the players had every right to take more classes if they wanted to, so I agreed that it was a good interim solution. I could tell Pruett was relieved.

As the meeting drew to a close, I told Pruett that he was not to speak with anyone on his staff, most notably McAllister, about this matter until further notice. My goal was to wrap it up as soon as possible so we could have some clarity moving forward, but I made it very clear that McAllister's days at Marshall were likely numbered. Pruett was OK with that, but as he stood up to leave he asked with concern, "Are we going to report this to the NCAA?"

I told him that we did not know at this point if any NCAA rules were broken, and we might be able to handle it in-house as an academic issue, but that it was way too early to tell. I told him I would keep him informed of the investigation, and he said he would get all of his players from the PE 201 class to enroll in Summer Session D immediately, in order to offset any potential problems. After Pruett left, Grose told us he thought it would be appropriate for Linda and me to meet with the president, J. Wade Gilley, later that afternoon. Provost Sarah Denman and Dean of the College of Education, Larry Froelich, would also be present.

Gilley told us that he was glad to be informed, but overall, he didn't seem too concerned. While Gilley had written some articles on intercollegiate athletic reform,[22] he was far from a reform advocate in my opinion. He mostly sided with athletic interests at Marshall, and took no affirmative steps nationally to change the system. Not surprisingly, he wouldn't be getting his hands dirty here either. As it happened, he had just accepted the president's job at the University of Tennessee, and most of his office was already packed for the trip to Knoxville. (Gilley would later find himself embroiled in controversy at Tennessee as allegations of academic fraud surfaced in the storied Volunteer football program in the fall of 1999. Gilley would soon resign from UT, in the wake of both this incident and the discovery of an inappropriate relationship with a female subordinate.[23]) The McAllister issue would not be his to deal with, though he directed Denman and Froelich to conduct a separate academic investigation of the allegations. Denman and Froelich agreed to not talk to or tip off McAllister until after we talked to him, and we all agreed that we would keep one another abreast of our findings.

Linda and I cleared everything for the rest of the week and set a schedule for interviews, with the goal of at least having a preliminary report by close of business in just three days, on Friday, July 9th. Time was of the essence because we wanted to prevent any leaks, and also wanted time to deal with any eligibility issues both inside the football program and with the other student-athletes that had been in the class.

Before we talked to McAllister and the football athletes, we wanted to speak with Missy Frost,[24] Robert Barnett, Louie Berndt, Mark Gale, Michelle Duncan, Frost's close friend and former Marshall softball player Laura McLaurin, and Arica Houvouras. At this point the order was not overly important, but we felt it would be better to speak with everyone else before we spoke with McAllister or the athletes, to confirm or refute what our suspicions were. We rapidly went through interviews over the next day and a half, starting with Missy Frost.

We reached Missy by phone in her hometown of Centerville, Ohio. She was very emotional when we called her and informed her why we needed to speak with her. You could tell that she feared something like this might happen, and was feeling guilty even though she had done her level-best to try to rectify someone else's transgression. Frost pretty much confirmed what Duncan had told me in our initial conversation, and said that although she suspected it would be best to contact me or someone else in athletics, ESSR department chair Barnett had assured her this was an internal academic issue and needed to go no further.

Next was Gale,[25] who stated that he confronted Derricott about allegedly having the test. Derricott told Gale that though very similar to the test, it was a study guide and was always referred to as such by McAllister and the players. Like Pruett, Gale told me he accepted that it was indeed a study guide and did not call me for this reason. He saw it more as Derricott spouting off than a real problem.

Houvouras will always be one I feel sorry for, as she was in the wrong place at the wrong time. She was a local Huntington resident who had returned to Marshall after beginning her soccer career at East Tennessee State, and really had no idea what was unfolding when she got a copy of the test from Romenello, the men's soccer player. She said she always thought it was a study guide, but admitted being surprised when the test, other than Missy's small changes, was exactly the same.

Next we reached Barnett, the former chair of the ESSR department, who was on vacation and also on sabbatical for the semester. He confirmed everything that had been said up to this point, and also said his feeling was that this was an internal department issue that did not need to involve the athletic department. I semi-admonished him, given that he had been an NCAA coach, reminding him that any time athletes were involved, I had to be notified to determine if NCAA rules had been broken. He apologized, but also said he believed he was following university protocol with regard to potential academic misconduct, even to the extent of the eventual awarding of A's to all who took the final exam. He did mention that he felt Bruce was too close to the athletes, and that if he wasn't leaving the school after his one year terminal contract, he would have spoken to McAllister about it.

So far, all of the explanations seemed plausible, but D-Day was fast approaching for McAllister. Late Wednesday afternoon, I called the interim chair of ESSR, Ray Busbee (who was acting in Barnett's absence), and informed him that I needed to speak with McAllister regarding a sensitive issue, and that he needed to be at my office door at 4:30 that day, no excuses. The word was quickly passed to Bruce, who immediately sought out Michelle Duncan to ascertain why I was summoning him. Michelle informed me that she played it cool, but said it had something to do with his spring class, the one Missy was a GA for. While I did not want Bruce tipped off, this revelation was not fatal because there was not a lot of time for him to prepare.

Linda and I arrived at my office, and Busbee and McAllister were waiting at the door. After we all sat down and exchanged pleasantries, McAllister immediately started talking quickly. "I think I can clear this up. Apparently there is a rumor that I gave a test out to football players and what it was in reality was a study guide…" I interrupted.

"Whoa, Bruce. Stop, let me say a few things before we start." I needed to tell him the purpose of the interview, the sensitivity and importance of what we were about to discuss, and needed his consent to tape-record. He agreed, and I spent a few minutes discussing what we had deduced up until that point. Not being a professional interrogator nor really trained in the practice, I wasn't sure how to go about it, but immediately started to muscle him and appeal to his love of the program and the athletes.

I told him that it appeared to me and Linda that he purposely gave the test to select football players to give them an academic advantage, a charge that he immediately denied. Then I brought up the meeting he had with Michelle a few days before, telling him that the impropriety of a faculty member soliciting grade information about football players made the subsequent allegation of distribution of the exam easy to believe. He continued to deny, and was beginning to get frustrated and defensive.

Linda forcefully chimed in.

"Bruce, we know it was the exact test, it was not a study guide." At this point, Busbee felt the need to come to his friend's aid, and questioned our authority to even interview him. I let Busbee know that we were working under the direction of the president, and if that he had a problem, he could talk to Dr. Gilley.

While that calmed Busbee down a bit, he still questioned why we were infringing on the academic freedom of a professor who could give out the test if he wanted to. I looked Busbee right in the eye and said, "It's true that that's his right ... if everyone got the test. Our investigation strongly suggests that is not the case." Busbee was silent. Now it was McAllister's turn to get animated, and I had to calm him down.

I asked, "Bruce, did the coaches direct you to do this? Did the athletes?"

"Nobody directed me, I do this in all my classes," he stammered.

I still had some belief that the coaching staff may have played a role in the incident, but my motivation at this point was to rid the department, and the university, of Bruce McAllister. His presence on campus and within the athletic department could only be poisonous. We were about to close and I decided to appeal to his conscience.

I said, "Bruce, if you did this alone and no coaches or players were involved, our penalties will likely not be as severe, but if you keep on denying this we will have a larger investigation that might result in suspensions, forfeitures, bad publicity. So if you did this ... is there something you want to say to me?" He continued to deny, but not as forcefully. He asked about player suspensions. I told him that we might have to suspend players until we got to the bottom of it, because if he did not do it, then maybe a player stole the test.

He hung his head. He continued to meekly claim that it was a study guide, and shook his head no. His eyes were beginning to glisten with tears. I knew we had him. Once I told him others could be penalized, his conscience finally caught up to him. If he indeed was acting alone and trying to endear himself to Pruett and the coaching staff, he would fess up, and I predicted it would happen soon. Linda agreed, but we both still wondered what Pruett and the other coaches knew, if anything. There would be more interviews on Thursday, most notably with the football athletes who were in the class.

I was in the shower the next morning, a little before 7:00 am, when my wife yelled into the bathroom that coach Pruett was on the phone and that he said it was urgent. This was not unusual, since Pruett would call at all hours and had seemed especially troubled by, and communicative during, the investigation. Earlier in the week, he had come to my house during the evening hours, as I was moving some furniture inside. Before I knew it, Bobby Pruett was helping me move furniture into my house, and the whole neighborhood was outside watching. Being head football coach at Marshall was certainly a lofty position in our little world, and the sight of him helping me with a couch was priceless.

I stepped out of the shower and grabbed the phone from my wife. As soon as I said hello, Bob said, "Dave, Bruce was just here, at my house, on my porch. He told me it was his fault, he was sorry for his mistake, and he is going to resign."

I couldn't say anything except, "Wow." Bob said that Bruce was crying and was remorseful, but Pruett told me he said, "Bruce, you have put me and my program in jeopardy, and you have to go." He said that Bruce tried to hug him and that he gave him a half-hearted hug and left. I asked Bob if Bruce said anything else, and he said he didn't.

On the surface, things were falling into place. I was bothered that he would go to the football coach to resign, and that no one would know exactly what was said on Pruett's porch, but I was convincing myself that McAllister did indeed act alone. Bruce's mental state was not that good in the wake of his wife's death, and I knew that the importance of the football program's place in his life could have prompted him to go too far. I also knew that coaches could be stupid when it came to gaining an advantage, but I did not believe Pruett and his staff would be stupid enough to direct a professor to distribute a final exam to a group of players. While it was plausible, it was not probable.

As I hung up the phone, I really thought this was good news. This may be just an internal issue after all and there may not be any NCAA rule violations, I thought. I was happy as I picked up the phone to call Linda and Layton. They both felt the same way. We determined to move forward with the interviews of the athletes, and to see if McAllister was going to follow through on his resignation.

The football athletes provided no different information than what we had found already. They were told they were receiving a study guide and they had no reason to believe that not everyone had it. We informed all of them to register for at least one more class during D session just to be safe, although part of me was beginning to think it was not necessary. That same Friday, Provost Sarah Denman called to inform us that Busbee and McAllister were heading over to Old Main, and that Bruce was indeed going to resign his position.

Later, Linda and I met with Denman and Froelich to finalize the items in the report. The conclusions reached in their investigation on the academic side were identical to ours. While in the College of Education offices my cell phone rang, and it was Cottrill telling me that a local lawyer by the name of Lafe Chaffin informed him he was representing McAllister, and that he would like to meet with us on Monday, July 12th in the morning in order to formalize his "confession." Cottrill felt that would be good, for us to get it straight from his mouth. I informed Linda and Sarah what was going on and we all agreed to wait on issuing the report until Cottrill and I met with McAllister after the weekend.

I certainly had a better weekend than the one before. In the span of less than three days we had completed an investigation, and McAllister was gone. I felt pretty good that we had managed to avoid a situation that could have been disastrous to the football program and university. The sports medicine staff was ecstatic that McAllister was gone. It seemed like we were near the end, and I went home for the weekend feeling a sense of accomplishment.

On Monday morning Cottrill and I made the short drive from campus to downtown Huntington and the law offices of Chaffin and Lowry, for what would turn out to be a short meeting. As we sat down in an expansive conference room, Chafin, an elderly man with wispy white hair, opened the meeting by saying, "I am here to represent Mr. McAllister. I love Marshall University, but I told him if there is anything he knows it is in his best interest to spit it out right now. So Mr. McAllister, please spit it out."

Bruce sat directly across from me at the conference table, and I never took my eyes off of him. He calmly said that he knew what he had distributed to players was the exam, and that he had given them the test in order to help them with their grades. He went on to say how sorry he was, and how he felt the only solution was to resign.

Cottrill spoke up and said, "Mr. McAllister, I need to know this in no uncertain terms … did you do this of your own volition? Did anyone cajole you, offer you anything in return, for doing this?" I felt it was best for Cottrill to drive the questioning, so I did not say anything. "Absolutely not," McAllister said, while raising his hand to reinforce the mea culpa. Cottrill said that was all he needed to know. I said nothing.

We all got up and shook hands. While Bruce was shaking mine, he told me again how sorry he was. I believed that he was, and I believed for the most part that he acted alone. While I still had suspicions of coach involvement, whether by Pruett or his assistants, McAllister had confessed and I felt a tremendous sense of relief.

With the confession in place, we now had to determine whether the incident rose to the level of a NCAA violation. I was unsure, but I knew it needed to be addressed and if it was a violation, we were going to report it, regardless of who protested. On the ride back to campus, I told Cottrill that while I had felt initially that we had a violation, I now believed this to be an internal academic problem that we handled according to university policies and procedures. I felt our investigation revealed beyond a shadow of a doubt that no athlete had knowingly received an impermissible benefit. I mentioned that there was precedent of the NCAA reviewing matters like this and rubber-stamping the efforts of the universities in question, but I did not think that we needed to contact the NCAA unless absolutely necessary. Not because we had anything to hide, but because it had already been adjudicated within my interpretation of NCAA guidelines. I returned to my office feeling safe that we did not need to report this.

But not everyone agreed, and word was beginning to leak outside the university about the incident. My former assistant, Dave Reed, who had just accepted an internship at the University of Cincinnati, had been talking too loudly about what had occurred to colleagues around the MAC. The news got back to MAC associate commissioner Rob Fournier, who told me Reed, probably just trying to feel important, had been spreading the word. This damaged our credibility, because the conference office had been tipped off that we might have a problem before we could determine for sure whether it needed to be reported. Now, thanks to Reed – who was a state away and really had no idea what was going on – we were playing catch-up with the MAC. I was pissed at Dave and told him so, but I wrote it off as youthful exuberance and as a stupid mistake.

Fournier called me on another issue later in the week and casually brought up that he had heard we were having issues. I told Rob we did indeed have a situation, but we believed that it had been handled properly. I gave him the thumbnail version of events, and he said he was not convinced that there were no NCAA rules violated. We went back and forth, until I said that we had not ultimately decided what to do, and that we would certainly report it through the appropriate channels if we ultimately concluded it necessary.

I was disappointed in Rob's view on the matter, but accepted that my opinion wasn't necessarily the right one, and that I needed to get more people involved so we could take the correct course of action. Now that the MAC knew, it was going to be checked out whether we wanted them to do it or not. Even if I was convinced there were no NCAA rules violations, we needed some outside confirmation. This wasn't about me, it was about Marshall, and ensuring that we continued to do things the right way.

Not surprisingly, Beatrice Crane didn't fully agree with my take on the incident either, though to her credit, she provided a constructive suggestion without being overbearing about it. Beatrice suggested we call in someone from the outside to evaluate the matter, just to cover our bases, and mentioned that maybe we should call the law firm of Bond, Shoeneck & King[26] to conduct a review. I was familiar with the firm because one of their attorneys, Rich Hilliard, was a former NCAA investigator who I had worked with during my time at Weber State, when we were up before the committee on infractions. Even though he was part of the team investigating us, I had a good rapport with Hilliard and was continually praised by him and the other investigators during those hearings. In spite of my deteriorating relationship with Crane and my initial concerns about bringing someone in from the outside, I told her that this was an excellent suggestion that would get us the outside verification we now needed.

Hilliard had subsequently left the NCAA and gone into private law practice when the organization moved its operation from Kansas City to Indianapolis. With his "local" knowledge of the NCAA process as a former investigator of 15 years, it was easy to determine that he could help us. I also wanted to leverage our friendship into having an ally fight for Marshall against the NCAA, if it came to that.

At a subsequent meeting including Cottrill, Grose, Denman, Pruett, Crane, West, and Wilkinson, I was given clearance to contact Hilliard and contract him to evaluate our report of the academic fraud matter. Grose raised the prospect of cost, but Cottrill figured it would be an hourly rate and that it shouldn't take more than a few hours for someone to analyze this. Cottrill, a lawyer himself, joked that lawyers would typically go slow and pad their hours anyway. We all laughed, but agreed to do this.

It was great reconnecting with Hilliard, who signed on at the rate of $120 an hour and seemed excited to work with me again. What I really did not compute at the time was the immense conflict of interest that firms like BS&K present when they work on infractions cases. Many who work for these firms, like Hillard, were once employed by the NCAA, and usually in enforcement, the very group they were now fighting against. It was a strange scenario, as many still interacted and carried on friendships with NCAA enforcement people. It was a professionally incestuous situation where backroom deals could and did happen frequently. Logically this arrangement is doomed to fail, and often results in both sides coming to a detente and agreeing to protect those who are deemed most valuable to institutions while shifting blame to lower-level employees like assistant coaches who will never fight back due to the damage it might do to their careers. Both sides benefit tremendously, in that the NCAA perpetuates the myth that it is actually policing itself and enforcing the rules uniformly, while these law firms get paid handsomely for their efforts. That there might be some collateral damage is really of no concern — saving face and public relations rules all.

Of course I did not feel this way back in 1999, when I contacted Hilliard to assist us. I believed the PR spin, so much so I would later pay for my staunch support of the system. In the beginning Hillard seemed to be a benefit for us and it was nice to have someone who on the surface appeared to be very supportive of my efforts. His initial impressions were more than reassuring, too. His analysis confirmed our own findings, and stated that any involvement by coaches and athletes was not persuasive. On the downside, he did say that in his opinion we had two secondary violations - an extra benefit for the football athletes, as well as unethical conduct on the part of McAllister. He advised us to self-report these items to the MAC in accordance with procedures.

I was nervous about going to Fournier, who I didn't always trust to judge Marshall objectively, but agreed that this solution offered good middle ground. We would report two secondary violations, and concurrently take strong corrective measures to include the professor resigning. All future hires - whether volunteer, work study, part-time, or full-time - would have to go through a compliance orientation, a situation that would only help my office long-term. In addition, we would not allow faculty members to hold any position in the athletic department ... another win-win for us. I confidently filed this self-report with Fournier in August, convinced that it would be accepted by him and we could finally move on.

More than a month later, just after the Marshall football team moved to 4-0 (including a monumental win at Clemson) with a 34-0 drubbing of Temple, I finally heard from Fournier and new MAC commissioner Rick Chryst on the issue. They said there were some additional questions they wanted answered regarding this situation, and that Fournier was going to forward the questions to me.

To say I was pleased to hear this would be a lie. I pressed them both into telling me what the problem was. We had this reviewed, we fired the professor, what could be wrong? After not hearing from the MAC for over a month following our self-report, I really thought this was over. It turned out Fournier wanted tons of information, and many of his questions took cheap shots at our investigation, including our retaining of Hilliard, and the fact we didn't ask Fournier for help. Fournier's ego and the feelings of others in the MAC toward Marshall were getting in the way of truly finding out if there were violations. The letter Fournier sent made it clear that he was going to make sure we reported something major, not just minor secondary violations.

To me, the MAC's queries were a combination of Fournier's hurt feelings for being kept out of the loop, and his attempt to exact revenge over the fact that Marshall had campaigned overtly for someone other than him to become commissioner when Jerry Ippoliti retired earlier that year. (Fournier had been acting commissioner for a period of months until Big East assistant commissioner Tom McElroy accepted the job. McElroy had a change of heart three days after taking the position and the league's second choice, Chryst, was named to the post).

Still, whatever the politics of the situation, we had to respond. I gathered everyone together again, and Linda Wilkinson, Rich Hilliard and I were tasked with answering Fournier's questions. The three of us were thorough and detailed in our response, and the conclusions were the same: we felt we had two secondary violations. We sent in this report hoping for the best, though that's not what happened.

It was not too many days later that Fournier sent Lance West and interim president Michael Perry letters stating that our situation was considered to be comprised of potential major violations, and that it would need to be reviewed by the MAC infractions committee at their October meeting. I was beside myself when I found out, but we were also not in any position to argue. We would have to go and plead our case in front of this committee, a committee that was usually hostile toward us. Crane was now a member of the committee, but based on my previous dealings with this group, I was very skeptical of Marshall getting fair treatment. The only bright spot was that Fournier was moving on from his position in compliance (he would become athletic director at Division II Wayne State in 2000), and in his place an old acquaintance by the name of Dell Robinson,[27] formerly of the Western Athletic Conference, would be taking over as Associate Commissioner. Unfortunately, Fournier had already set things in motion and the MAC committee was going to see it through.

My skepticism was growing, but Hilliard felt we had a shot at convincing this committee to accept our findings. I was worried, given the prevalent attitude toward Marshall in the league, that the MAC hearings in Cleveland would be little more than a way station en route to a larger-scale NCAA investigation.

I was right. Though our trio was better-prepared to present our case than the group of ADs and FARs was at interrogating us, the results of the hearing were a fait accompli. Fournier had pounded such an anti-Marshall sentiment into many members of this committee that we probably never had a chance. In spite of our best efforts, the MAC Infractions Committee informed us they were not going to make a determination, and our report was being forwarded to the NCAA Enforcement Staff for their review. I was disappointed, but

Hilliard thought that once we took the fight away from the MAC and its prejudices, and into the NCAA arena, we would have a real chance of avoiding major violations.

In January of 2000 it became official. To open the new millennium, and only days after Marshall football had capped off the 1999 season by going a perfect 13-0 and destroying BYU in the Motor City Bowl, new university president Dr. Dan Angel received a preliminary letter of inquiry from the NCAA. This meant, in layman's terms, "We are not saying you did anything, but we are coming to find out for sure."

The NCAA investigation was on, and there was no stopping it now.

CHAPTER 12:

THE MASTERPLAN

IN JANUARY OF 2000, just as the NCAA was notifying Marshall that it would soon be paying the university a visit, Randy Moss was finishing up a brilliant second season with the Minnesota Vikings.

Not yet 23 years old, the former Marshall star had led the Vikings back to the NFC playoffs during a 1999 season in which he caught 80 passes, scored 12 touchdowns and set a franchise record with an eye-popping 1,413 receiving yards.

All of the questions and concerns about his character that had followed Moss into the league - and there had been several - had by now been dwarfed by his stunning on-field exploits, and the 19 NFL general managers that had passed on Moss in the 1998 Draft (including the brain trust of the Cincinnati Bengals, who passed on him twice) before the Vikings nabbed him at No. 21, were at this point looking mighty silly.

Moss had been kicked out of two of the most storied programs in college football for his behavior off the field, and it was those incidents that many of those NFL people just couldn't bring themselves to forget. After being called "the greatest high school athlete I [have] ever seen" by head coach Lou Holtz, Moss signed a letter-of-intent to play for Notre Dame in 1995. But before he ever got to campus, Moss was charged with criminal battery stemming from a racially-fueled fight at his high school, DuPont High, which left one person hospitalized. Moss pled guilty and received probation along with a 30-day suspended jail sentence, prompting Notre Dame to revoke his scholarship offer.

Moss transferred to Florida State, a school with a reputation of looking the other way on boorish behavior, but Moss couldn't keep clear of trouble in Tallahassee either. In 1996, Moss violated his probation by testing positive for marijuana, and was sentenced to an additional 60 days in jail. Florida State showed him the door.

After striking out at two legendary I-A schools, Moss was all but radioactive in the world of college football, the most infamous college football player who had never played a down of college football. That was when Marshall, a school roughly an hour from Moss's home in West Virginia, came calling. Marshall was still a member of I-AA, and NCAA rules wouldn't prevent him from playing in 1996 as they would have if he chose to transfer to a I-A school. The fact that the university would be a member of I-A by 1997 was immaterial.

With the Thundering Herd, the star 6-foot-4, 200-pound receiver with blazing 4.25 speed would find a soft place to land. And there wouldn't be a whole lot of hue and cry from the university community over Moss' arrival. After all, the team's history of taking student-athletes who were "damaged goods" had led to a lot of winning football during the 90's.[28]

Some of the players Marshall University brought to its football program had disciplinary issues in their background, and needed a second, or in Moss' case a third, chance at playing college football while pursuing the seductive dream of a pro football career. But more often, the questionable kids the school was admitting were good, decent young men who happened to be major academic risks with very little chance of succeeding in a university atmosphere that exploited their abilities without offering much in the way of a beneficial education in return.

When Jim Donnan arrived in Huntington in 1991, He did not come to be a caretaker or Father Flanagan, he came to win football games. Donnan thought he could build Marshall into a national power, and theorized that bringing in top-flight athletes, regardless of academic standing, would be the quickest way to make the Herd a I-AA powerhouse.

Donnan had a simple strategy - bring in players that could play anywhere, but could likely not get academically eligible anywhere. New NCAA rules at the time made it difficult for the larger, more accomplished institutions to bring in athletes who did not meet the new NCAA initial eligibility standards.

Enter Marshall University, a school with higher aspirations than being a glorified community college, at least from a standpoint of athletics. The football program had begun to win some games under Stan Parrish and George Chaump, and had also started to generate some regional and local buzz. Donnan was brought in to capitalize on that, and the administration gave him the green light to bring in the players he needed to win. His ability to do this would be made easier by the fact that Marshall had an "open enrollment" policy. Even more important than that factor was the arms-wide-open acceptance of "Props."

Prop was short for Proposition 48, the legislative proposal, and later-approved rule (NCAA 14.3), that designated athletes who due to academic shortcomings were ineligible for practice, competition, and athletic financial aid during the initial year of residence. These athletes, also called "non-qualifiers," could come to college if they met the university entrance requirements or special admission exceptions, but could not participate in athletics during the freshman year if they did not meet NCAA initial eligibility standards.

Many institutions would not accept non-qualifiers on their campuses and/or let them be affiliated with football or any other team. The larger and more established football-playing institutions such as those in the Southeastern Conference, had the luxury of being able to turn away blue-chip athletes if they were academically deficient. These schools could always find someone as good or better to fill the slot.

But mid-major schools like Marshall did not have that luxury. For Donnan, Pruett, and to a lesser extent the basketball program under former head coach Billy Donovan and his successor Greg White, these players became the lifeblood of their sports, and directly impacted the fortunes of both the teams and their coaches.

These non-qualifiers, numbering well over 100 covering the span of a decade-plus, were brought in with regularity to Huntington and warehoused for a year to meet academic requirements in preparation for hitting the field the next season. These athletes could not practice or receive scholarship money, but they could attend team meetings and functions, receive academic assistance via the athletic academic advising center, and work out in the athletic weight room.

Many of the names on the self-report following the Motor City Bowl – the players who weren't listed on the official travel list - were current and/or former Prop 48 athletes. The football coaching staff, specifically Coach Pruett, could not seem to remember who was or was not on the team. Like his predecessors, Pruett gave his staff free reign to invite props to campus, and if these kids finished the academic year eligible, they would be brought onto the team.

Pruett confirmed this practice soon after my arrival at Marshall, and emphasized he saw nothing wrong with "giving a kid a chance." When I informed him that these kids were as much a part of the team as anyone in the eyes of the NCAA, and that they had to be on the squad list and monitored, he was incredulous. Pruett claimed not to have known the rules previously, and mentioned that my predecessor had told the coaches they did not need to worry about the props. I initially gave the staff the benefit of the doubt due to changes within the compliance program, but made it clear that the days of just inviting props to campus was over, and there was now a strict roster management/monitoring process and all additions and deletions had to come through my office. The roster issue may have been my cross to bear, but the kids in the prop category had much tougher challenges.

Since 99% of the props that Marshall admitted in all sports were disadvantaged African-American males, there was a constant concern as to how these young men would finance their educational costs. Money from parents or family members was typically non-existent, as were academic scholarships and other university aid. Most qualified for federal aid in the form of Pell Grants and student loans, but there was still a funding gap. Meanwhile, football and men's basketball needed these players in order to compete, and the coaches weren't allowed to just hand them a wad of cash to help make ends meet.

The most logical thing for them to do, since they did not have practice and game responsibilities during their first year, was to get a job. Of course, with the NCAA involved, it was never that simple.

In 1997, the NCAA membership voted to overhaul existing NCAA employment legislation and allow college athletes to hold a job during the academic year. The stipulations were many and initially very misunderstood, so much so that implementation of the new rules was delayed an additional year to be revised and studied further by the membership and specific committees.

The basic intent of the legislation was to allow those athletes who had completed a year of residence (finishing the first academic year) the opportunity to work up to the value of a full scholarship, plus $2000. This meant a full scholarship athlete could earn a maximum of $2000, while a partial scholarship athlete could earn $2000 plus the difference between the scholarship money they were receiving and the value of a full scholarship.[29]

Freshmen on full scholarship could not work, and those on partial rides could earn only up to the value of the full scholarship - not the additional $2000 that sophomores and beyond could earn. Freshmen walk-ons - the category that the props fell into - could earn up to the value of the scholarship, but could not earn the additional $2000 until after their first year of residency.

That was not all. There were also stipulations on where student-athletes could work, and how they got the job. If the job was in the athletic department, the money counted as scholarship dollars, and would cut into the school's limits for number of scholarships. The same went for players who got jobs in which "athletics interests intercede[d]" in helping them secure employment. If a coach, or other athletic interests such as boosters helped you get the job, the earnings were to count as scholarship dollars.

In Marshall's case, none of the props were counting against NCAA scholarship limits, and none of their earnings was counting against the university's funding of scholarships. As I would come to find out, almost by accident, while preparing for the NCAA's visit in early 2000, Marshall was skirting these rules, and had been for some time. And though it might have been a stretch to argue that the Bruce McAllister situation provided the football team with a tangible competitive advantage, it would soon become clear that the relationship between Marshall's Prop 48 athletes and an impermissible off-campus employment arrangement had been a vital component of the team's recruiting, and by extension success, over the past decade.

The seed of my discovery of the prop job program had occurred in 1998. It was at that time, after putting out dozens of other fires within the compliance program, and after the NCAA had clarified the new job rules, that I was finally able to achieve the goal of getting a program for the monitoring of athlete employment off the ground. Knowing I needed some help to get it started, I was able to hire Keri Simmons, an injured women's basketball player at Marshall, to pitch in. Keri was with me for only a few weeks, but did a masterful job with very little guidance. She developed a first-class employment brochure and monitoring forms, and implemented specific protocol to handle the development, maintenance, and monitoring of the program.

Unfortunately, Keri left me after just a couple of weeks, taking a great opportunity to become an assistant women's basketball coach at College of Charleston. I was left alone again wondering how I was going to cover all of the bases relative to athlete employment monitoring, but knew that unless I found a way to get it done, Marshall was essentially a ticking time bomb.

Little did I know that the bomb had already exploded, it was just being covered up.

After Keri had helped develop the program, it was time to go to the coaches and start informing them about the employment procedures, given that the new rules were finally going into effect. I wanted to start with a football meeting, and I needed the entire staff there. Pruett agreed and asked me to come in on a Sunday, during fall football practice, since it would be easier to get all the coaches together. I agreed and worked on my presentation, which included the NCAA-provided video and several written documents. Following the video, I proceeded to go over any scenario I could think of to illustrate how this was going to be monitored.

On top of prior approval from my office, all employment for players would be monitored by my then-newly-hired graduate assistant, Dave Reed, and the monitoring process would require forms from the employer, employment spot-checks on-site, and review of pay documents (we required payment in check or money order).

Pruett spoke up, "What about the props?"

I stated clearly what I had always stated to all coaches with regard to prop athletes and for other athletes. Props could work, but they could only earn up to the amount of the full scholarship, the employment could not be specially arranged, the players had to be paid the going rate for like services, the job could not be promised in recruiting, and most importantly — all jobs, for all athletes had to be cleared by me first. I was clear and unambiguous on this - multiple times.

"By the way," I asked, "Do we have any props working now?" It worried me a bit that Pruett had asked the question, and I wanted to make sure there was something I hadn't missed. Pruett stated that the props worked during the summer earning money, but that he did not really want them working the academic year so that they could concentrate on academics and get eligible. But Bob still seemed a little unclear about this issue, and continued to press me on the prop issue.

I emphatically stated again that all rules applied to the props that applied to the rest of the kids, and that all employment had to be certified by me prior to any commencement of work, because there might be nuances to take care of in the case of each individual. I added that if any props were working, they needed to report to me immediately. I was paid no visits by any football players, props or otherwise, in the ensuing days.

A few weeks later I held a meeting with the entire football team, including all of the props on the squad list, and told them the same thing I had told the coaches. I emphasized that employment would only be approved if it was at the going rate for like work performed, with no special arrangements. I also mentioned that Dave Reed and I would be monitoring all employment activities. No player said anything at that meeting that raised any red flags, and I thought little more about the prop-job issue, or any props working, for that matter, until weeks before the NCAA was due to make their visit.

As February of 2000 approached, the investigation was drawing near. I continued to follow all directives from Rich Hilliard as far as planning for the anticipated week-long visit of the investigators. I was told by Rich that the NCAA investigator assigned to our case would be Cris Sexton, who had recently been promoted to Director of Enforcement, along with a new investigator by the name of LuAnn Humphrey.

Sexton and Humphrey were both assistant district attorneys by trade, Sexton in South Carolina and Humphrey in Indiana, and both had tired of the prosecutorial grind and found that working at the NCAA was more fulfilling and fun. Like many NCAA enforcement officials, neither had ever worked in a college athletic department, and it didn't seem to me that either was very well-suited to investigate Marshall considering the nuances of intercollegiate athletics with which they were very unfamiliar, for all practical purposes. To me, this has long been a major flaw in the system, as it is tough dealing with people who have virtually no understanding of your day-to-day responsibilities.

Sadly, this was par for the course with the NCAA national office, a place I had come ever-so-close to working myself. The NCAA is infamous for hiring very inexperienced individuals for very important jobs in the name of diversity and equal opportunity, and it appeared to me that both Sexton and Humphrey had their positions because of this practice. There were more seasoned investigators on the NCAA enforcement staff in 2000 then these two and certainly better people they could have hired for these positions, and in that respect, I felt that Marshall had already received the raw end of the deal.

Hilliard wanted me to contact Sexton and Humphrey directly to establish rapport, and ensure that they had everything they needed for the upcoming visit. I had already exchanged cordial e-mails with Sexton when Humphrey requested that I call her to chat about an itinerary for the visit. In late January 2000, I telephoned Humphrey at her office in the new palatial NCAA headquarters in Indianapolis. We had a very pleasant conversation.

Humphrey briefed me on the interview schedule, and I asked what they might need in terms of hotel rooms, transportation, etc., all of which she politely declined. All I was to do was notify the students, coaches, and others involved with the McAllister investigation of their required presence to be interviewed, and to supply a venue to do the interviews.

With that out of the way, we swapped war stories. I knew that Humphrey was a former officer and Judge Advocate General in the Air Force, and when I told her I used to be an Army officer myself, she seemed genuinely interested in my history. I was beginning to feel a sense of relief, thinking that we would have a fair, impartial observer, and that my development of goodwill during that initial phone call could only help. But as the phone call was wrapping up, LuAnn mentioned she had another thing to talk to me about. I was intrigued. Humphrey said, "Dave, just so you know, we have become aware of other issues that we need to look into."

My heart sank, and I asked, "What issues are you talking about?"

She stated that she was not permitted to discuss these issues due to NCAA rules and investigative procedures (which was not really the case, the fact is she wasn't *obligated* to discuss these details) but that we would find out upon their arrival in Huntington the next week.[30] I asked her if the alternate issue concerned the recent arrest of one of our football players, Carlos Smith,[31] who had been charged with felony unlawful wounding in a racially-motivated attack on a city police detective's son. Marshall football players getting in trouble with the law was nothing new, and I thought the NCAA might have the same suspicion I did, that Pruett was currying favor with local police and prosecutors to ensure his players were given breaks in situations where the normal student would not. This would be a very blatant violation of NCAA extra benefit rules.

I asked LuAnn directly and she said she couldn't confirm nor deny that the Smith arrest was the new issue. I thought, "My God, it has to be something about Randy Moss or some other hotshot. It has to be something big." For the first time in the investigation process, I was worried. I had some concerns in the past, but now I was really worried about what might happen. The NCAA hadn't even begun their formal investigation yet, and here they were with other issues already. This was certainly not good news. Every positive feeling I had was now gone.

I immediately called Layton Cottrill to tell him about the conversation, then called Hilliard to pass the information on to him. Hilliard said he would sniff around to see if he could find out anything, but he cautioned us against getting too worried because this was a normal tactic of the enforcement staff, and many times the other issues were nothing more than pie-in-the-sky accusations from rival fans or internet chat boards. Hilliard's reaction made me feel better, but I still decided to call a meeting of the minds.

Cottrill, Pruett, Lance West, Ed Grose, Sarah Denman, Linda Wilkinson and me met in the university administration building for a conference call with Hilliard. Rich was very convincing, saying that we needed to keep our eye on the ball and focus on what we did know, which were the academic fraud allegations and Bruce McAllister's actions. Everyone in the meeting agreed that focusing on issues that might turn out to be irrelevant was counterproductive, and that we would address the additional issues if they turned out to be a problem.

I felt somewhat reassured, and continued to work with Hilliard, Sexton, and Humphrey through the first week of February 2000 on preparing for the upcoming visit, which was now less than two weeks away. Hilliard and I made a decision that the NCAA interviews would be conducted without legal counsel present. We felt we had nothing to hide, and did not want to give the appearance that we were trying to spin anything. Hilliard had experience in these matters, and I deferred to his thinking, though we would eventually come to regret this decision.

CHAPTER 13:

MISDIRECTION

THE MORNING OF TUESDAY, February 9th started like any other day, catching up on work, emails, returning phone calls, putting out the latest fires, and checking, auditing, and educating. It was a miserable day weather-wise. Outside my window was the semi-rare sight of heavy snowfall in the southwestern part of West Virginia, and I was happy to be working inside my office instead of outside in the cold. Just like the weather outside at the time, my day would go from bad to worse.

My phone rang and it was Lance West, talking to me on speaker phone. This was never a good sign, because it meant that someone else was in the room with him. "Good Morning Coach!", West said in his usual cheerful, phony way. After we exchanged pleasantries, I asked what was on his mind this snowy and wet morning. He said in a little more serious tone, "Coach, I have Beatrice and Coach Pruett here with me." This was a major red flag. When Beatrice and Lance were calling from his speaker phone, it meant an ambush was imminent. This was a very typical tactic of Crane to put me on the defensive and make me look bad.

"We are pretty sure we know what the other issue is," Lance said, referring to LuAnn Humphrey's vague hint.

"Oh really?" I responded, "How is that, considering they said 'issues?'"

Lance shot back, "Why don't you just come over here, coach, so we can talk."

The coy routine was not sitting well. "Why don't you just tell me what you think the issue is, and how do you know this information?"

Lance wasn't budging. "Coach, please come on over," to which I agreed.

I hung up the phone, and felt that sense of dread that seemed to accompany me everywhere these days. Since they wouldn't tell me over the phone, and since they had already discussed the matter absent my presence, was this something that was going to be pinned on me? I knew this was not a good scenario, so I searched quickly for a tape recorder but could not find one small enough that could be hidden. In desperation, I called Linda Wilkinson and asked her to come to the meeting as a witness, and she agreed.

As we were walking through the now-heavy snowstorm to the Football Stadium Facilities Building, where the football staff and the rest of senior athletic administration offices were located, I explained my concerns to Linda.

While being three blocks west of the football program and other senior staff may have had its advantages, the arrangement had also allowed Beatrice to undermine me on matters of compliance. Crane was always available to Coach Pruett as she knew the value of associating with the powerful, so Pruett and many of his staff became adept at going to Crane for NCAA interpretations, especially if they did not like or agree with my interpretation of a particular rule. It seemed Crane and I rarely agreed, and this became an ongoing problem. I never had a problem with Crane raising questions, but when she overruled me without consulting me, this was a violation of our internal policies and made our department incredibly dysfunctional and that dysfunction was amplified by a lack of leadership to mitigate the situation.

I demanded to West over and over again that interpretations must come from one place and one place only. Given the nebulous nature of many NCAA rules, a coach or administrator could certainly find the answer they wanted if they kept on asking people, plus the question a coach asked me might be completely different from what they asked Crane, even though it may be about the same subject. West assured me that he would tell Crane to cease, but it never really happened.

Now, I told Linda, I feared that Beatrice was once again offering her own interpretations, and questioned how she had this potentially important piece of information when I knew nothing about it. I told her that I was sure something was going to be pinned on me considering how Crane seemed to never forgive me for my stance on her relationship with Thompson, and that Pruett had gone to Crane because he knew she would be a willing accomplice due to the friction that existed between us.

Linda, being ever so optimistic, told me to wait and see what happens, though she did acknowledge that one needed "to watch their back" around

Crane because her interests concerned herself, first and foremost. I couldn't have agreed more with Linda's take on the situation. As Linda and I walked into West's office, everyone exchanged pleasantries and took their seats around West's large desk. West attempted to look in charge, sitting in his oversized high-backed chair behind his large oak desk and said, "Dave, we believe we know what else the NCAA is looking at. Beatrice why don't you tell Dave and Linda what you know."

I was already fuming, because this was all done behind my back when I was only a phone call away. I glared at Beatrice, because I knew exactly where this meeting was going. This was an ambush plain and simple. She knew something, and she was going to make damn sure that it was dumped in my lap to make me look stupid, in turn making herself look better. I wanted to scream, but I felt I needed to get the information first, and to ascertain what I was up against before I flipped out.

The story Beatrice told was downright laughable, and as I suspected, the joke was on me. She said that she "just happened" to be walking by Coach Pruett's office the night before, and he "just happened" to ask her to come in for a chat. According to Crane, Pruett was despondent over the other potential issues that LuAnn Humphrey had alerted me to, and could not figure out for the life of him what they were. So, they started "casually chatting" about several potential vulnerabilities within the football program, and Pruett "just happened" to mention a little employment program for the Proposition 48 athletes, during their initial year of enrollment. But Pruett had told Crane there was no way this could be what the NCAA was looking for, because, "Dave says there is no problem with it."

My jaw dropped, but before I could speak, Crane announced to the group assembled in West's office, "I think there is a problem with it, props cannot work, and I was concerned because David let props work the ESPN game a few months back."

I scanned my memory bank. In the fall of 1998, I had approved ESPN's employment of several then-current Marshall student-athletes, including Prop 48 athletes in their first year, to be paid a total of $50 to work the telecast of a Thursday night football game on campus. Also assisting in the same capacity were several team managers, members of the athletic staff, and other Marshall students who did not fall under my purview within NCAA compliance. At the time, I had determined that since we hired the props like everyone else, and that it was not a special arrangement, it was permissible for them to work the game. Now, though neither Beatrice nor anyone at Marshall had questioned it at the time, at least to me, she was saying that since we did the hiring at ESPN's request, the one-night jobs constituted special assistance from the athletic department. But even if my interpretation on that matter had been incorrect,

Pruett was apparently using what was at best an innocuous secondary violation as justification for a Prop 48 work program that I knew nothing about until the snowy day I was summoned to West's office.

Crane claimed that she raised a red flag about the ESPN game employment because she saw Associate Athletic Director Mike Bianchin, who was a former graduate assistant coach under Pruett, preparing employment forms for an athlete she knew to be a Prop 48 athlete. I always thought Bianchin lucked into his job because Pruett wanted him hired, and this job was offered as a consolation prize to Mike and his fiancé, assistant women's volleyball coach Glenna Easterling because Pruett did not hire Bianchin for a full time coaching job as previously promised. I never liked it when people were hired who hadn't paid their dues, but overall I thought Mike did a decent job considering his youth and inexperience. Once the athlete left Bianchin's office, Crane inquired about his presence. Bianchin explained that several props were going to work the ESPN game the next night performing various duties, and he was just ensuring that proper forms were filled out as required by the compliance office.

When Crane said to Bianchin, "Props cannot work at all during their freshman year," Bianchin stated that I gave him the green light for the props to work. Beatrice said that I was wrong, and told Bianchin to call me to inquire again. Mike did not feel that was necessary, and in his case with good reason, as it was later determined that Bianchin himself worked with Prop 48 athletes while he was a graduate assistant football coach, and had full knowledge of other impermissible work programs for prop athletes. Bianchin, it would turn out, knew that athletes working in other places were not turning in employment forms, were making well above the standard wage, and that it was not approved by my office. Yet he said nothing, in an effort to protect himself and the football program.

Calling me, Bianchin likely reasoned, could be the start of the peeling of an onion he didn't want unraveled. (Also, as a staff member, Bianchin had been required to sign a yearly form stating that he was not aware of any NCAA violations. The same went for Pruett and everyone else on staff. It would become clear that all of the above misrepresented themselves on official NCAA forms several times, a violation of the NCAA rules on unethical conduct. Amazingly, nothing happened to those who falsely signed the form, and the NCAA would never interview Bianchin in spite of my repeated requests to do so).

Crane, according to testimony she later gave to NCAA investigators, then forcefully told Bianchin, "Humor me and call him." That Crane would not call me directly and handle this professionally was par for the course, and she saw another situation to attempt to make me look bad and she wanted to take advantage of it. Reluctantly, Mike made the call. He was on speaker phone and I did not take the time to ask him to use his extension. Unbeknownst to me, Crane was listening in. Mike said he wanted to make sure, just to be safe, that the props could work the ESPN game. I went through my standard spiel on employment, approval, and rate of pay. I also took special care to make sure other non-football athletes and other non-athletes were working. Bianchin confirmed this and said he had no problems at this point. I reminded him that I needed the employment forms on file before any work commenced. Crane said nothing, nor did I have an indication she was in the room. She should have spoken up if she had a problem, as I would always listen to any concerns she had, despite our personal friction. She would later tell the NCAA that she felt "comfortable that everything was checked out." Yet only a few weeks later, after being prompted by Pruett, she determined that the ESPN props must be the "other issue."

Pruett had played it masterfully. He had covered himself months before by asking the question that would get him a favorable interpretation, namely, "Can props work?" to which the correct answer is yes. The caveat being, as I and Dave Reed had told Pruett and all the coaches multiple times prior, that all employment must be approved by my office, and that we would make the decision if it was ultimately permissible. Apparently, somehow a coach that remembered the most minute details from football games played years ago, conveniently forgot this simple and very public policy. Pruett's amnesia was back. Too bad his old buddy Bruce McAllister wasn't around for a brain massage. Sadly, in NCAA investigations, the finality and public scorn that an institution faces often moves many presidents, AD's, and coaches to make very bad decisions to protect their own self-interests and that of the brand. The infighting at Marshall had been brewing close to the boiling point for many months and once it was about to explode, many went on defense by playing offense, and directed their public and private ire at me since I was an easy target.

Though I had no idea of its extent at this moment, I knew that Pruett must have been complicit in a jobs program for props, that he was worried that the NCAA knew about the jobs program, and that he wanted to distance himself. The ESPN issue was his "get out of jail free" card, and he had Beatrice Crane leading the charge to connect me to this impermissible employment.

I had fallen for the classic coach trick, and I should have known better. I clearly gave Pruett the information he wanted to hear on athletic employment, and now he felt protected if the program was ever exposed. He had plausible deniability, and was now wearing me as his bulletproof vest.

I was getting ready to explode at this point, but Beatrice's tale was far from over.

After deciding the prop-job issue was what the NCAA must be worried about, Crane picked up the phone. Instead of calling me, she dialed Marshall general counsel Layton Cottrill, who allegedly told her to "check it out." Apparently, checking with the person the university had hired to interpret such matters - me - was out of the question at this point. I believe, and Cottrill told me as much, that Crane vehemently resisted talking to me since she felt I already made the wrong interpretation but Cottrill should have also involved me in the discussion and was flat out wrong not to do so.

So Crane instead called her former assistant, Jennifer Smith,[32] the associate athletic director for compliance at Michigan State, to enlist her opinion on the matter. Besides being one of my pet peeves, calling another school to air our dirty laundry was strictly prohibited by departmental and university policy, yet Crane was notorious for this. Crane gave Smith the 10 percent factual story that she and Pruett had hammered out, and asked, according to Crane, "Can props work during their first year of enrollment," to which Smith apparently laughed and said, "of course not."

But the evening would get more interesting still for Crane and Pruett.

In an apparent case of impeccable timing and incredible coincidence, just as Crane and Pruett were debating what to do next (perhaps following protocol was next on the agenda?), a "secret source" allegedly called out of the blue to reveal that the NCAA was really coming to Marshall to look into an impermissible employment scheme involving non-qualifying athletes. On top of that, the source said, it was the main topic the NCAA had problems with, not the academic fraud issue.

I could not take it any longer, and forcefully spoke up. I told Crane that she was off her rocker if she thought Prop 48 athletes could not work, period. I reiterated the facts … that these athletes could work as long as they were being tracked, being paid the commensurate rate of pay for like work performed, did not earn more than $2000 above the value of a full grant-in-aid, and if this job was not a special arrangement for just certain athletes, meaning they must have been hired like everyone else. I kept saying it over and over and she just shook her head no. I went on to say that unless these jobs were used as recruiting inducements, I failed to see how this situation could constitute a major violation.

Now Pruett spoke, finally giving me some insight on what types of jobs we were dealing with. He said that Marshall Reynolds, a powerful booster who was well-known on campus, hired everyone who walked through the door of one of his businesses, McCorkle Machine Shop, and that this was not a special arrangement, the kids were not recruited with the promise of jobs, and as far as he knew they were paid what others earned.

He also said he was under the impression that this employment had been approved and was being tracked by the compliance office. I stated that I never approved any props working, except for the ESPN game in 1998. I added that I was unaware whether Dave Reed had knowledge of the McCorkle jobs, but I was reasonably certain he did not.

At this point, I finally decided it would be best to try to calm everyone down as it was simply getting out of hand. I didn't feel the need to panic before all the facts were known and I stated in a very reassuring way, "We are not getting anywhere arguing, and we simply do not know all of the facts."

It seemed to be the best course of action, but panic is what everyone else was doing. Beatrice continued to say that this was a major violation, and insisted it was the main reason the NCAA was coming. She was adamant that we self-report (meaning I would blow the whistle on myself) immediately in order to beat the NCAA to the punch, a notion I shut down because you cannot write a self-report without a clear handle on all of the facts. Also, I was not going to throw myself in front of the train without doing a thorough investigation.

I was getting frustrated, and demanded that if I was supposed to report this and admit to a mistake that I knew I hadn't really made, she had damn well better reveal her secret source. I told her that it was complete bullshit that she went behind my back to get information that might have been flawed, and then presented it to me in this way.

Crane adamantly refused to reveal the source. My frustration was beginning to show.

"Give me the fucking name," I screamed, "If the NCAA is talking about our case with unconcerned individuals, then they are violating their own bylaws and rules of confidentiality!"

Beatrice just looked down at the floor and would not answer. Pruett tried to put his hands on my shoulder to calm me down, to which I said, "Don't ever fucking touch me, coach," and pushed his hands away. Linda was horrified at the course of the meeting and was shocked into silence. I then looked at Lance, who as usual was not taking charge, on the possibility that he may order Beatrice to reveal her secret source. I said, "God damn it Lance, she is violating policy, tell her to give me all of the information and the name of the source."

Lance just barked, "Watch your language, Dave."

I looked around the room, and knew it was over. They had their patsy. No one was coming to my defense, and everyone seemed content with this backdoor move by Crane and Pruett to pin the blame on me for consenting to a program that I had obviously known nothing about. I wanted Beatrice, the leader of this witch hunt, to know I was fully aware of what she had done.

"You god-awful bitch. What Rick Thompson said about you was true." I meant to say it, and said it with pure conviction. She stormed out in tears, crying, "I am going to quit," to which I responded, "Don't let the door hit you in the ass." Pruett raced after her and both ended up in her office across the hall with the door shut.

I continued to berate Lance for his handling of the situation. Although he was my boss, I felt he needed a dressing down for his pathetic handling of this situation, and for how he knuckled under to Pruett and Crane. In his usual fashion, he tried to smooth out the problem by saying, "Things may not be as bad as they seem." I just laughed condescendingly. How could it not be bad when my own football coach maintained a potentially impermissible jobs program, and he and the Senior Women's Administrator were conspiring to blame me for it?

Linda Wilkinson briefly came to my defense by telling Lance the situation was being handled in the wrong way, and that Beatrice needed to come clean with this source so we could assess the information. I was pleased Linda was finally helping. Lance stated that the source was not important but the information was, a statement that all but assured me that Lance himself knew the source, and that he simply had no grasp of the severity of the situation or what his job was as athletic director. As I complained about the predicament, Pruett charged in the door with an email that had the address line torn off, purportedly from Beatrice's source.

I looked at the email, and it basically said that Proposition 48 athletes could not work during the academic year, in their first year of enrollment … if they were assisted in getting the job by the athletic department. Hey, that sounded familiar. Kind of like what I had been telling the coaches, including Pruett, for months.

I had my fill of this garbage. I told West, Pruett, and Wilkinson that I was going to call the MAC office and Rich Hilliard to determine if we had a violation and if we did, whether it was major or secondary. I said that if the ESPN issue constituted assistance, then we would have at worst a secondary violation. In addition, since we had people working for Marshall Reynolds, and it appeared that proper policies were not followed by the coaching staff in reporting this program, I theorized that we might have a violation due to a lack of monitoring. But if Pruett was telling the truth, and the kids got the job on their own, it had not been promised during recruiting, and they were paid like all other workers for like work performed, then we may not have a violation at all. Beatrice's assertion was that props could not work, period, and I knew she was wrong. I left seething over the circumstances that had resulted in the meeting, but was still cautiously optimistic that, at worst, we had only secondary violations.

As Linda and I walked back toward the Henderson Center in the cold, we were both emotionally spent. I was near tears complaining to Linda my dismay at how two colleagues could turn on me like that and make those accusations and assertions without any facts and without warning. All of the policies and procedures I had put into place were flaunted and no one was there to back me up. Linda agreed with everything I said and stated she was stunned at the actions of Pruett and Crane. She felt that both should be disciplined for not following procedures, and that Lance needed to get the information on the secret source. At least Linda made me feel like I was not out of my mind.

There was another part of me that wondered, "Did I somehow cause this? What did I do wrong?" I was beginning to question everything, and doubt my own abilities. My loyalty to the organization made me give Pruett a partial benefit of the doubt. Maybe he did misunderstand me, maybe I wasn't as thorough as I could have been, but surely he was not going to finger me for something I clearly did not know about nor authorize. My angst was mainly directed at Crane for her role in exacerbating the situation before we knew what we had on our hands.

After I calmed down a bit, I pressed on to find out if we actually had violations, as well as much larger problems than we needed one week before NCAA investigators came to town. The first person I called was Hilliard, who had over 20 years of NCAA compliance experience and was a nationally-recognized expert on NCAA violations and infractions. Based on the information we had, he answered quickly by saying, "I don't think that is a problem at all." We discussed what qualified as intercession by the athletic department, and were both convinced that based on Pruett's statements, the jobs for Marshall Reynolds did not qualify as athletic assistance.

Hilliard then contacted Pat Britz, who worked for the rules and interpretations wing of the NCAA national office called NCAA membership services. Meanwhile, I called Dell Robinson, Associate Commissioner of the MAC. Both seemed to confirm what we were thinking, based on the information that we all had, though Britz sent an email to me and Hilliard the next day indicating that we might have a problem.

Britz said that upon further review, it appeared the football and basketball coaches did intercede directly to get the jobs for the athletes, or at least enough for it to be a violation. Britz went on to say that, "…while I am certain things like this are going on, it is not permissible based on the legislation."[33]

This was not great news by any means, but I still wanted more confirmation. I forwarded all of the information to Steve Mallonee, Director of NCAA Membership Services, and probably the person that knew NCAA rules better than any other. He supported Britz by saying it appeared the athletics department interceded, without saying what defines intercession. He went on to state that it was permissible to assist directly during the summer months and holiday breaks, but not during the academic year.

A light bulb went off in my head. Maybe this was a huge misunderstanding.

Could it be that Coach Pruett got information from me about holiday breaks and not during the academic year? Maybe this was just poor communication, and no one intended to do anything wrong? I was rationalizing the situation because I could not believe anyone at Marshall would intentionally railroad me, even Pruett.

Hilliard and I huddled and determined that we needed to find out all of the facts quickly and file a self-report prior to the investigators' arrival on campus. We theorized that even if the athletic department had broken the rules by providing assistance, we could still be OK if the athletes were paid for like work performed, and if we could prove that no one intended to violate the spirit or intent of the rule.

Hilliard's plan was to get confirmation from the employer on rate of pay, circumstances of hiring, work performed, time, dates, etc. This would include statements by Pruett, Reynolds, myself, and the athletes. Rich thought that we would be able to get by with several secondary violations if responsibility for the employment program was ferreted out to everyone. His plan was to suggest in the self-report that I gave an incomplete, but substantially correct interpretation, Pruett believed that interpretation and acted, but did not ensure the athletes registered the employment nor turned in check stubs, and the athletes did not follow through as directed in the Student Athlete Handbook and via several meetings, thus the layers of protection broke down.

Since Pruett maintained these jobs were not promised by anyone during recruiting, and the jobs were brought up to give economically disadvantaged kids a chance to earn pocket money until they were academically eligible for an athletic scholarship, we thought we might be cast in a more positive light.

I was optimistic.

Unfortunately, as with so many pieces of my experience at Marshall, I based my optimism on a faulty premise. Namely, that Bobby Pruett was capable of telling the truth.

Chapter 14:

The Big Dig

It seems every college athletic program, or at least every successful one, has one significant booster. This person, like Bobby Lowder at Auburn or T. Boone Pickens at Oklahoma State, has the ability to bankroll an athletic department's efforts to hire the best coaches, subsidize the building of facilities and overall, simply do what it takes to win. Many times this person becomes the de facto athletic director of the institution, since he who holds the purse strings has the ability to exert tremendous influence and authority over the goings-on with regard to an athletic program, most notably the sports of football and men's basketball.

At Marshall, this man was Marshall T. Reynolds.[34]

Despite growing up, in his words, "too poor to pay attention," by 1999 Reynolds had made a fortune as one of the United States' top commercial printing magnates. In was in 1964 that the 26-year-old Reynolds, along with his partner John Harrah, purchased Chapman Printing Company from proprietor John Chapman. By 1972, Reynolds had bought Harrah out, and purchased five more printing companies during the decade. Reynolds made more acquisitions in the 80's, including a hotel and a bank that he would eventually sell for $28 million, until, in January of 1993, Reynolds' holding company Champion Industries became a publicly-traded company on the NASDAQ index.

More than that, Reynolds was a community hero. His efforts at creating jobs and supporting Huntington earned him a spot on the city's Wall of Fame and a series of plaques inside the aging Huntington Civic Arena downtown that honor important people in the life of the city. While a hero, his money and power made him a man few people dared to cross and he struck fear in the heart of many a Marshall University president and local politician. Reynolds also had a passion for sports, and his profile in and around campus at Marshall first began to get noticed in the 80's, courtesy of a close, personal relationship with then-men's basketball coach Rick Huckabay.

The Herd's success on the hardwood during that era, and rumors about how they got so successful, brought NCAA investigators to Marshall. The relationship between Huckabay and Reynolds would come under the microscope, although it was other boosters that were named in the report that landed the Thundering Herd on probation. Still, many in Huntington believed that Reynolds was the "bag man" for the men's basketball team. Case in point: when Huckabay was forced to resign under pressure, word around town was that Reynolds bought Huckabay a nice new car in which to drive away, along with forcing then-Marshall AD, Lee Moon to go the NCAA to personally plead Huckabay's case and for leniency in his punishment. All rumors, but enough smoke that there was likely some truth to his heavy-handed involvement in athletic affairs at Marshall University.

But the Marshall coach who really benefited from Reynolds' philanthropy was Jim Donnan.

Along with Moon, Donnan approached Reynolds in 1992 and asked if he could help in employing some of the Prop 48 athletes whose numbers were growing during the coach's first years on the job.

The details of the arrangement made that day in '92 are unknown, and the selective memories of people involved are interesting. Moon flat-out denies such a meeting ever happened, but Donnan and Reynolds claim a meeting discussing this subject indeed occurred. What is clear is that Reynolds agreed to let the Prop 48 athletes work at one of his local businesses, McCorkle Machine Shop, on weekends doing "GI" kind of labor - sweeping, cleaning, and taking out the trash.

On the surface this appeared to be a legitimate arrangement. All the athletic department would do is tell these kids they could work at McCorkle if they desired. All they had to do was show up, and the managers would hire anyone, including any athlete, who came through the door for weekend work. It appeared they would be paid the going rate for these services, just as non-athletes would. There exists no proof of this program prior to February 2000 - no paperwork, and no verification. However, the program could have actually been permissible if the kids got the job as previously described, if they actually worked, and if they received the going rate for like services.

As I was to find out in February 2000, when I first began investigating what was commonly but quietly known as "the Saturday Program," the façade was far different from the reality. Actually, I wouldn't have found out much about the program had I been permitted to resign.

The night of the ambush meeting in Lance West's office, I told my wife the entire story and said, "Maybe it is time to get out of Marshall." I slept on it, for what little time I actually did sleep that night. My head was spinning, and I felt myself hyperventilating and sweating. I was convinced I was nearing a nervous breakdown. I kept retracing the day, wondering how people I trusted could turn on me so quickly, and alternating between thoughts of self-doubt and self-assurance.

I got up the next morning and told my wife I was resigning from my job. After the way I was treated, how could I ever trust the people I worked with? How could I ever work at Marshall again? I was convinced it was time to go, and that my family and I would survive and even flourish. The move would give Marshall the convenient option of blaming me for everything, but that wasn't much different from how I was being treated anyway. I knew I couldn't control outside perceptions, but there was solace in knowing the truth. Without trust you have nothing, and the athletic department at Marshall was as low and dysfunctional at this point as ever.

I fought back tears as I drove to work in my nice, free courtesy car for what might be the last time. I parked in the same lot that I had for the past four years, and walked across 3rd Avenue for what I thought was the last time. I was humbled, thinking that it was strange that it would all end like this and that my dream would be over, but that life would go on. When I sat down at my desk, I could not hold back the tears as I typed my resignation letter.

While finishing up the letter, my phone rang. Coincidentally, it was Lance. In his typical nice-guy fashion he said, "Hey coach, how you doing? That was a pretty tough day for us yesterday." Despite my ambivalent feelings toward Lance, I must say his words were somewhat calming, a tone that might have been helpful the day before.

I said, "Well, I have certainly had better days, Lance."

"Coach, we will get through this like everything else and..," Lance said, as I interrupted him. My voice began to tremble, "Lance you need to know that I have just finished my resignation letter. I feel it is best and I simply cannot work under these conditions anymore. If you guys want a scapegoat, you have one."

The phone line was dead quiet.

Lance then said after a pause of a few seconds, "My God Dave, no, please no!"

He went on to praise me and state how far the compliance program had come and how valuable I was to the department and university. It was nice to hear, but too little too late in my opinion. I was resigning, I had enough. He asked me to take a little time to reconsider and I told him I would, but my mind was pretty much made up.

I figured Lance would begin working the phones following my revelation, and as expected, my phone soon started to ring. The first person to call was Layton Cottrill. Cottrill was a man I liked and respected, at least at first, and I thought he felt the same about me. He certainly seemed to be my biggest fan at times, even at this dark hour. He asked how I was doing, and I told him I was resigning. "Don't do that, Dave, Jesus, are you fucking crazy, how do you think it would look to the NCAA if you resigned?" I responded that I could not work under these conditions, with the constant interference of Pruett and especially Crane, and with Lance either unwilling or incapable of reining them in. The situation was not just becoming untenable, it was simply over.

Cottrill yelled, "I have about had enough of that fucking blonde bitch. She is lucky we gave her a chance after she screwed up everything at Louisville. Listen Dave, you didn't do anything wrong," he continued. "Everyone, including me, is at fault here. That motherfucker Marshall Reynolds is probably the real culprit. We do not need in-fighting here when the NCAA is at our doorstep, and we certainly do not need my compliance guy to resign right now!"

He was convincing, and it was clear that he wanted me to stay both for the good of the university and the good of my own career. His opinion was important to me, and his words mattered. He told me to go home, relax, and think about it, and I told him that I would. The phones at Marshall had caller ID, so I was able to see who else was calling as Layton was attempting to talk me off the ledge. I saw that Lance called back, as well as Pruett and the university's senior VP for operations, Ed Grose, probably to weigh in on the news I was planning to resign. Protocol dictated that I called Grose first. He and I had a fairly decent relationship at the time and he, like Cottrill, had always backed me up on issues of compliance, whether they were my fault or not.

Grose told me he had heard I was thinking about resigning. Like Cottrill, he was very reassuring, though unlike Cottrill he deflected my criticism of Crane and Pruett by saying we were a team, needed to stick together, and that this was no time to fight. He also seemed unconcerned about this secret source and the methods Pruett and Crane used the day before, but went on to praise my dedication and work ethic. He urged me not to resign, and said that would be the worst result for everyone. He said that he was ordering me (in a nice way) to take a few days off and not think about anything university-related.

I hung up feeling better, and then checked my messages. The first was from Lance, again almost begging me not to resign and praising my efforts and accomplishments. Pruett also left a message, starkly different from his stance the day before. He first asked me not to resign, then went on to say the program was the cleanest he had been a part of and that I was excellent at my job. Linda Wilkinson also called, pleading for me to reconsider.

A big piece of me knew that this groundswell of support was self-serving on the part of those who phoned me. Obviously, my resignation wasn't going to look great to the NCAA, and it was highly preferable to have me on the inside of the situation, working for Marshall, rather than sitting on the sidelines or working against the university. I knew this might be a snow job to set me up as a fall guy later, but I also knew that if I could help Marshall navigate the situation, my career didn't have to fall to pieces as it surely would if I resigned. Also, my ego was pretty much shattered by this point, and having the upper university administration, and the exalted football coach, fall all over themselves to keep me as Assistant AD for Compliance was flattering. I did not immediately say I was staying, but was now strongly considering retracting my resignation. I still had my family to think about, so I was leaning toward staying.

There were still more pressing issues. There was an afternoon conference call scheduled with Hilliard and the very same brain trust who spoke to me about the potential resignation. This meeting would be the first time I would see Crane face to face since the debacle the day before. I was spent from the roller coaster of emotions and I felt my body getting sick. The flu was going around and I was starting to get smacked hard by the virus, no doubt amplified by the stress of the past few days. Later in the afternoon, before the meeting, I called Lance and told him I was retracting my resignation, on the condition that I never deal with a situation like the day before again. I also pleaded with him to rein in Crane and keep her off my back so I could do my job. He agreed with my assessment and seemed overjoyed that I decided to stay.

That afternoon I joined West, Pruett, Crane, and Wilkinson at the meeting. We met in Old Main Administration Building with Cottrill, Grose, and Provost Sarah Denman. Cottrill started the meeting by dressing down all of us because we let this happen. Surprisingly, his angst seemed to be directed more at me than anyone else, but he made a point of looking straight at Crane during his tantrum. I was pleased that he at least directed his voice to Crane and said, "where were you [on this issue] when you were in charge of compliance?" Yet, Cottrill didn't go after Crane for her secret source, which was strange since he expressed his dismay and anger over it the day before. I just did not have the energy to pursue it again and my flu was getting worse by the minute. My body was spent because of all the aggravation and emotion and I just wanted to go home and rest. My fighting for my program and its policies and my personal issues were over for that day.

For one of the few times during the NCAA investigation, I mainly listened during the meeting. We then teleconferenced Hilliard in to the meeting. Hilliard explained where he thought we were with the jobs program and how he planned to explain it to the NCAA. The plan was to parcel out blame to literally everyone. Meaning me for not giving a "complete" interpretation, Beatrice for not following policy and seeking outside, inaccurate information, and for not discovering the program on her watch, Pruett for not following compliance procedures in reporting the jobs program and income earned, and everyone else for consorting with Marshall Reynolds and not reining in what appeared to be a renegade booster. The lion's share of the blame would then fall at Reynolds' feet by portraying him as an out-of-control booster who knew the rules and took an innocent jobs program to an impermissible level. Everyone signed off on the plan and everyone except for Pruett, who still tried to maintain he had nothing to do with it, believed it was an accurate description of what happened.

Without knowing the full extent of the violation, something I would not completely uncover for another year and a half, I agreed to this plan. I knew I was not blameless in this and I had to look in the mirror for at least part of the problem based on what I knew at the time. My standards for myself are higher than anyone else has for me. I felt that even though there was a solid compliance program and this breakdown should not have occurred, I needed to own up to not giving a complete interpretation -regardless of what I knew. The military, and my own personal ethics and morals, taught me that you own up to mistakes so you can learn from them and make sure they do not happen again in the future. My instinct was to be loyal, since everyone was taking part of the blame. My part of the blame, albeit very small and in many ways irrelevant, was still a mistake and I needed to be straight up about it. Surely the NCAA would look at that in a positive light. The bottom line was that I was convinced at the time that no one, including Pruett and Reynolds, intended to violate anything and if there was no direct intent to circumvent NCAA rules, we could get out this relatively painlessly. I started feeling better and I was optimistic we would be fine.

A couple days had passed since the debacle in West's office, and the meeting in Old Main. Pruett was being supportive of the plan and on the surface, supportive of me. Crane was now keeping her distance and I was ready yet again to fight for Marshall University. I needed to get on track and write a self-report and continue to prepare for the NCAA visit. Self-reporting, self-detecting, and self-correcting of NCAA violations are considered mitigating factors by the NCAA Committee on Infractions in deciding sanctions. Hilliard was firm that we needed to get out a self-report as soon as possible to get credit for it. I agreed and wanted to put our defense plan into action. I was actually feeling that we may have stopped things before they really became bad.

I now had only three days to get the self-report done and in the hands of the NCAA investigators, Humphrey and Sexton. I met with the football and basketball coaching staffs to determine who worked in the program, and of those who worked in the program, who was still on campus with eligibility remaining. It took a couple of days, but I was able to get what appeared to be a full list with the help of Reed.

The most pressing matter was that men's basketball player Monty Wright was listed as one of the athletes who worked, and he had a game against Kent State that weekend. Since he was involved in the impermissible jobs program, he was technically ineligible to compete for Marshall University until we appealed his eligibility status through the NCAA student-athlete reinstatement process. This, of course, raised the ire of head men's basketball coach Greg White and his staff, who claimed that this program was approved all along by my predecessors. To his credit, White didn't contend at the time, as Pruett had, that I had given explicit approval. He also stated that he was present with Moon and Reynolds at a meeting where this arrangement was discussed, and he felt it was something that had been going on and was approved. Regardless of the circumstances, the toothpaste was out of the tube, and we had an immediate eligibility situation with Monty Wright. Wright was not considered one of the stars of the team, but he was a key reserve, and at this moment the coaches made it seem like he was the most valuable player on the team.

Whether Wright should be allowed to play while we fully investigated the program was a judgment call. Since we still did not know what the extent of the violation was or if it was even a violation, I determined that Monty Wright should be able to play. To me it made no sense not to let him play, especially if it turned out to not be a violation. Then we would be benching a player for no reason. I told Greg White that Monty could play. I was still physically and emotionally ill and had to go home and rest. I thought at least we could all decompress for the weekend and have a fresh look once the NCAA comes back with an interpretation. I drove home, got in my pajamas, and literally collapsed on the bed.

As I drifted off to sleep, the phone rang. It was Lance and Beatrice. Jesus, this was all I needed now. Lance said he was uncomfortable with Monty Wright making the trip to Kent State due to the potential violation. I was fuming again. I said, "Lance, how many times do I have to tell you that we do not know if it is a violation? If it is determined we have a problem THEN we hold him out and petition for reinstatement."

Shockingly, Beatrice agreed with me and felt we may be overreacting. I told Lance that situations like this are why Athletic Director's get paid big bucks. I told him it was his call and I hung up. Monty Wright was not allowed to make the trip to Kent State that weekend, much to Greg White's consternation. I said my piece and left it to Lance to make the decision, though amazingly I later found out he had told White that I was uncomfortable with Wright making the trip. The guy just was incapable of making a decision.

I had gotten over my horrendous bout of the flu and came into the office that Monday about prepared for anything. It was that day when I received the final confirmation from Hilliard that we had to report the jobs program as a violation, because it appeared that the kids were assisted with getting the jobs by members of the coaching staff. I was deflated. Monty Wright had the unfortunate luck of being the first athlete involved in the prop job debacle to need an eligibility restoration request filed with the NCAA. We were not overly worried about the football players because it was only February, and Wright was the only one who needed to play right now.

I called Monty into my office and told him I was sorry that he was not allowed to make the Kent State trip (a game Marshall lost). I informed him that my choice was for him to go because we just did not have all of the information to ascertain if we even had a violation or not, but that I had been overruled by the athletic director. Wright was very soft-spoken, but I could tell he was hurt that he seemed to be the only one suffering. I patted him on the shoulder and said, "I need you to answer a few questions, and then I will tell you what we have to do to get you back out on the floor."

I asked Monty if he had ever worked at McCorkle Machine Shop to which he answered yes. I asked him who told him about the job and who hired him. He said that he was instructed by assistant men's basketball coach Steve Snell to report to McCorkle Machine Shop on Saturdays, to ask for a guy named Russell, and to identify himself as a Marshall basketball player. He explained that he worked on certain Saturdays when he needed a few extra bucks. I asked how much he earned, and he said that he could not remember, but that "it wasn't much, maybe five or six hundred bucks." I probed a bit further and was not really getting anything specific. Monty had always been a very introverted individual, but getting good answers seemed to be like pulling teeth. He could provide no check stub, nor exact days of work, and he seemed unsure of the identity of anyone else he worked with except for two other basketball players, William Butler and Forrest Kirby, along with quite a few football players. He also thought there were others working that were not Marshall athletes.

He consistently said he felt he worked hard and that he hated the job. I then pointedly asked Monty why he did not tell anyone he was working, especially since information like that is constantly requested by my office via the coaches or directly to the athletes. Monty just quietly said, "I figured the coaches were handling that and I didn't think I had to tell anyone because I was a prop." I realized that I was not going to get all of the information I needed and I could tell Monty was extremely nervous. I felt pity for him.

I contacted Hilliard and told him that I could not get much specific information from Wright. I went on to say that I needed amounts, dates worked, etc. or I could not get his eligibility restored. In a subsequent meeting that day, Hilliard, via phone, did not want me to contact Marshall Reynolds directly, a point echoed by Cottrill, who in turn told me to be very careful when dealing with Reynolds and to not call nor contact without permission from him. Pruett also weighed in saying he would contact Reynolds himself and get the information on hours and wages. Pruett stuck to his familiar mantra, saying, "They were hired like everyone else and paid like everyone else, shucks, I don't know what the big deal is."

I was very apprehensive about Pruett calling Reynolds, and uncomfortable that I did not have the authority to interview Reynolds myself, but since Hilliard and Cottrill supported it, I acquiesced.

Pruett called the next day and informed me that Reynolds reassured him that these kids got the jobs on their own, he hired people other than selected Marshall athletes, and that they worked hard and were paid something like $4.50-$6.00 per hour. Pruett went on to say that I needed to talk to one of Reynolds' underlings, J.J. Hatfield. Hatfield, according to Pruett, was the person in charge of the jobs program and he had all the information I needed. Since Reynolds was the top CEO, he was far removed from the day-to-day dealings of transient workers.

When I called Hatfield, I was immediately put through by his secretary. He was obviously expecting my call. After we exchanged pleasantries and I started to explain what I needed, he stopped me and said that they probably did not have records of that information because they normally paid transient workers in cash based on an hourly wage. I implored him that I needed some verification. He said that they may be able to find some records, but it would take time since Reynolds' companies employ hundreds. I explained the Monty Wright situation and Hatfield said he could not specifically recall Wright working, but that anyone who worked as a transient, worked only on Saturdays at a rate around $6.00 an hour and pulled a shift 10-12 hours long. He said that he would talk to the direct supervisor, a former employee named Eric Eckhart, for verification of the information I needed, but Hatfield stated that anything given to me would likely be "created bullshit." I told him I needed exact records regardless of where it led us. He explained that Eckhart was the person who supervised the transient worker program since its inception years before, but that he had since moved on to a new job in Indianapolis. I asked about the name Monty referred to, Russell. Hatfield explained that was Russell May, a former employee who apparently left disgruntled from Champion Industries a few months before, and that he was unaware of where May was working now. I thanked Hatfield for the information and told him that I would be in touch to follow up on the verification information.

This still did not solve my Monty Wright problem, and I was beginning to get pressure from the men's basketball staff about his status. Also, it would only be a matter of time before the press became aware that he was not suiting up for games. I called Laura Wurtz of the NCAA reinstatement staff, who said that I could get Monty reinstated based upon what information I had at that time, and base a repayment schedule on that amount. This meant that Monty could play immediately once I made a good faith estimation on his earnings, and produced a repayment schedule. The money would go to a local charity. It was sad that Monty had to pay back money that at the time seemed to be earned legitimately and through NCAA rules, but it was determined that he had received improper assistance in securing employment, so it was a violation.

However, I had not given up the fight. I had to do the repayment proposal so he could play, but once his eligibility was restored, I planned on filing an appeal so that his repayment would be delayed pending the appeal decision. Wurtz expertly guided me through the entire process and made it effortless. I appreciated all of her work with me on getting this done, and I was extremely confident that we would win on appeal. I still felt that it was an extreme reach to call these jobs violations, much less major violations.

Wright told me he worked six or seven Saturdays for 10 hours a day. I decided to estimate high and say that he earned $420 for the time he worked, prior to any taxes being taken out. Since Wright had a little over two years of eligibility remaining, I could spread out the repayment over the next 27 months. Not too bad, plus he did not even have to start repaying until our appeal was denied, which I was certain would not happen. So the crisis was averted temporarily.

With that episode behind us for the time being, it was time to get ready for the visit by the NCAA, and start thinking in terms of the McAllister academic fraud issue first and foremost. I was eminently more worried about the academic fraud issue than the jobs problem, because the facts were clear on the former issue. Hilliard and I both felt, based on Wright's and Hatfield's comments, that we were in pretty good shape and the jobs issue would be a minor violation at best. On that front, our ignorance was bliss.

CHAPTER 15:

A SCAPEGOAT EMERGES

It was overcast on the day in February of 2000 when NCAA investigators LuAnn Humphrey and Cris Sexton arrived on campus at Marshall University. The dark clouds were a bad omen, and also boding poorly was the fact that Humphrey and Sexton went to the wrong building for their initial intake meeting. Instead of heading to the Old Main Administration Building, they inadvertently showed up at the football offices, and met the one person I really wanted to keep them away from - Bob Pruett. Pruett immediately decided they needed a stadium tour and neglected to tell us the investigators had arrived. We were on pins and needles looking for them, wondering if they got lost.

Eventually, the investigators were located and were brought to Old Main by Pruett, where the assembled group - including Cottrill, Grose, West, Wilkinson, Hilliard and myself - proceeded in our attempt to kill them with kindness. Hilliard had been on the other side of several of these NCAA investigations, and told us such friendliness and cooperation would be a good approach.

Joyce Luann Humphrey, at the time a woman in her mid-40's at the time, had a much older, almost grandmotherly look to her. That said, the former Assistant District Attorney for the City of Indianapolis also had a pronounced mean streak that had served her well professionally. She was excited to get out of the daily grind of the DA's office and have some fun working in sports. Like Sexton, she had never worked a single day on a college campus, and the Marshall case would represent her first lead role on a major infractions case.

From the outset, it was clear that while Sexton was there to monitor and assist as needed, this investigation was in the hands of Humphrey.

The schedule for the first afternoon consisted of an interview with Missy Frost, the former assistant softball coach who had discovered the existence of Bruce McAllister's "study guide," and several procedural issues for Rich Hilliard and me. It was at this time that we were to learn for certain what the "other issues" were that Humphrey had alerted me to in our phone conversation the previous month.

After going over some initial and innocuous procedural items, it appeared that we would break for lunch before the interview with Frost would begin. But first, Humphrey indicated that she had some questions for the group. Little did I know, she was about to go for the jugular, specifically mine.

"Mr. Ridpath, why did you not self-report the McAllister incident earlier?"

Humphrey's tone was condescending, and caught me off guard in light of her previous, professional approach. Considering we were supposed to just be setting the table for a week of interviews, I was wholly unprepared for her interrogation. I looked at Hilliard and Cottrill, neither of whom seemed interested in assisting me. So, I began to answer.

"It's simple, LuAnn, and I maintain what I have said all along. We self-reported this the moment we knew, for certain, it was a violation. It makes no sense to self-report what might be a violation until you know for sure, so in accordance with the principles of the NCAA and Mid-American Conference, we conducted a thorough investigation, secured McAllister's confession, had it reviewed by Rich Hilliard, and self-reported."

"Why did you not involve the MAC in the investigation?" she shot back.

"We didn't have to, nor care to," I said. The tension in the room had become palpable, yet no one on the Marshall side was coming to my defense.

"Why didn't Coach Pruett or someone on his staff call you immediately when they heard about this test being out?" Humphrey snorted. I snapped back, "You have to ask them, but our position is clear, the coaches heard that it was a study guide available to everyone ... case closed."

Humphrey had a very skeptical look on her face, and laughed sophomorically at my responses, which was getting under my skin. I understand that there are techniques to use when interviewing people, but this was out of line and not in practice with NCAA protocol. If I was being officially interviewed, I needed to be appraised of my "rights" if you will, my obligation to tell the truth and cooperate, and most important, my right to have counsel present which I was never informed of. They clearly wanted to catch me off guard and set a trap. I started to suspect, after the NCAA had been on campus for less than an hour, that this was less of an investigation than a witch hunt, with a predetermined witch who looked a lot like me. I would learn much later that these types of techniques are used by the enforcement staff to expedite investigations, even if it means never really getting to the bottom of things.

The meeting broke, and Rich and I stayed behind to get ready for the Missy Frost interview. I saw Cottrill and Wilkinson briefly, to talk about what just transpired. Linda was shaken up, and stunned by the turn of events. Cottrill urged us not to panic and stick to the plan, sentiments that Hilliard echoed. Rich added that this was typical NCAA technique, and we needed to be cooperative, although he conceded that Humphrey's "tenor and tone" towards me was overly harsh and not common practice when beginning a week of interviews. However, he dismissed it to the growing pains of the new investigator.

Soon, I would realize I was not alone in feeling Humphrey's wrath, because Missy Frost would be joining me on the firing line. Missy was the epitome of a "student-athlete" when she competed in softball at Marshall as an undergrad, later being hired as a graduate assistant coach, and was the type of person any parent would want their son to marry. She had shown courage and integrity in dealing with the McAllister/test issue, and it was clear to me that if not for Missy, the fraud could have been much worse and McAllister likely would have continued providing impermissible academic assistance to football players. To me, she was a hero. To the NCAA, she was a villain.

Humphrey began hammering her, painting Missy as someone who was trying to execute a cover-up, and accusing her of protecting the athletes involved as well as McAllister. She even went as far to suggest that Missy was having a "romantic entanglement" with McAllister. It was getting pathetic, and Missy needed help as she was getting justifiably frustrated with the tone of the interview. Again, I looked for Hilliard or someone else to step in, but no dice.

I was sick to my stomach, thinking about how we had previously convinced Missy and all of the student-athletes involved that they didn't need to be represented by their own counsel at these hearings. The idea was that we wanted to show complete cooperation, and not give any appearance that we were hiding something, so the fewer lawyers involved, the better. Rich Hilliard had been present at several prior meetings, including one with Missy that very morning, in which I assured everyone involved that they would be protected by Marshall. Rich continually stated that he was there to advance the interests of the university, and that included protecting and giving counsel to members of the institution.

Now, apparently a cat had his tongue. I repeatedly looked at Hilliard for help during this unwarranted pounding. He said nothing, even when I urged him. Although I knew it wouldn't be received well, I would have to become

Frost's de facto counsel. I began to defend Missy and challenge the tactics of the investigators, especially when they kept asking the same questions over and over in different ways just to get the answers they wanted. It was truly unbelievable to watch this play out. Frost, who was obviously under extreme duress, led me to basically admonish the NCAA for their inappropriate investigative tactics. It became so heated that at one point, I told Humphrey and Sexton that the hearing wouldn't be resumed until Missy had either outside counsel and/or her parents in attendance. I knew that Missy wanted to work in intercollegiate athletics as a career, and this "investigation" could become damaging to her future goals. Not to mention that she did absolutely nothing wrong. This stance did not go over well with the investigators, who were obviously not accustomed to someone challenging them and their authority. However, I believed I was fighting for the institution as I was instructed to do by my superiors, and I certainly was not going to let these jackbooted investigators run roughshod over innocent people. Missy Frost certainly did not deserve this kind of treatment and I was not going to stand for it.

I was stunned at the turn of events. In my mind, the two people who were actually trying to prevent violations and protect the integrity of the university's athletic department were being targeted by Humphrey and Sexton, possibly because we were the most convenient scapegoats for a couple of inexperienced investigators, or because it would just move the investigation along in an expedient fashion. As Hilliard and I walked down the hall following the session, I began to dress him down.

"What the hell is going on Rich?" I said.

"Just calm down, Dave, they are just gathering info," Hilliard said. I just could not accept that answer, and I told Rich that I would not let them harass and belittle someone like Missy, a person without whom we would not even have a leg to stand on. I told him he better come to our defense because I'd told everyone that they did not need counsel at his urging. Hilliard again assured me that the action of the investigators was typical protocol, but that he would be there when needed. My trust in him was waning, but he did have experience in these matters, and I put my faith in what he was saying even as I was becoming more and more reluctant

Once cooler heads had prevailed, and the interview with Frost was mercifully over, Hilliard, the two investigators and I convened for the moment I had been waiting for. I would now finally find out what the "other issues," which had caused much tension and distress really were. Cris Sexton would handle this portion of the investigation, and began by bringing up the self-report on the prop job issue, which she revealed was the first the NCAA had heard of it, and was not the issue we had feared. I was now grinding my teeth so hard that enamel powder was coming out of my mouth.

Beatrice Crane had been dead wrong, just as I had suspected all along. Her inappropriate and dangerous actions put the institution in a poor defense position, made us look foolish, and certainly like an institution that did not have control over its athletics program. I was furious, and yet strangely relieved and somewhat vindicated. Beatrice's "secret source" it seemed had either been fictional, wrong, or she was flat out lying. Whatever it was, it dug us a hole we would never get out of and demonstrates why strict policies and procedures must be followed by all in NCAA investigations. Sexton and Humphrey also expressed deep concern over Crane's assertion that the information she was claiming to be true was leaked by the NCAA enforcement staff itself. This was something that both vigorously denied and doubted happened.

Sexton and Humphrey then went over the information they had, and though it certainly was issues - plural - what they had was pretty pie-in-the-sky stuff obviously obtained from "whistle-blowers" with no credibility. I could hardly contain my glee as Sexton ticked off her list:

1. Chad Pennington's family being provided with a skybox and impermissible perks.

2. Something (her word, not mine) with the courtesy car program for football and basketball coaches. No specifics.

3. Illegal employment of athletes at a local nightspot called the Wild Dawg Saloon, owned by university booster Mike Kirtner.

4. Free food and drinks allegedly provided by Kirtner and his staff to Marshall athletes at the Wild Dawg.

"Is that it?" I chuckled. "This is what we have been worried about for two weeks?"

"It disturbs me that you are responding like that," Sexton said.

"Jesus, Cris," I shot back, "There is nothing there. Chad's family has not received any perks. Chad's uncle owns a skybox and his Dad is an alumnus. Anything that they receive falls under a previously-established relationship." (The NCAA did not consider such things a violation if a student-athlete's family had an existing relationship with the school prior to the student-athlete's recruitment). I asked her to tell me more about the courtesy car program because I believed it to be well-managed, with no cars given to student-athletes. She could not provide any more information. There was nothing there either.

The issue over employment and perks at the Wild Dawg was more than humorous to me. Mike Kirtner, while a loyal booster, was a scared rabbit when it came to doing things within NCAA guidelines. Not that his stance was bad, but it got a little tiresome when he called me all the time, making sure obvious and simple things were permissible to do. In hindsight, I wish there were more

Mike Kirtners covering all of their bases. I knew that Kirtner would have never employed a single athlete without my consent, and he was famously frugal with his money even though it appeared he had a lot to play with, so free perks were out of the question … for anyone.

Though still concerned over the tactics of the investigators, part of me felt a small victory once this session had adjourned. I was certain that these petty issues would not amount to much, and that we were back where we started dealing with an academic issue, as well as a prop-jobs issue that we had yet to grasp because of where Beatrice put us.

The first day was over, and as Hilliard and I walked back across campus toward the Henderson Center where the Marshall men's basketball team was playing Ohio University, I could not contain my anger at Crane and where her actions had led us, and I vented at Hilliard. Hilliard agreed, saying over and over that she should be fired, held accountable for her actions, and how she hurt the university.

I was now convinced that so much information was on the table that the powers that be would finally do what they should have done sooner, and fire Beatrice Crane. The damage she caused by her arrogance and wrong interpretation was almost irreparable. She seemed more concerned about being right and proving me wrong than she did about the institution and the athletes that paid her high salary. I even found myself in agreement with Sexton and Humphrey who were both disturbed about Crane's refusal to reveal where she got the information - a clear violation of the NCAA's cooperative principle.

The NCAA was in town for four more days, so I knew it would be a tough week. An interview with Michelle Duncan, who had brought the issues with McAllister to my attention, was on tap along with hearings including Coach Pruett and several students - athletes and non-athletes - that were students in the PE 201 class in question. While I should not have been surprised, the investigators went after Duncan with vitriol. Again, I found myself verbally sparring with the investigators, because I knew Duncan did nothing wrong and I wanted to protect her. After her interview, I told her to get counsel also.

I would ultimately advise Pruett the same. Although his interview wasn't terrible, I had to throw him more than one life raft, because some of his answers didn't match what was in the self-report. The NCAA did not go after him as hard as it had Missy Frost, which bothered me, but they painted him into a corner enough to make me wonder whether he was a target too.

Now it came time for the students from PE 201 to be interviewed. I believed that the investigators would save their Gestapo techniques for those with an athletic affiliation, but I was wrong. Humphrey berated the non-athletics students, all of whom stated that they did not get a copy of the "study guide," though some said they knew one had been distributed among football players. Once Humphrey had made a couple of students cry in her interrogations, I had to put a stop to it. After one student got particularly upset, I demanded that the interview end immediately. I took Humphrey and Sexton outside and angrily asked that they adjust their techniques, especially when it came to students who were not affiliated with the athletic department. I made it clear that any continued harassment of students would be turned over to our equally fierce Dean of Students, Dee Cockrille, who I knew would not allow any harassment of students by the NCAA.

The investigators soon moved on to the football athletes. Several were interviewed, and their message was consistent: they thought they received a study guide, and they thought everyone in the class had it. The answers of the players were in line with what came from the other students. Although the athletes were pressed hard by the investigators, it was shaping up just as we reported it. McAllister acted alone, and there was no culpability on the part of the players because they were unaware they were receiving an advantage. Even if they had, Missy Frost had changed the numbers on the test in an attempt make it different. On top of all that, all students made the same grade, which was a decision made by an academic chair, and not the athletic department. It was hardly the ideal way to handle such a situation, and I had heartburn with many people over the way it was handled before it got to my desk, but I was beginning to feel that we could get out of this with secondary violations.

That said, the interviews with Pruett and associate head coach Mark Gale led me to suspect, likely along with the NCAA investigators, that the staff knew more about, and was doing more to promote, McAllister's activities than they initially let on. But try as they might to uncover any details that would lead them down a path to some deeper conspiracy on the McAllister/test issue, the NCAA investigators failed to come up with anything, beyond circumstantial evidence that jibed with our self-report. After their first visit, the NCAA would come to Marshall five more times, interview more than 150 people, engage in countless phone calls, interview summaries, harassing of witnesses etc. and they could not find anything more than what we self-reported.

Meanwhile, though the situation hadn't seemed to pique the interest of the investigators at this stage, I began to dig deeper into the prop-jobs issue. Unfortunately, the panic that Beatrice and Pruett had caused us just days before the NCAA was to visit led to us filing a self-report on the jobs issue prior to my office being able to do more than a cursory investigation. The thought was that if the NCAA was gunning for us over this situation – as Beatrice had convinced her cronies both inside and outside the department that they were - blowing the whistle on ourselves beforehand could help mitigate some of the damage. But now, irrespective of the fact that the self-report had been perfectly needless at this point in the investigation on this issue, we were in the position of having to alter the report as new findings came to light. Which they did, at almost every turn, once I started to investigate more fully.

The problem was the paper trail, or lack thereof. Coach Pruett and Marshall Reynolds were firm in their contention that these were transient jobs, open to anyone, and that the players were paid the going rate. The student-athletes I interviewed who were involved in this enterprise were echoing the same. But Reynolds was not providing me with any tangible evidence to support this contention - Hilliard and Cottrill wouldn't even allow me talk to him directly, I could only submit written requests approved in advance by Hilliard - and I was being given different rates of pay by all of the various Reynolds underlings to whom I spoke. What was becoming clear, however, is that the money being discussed was much greater than the $6.00 per hour that had been indicated when we filed the self-report. The number was now more like $12.50 per hour.

What Reynolds told Hilliard was that players were actually paid $100 dollars cash per day for two days of manual labor at Chapman Printing, one of Reynolds' businesses. He said that all workers who showed up worked eight-hour days both Saturday and Sunday, that no taxes were taken out (citing a loophole in West Virginia tax law that Reynolds used to his advantage) and thus there was no reason for the business to keep records of the arrangement.

To me, all of this sounded mighty fishy, which meant it sounded much worse to the NCAA. This was the late 90's in one of the poorest cities in West Virginia. The notion of earning $100, straight cash, for a day of manual labor, should have produced a line at the door of Chapman Printing that stretched from Huntington to Wheeling. But Reynolds was firm, and when I asked him to give me one name of a non-athlete who did the same work, he said he would produce "several." I wanted to believe him, because if what he said was true, our problems could be minimized somewhat. There was still the issue of athletic department interests allegedly and improperly arranging the jobs for the student-athletes, but if we could get a repayment plan started for the players in question, there was no reason anyone had to be ineligible or we had to worry about anything along the lines of major violations.

I was being optimistic … and naïve.

CHAPTER 16:

WADING THROUGH

In June of 2000, roughly four months after they had first visited the Marshall University campus, the NCAA investigators were finally ready to start their interviews relating to the prop-jobs issue. By this point, at Hilliard's behest, we had devised a strategy for how to respond to the NCAA's findings on the matter, which we fully expected to jibe with what was in the self-report. The idea was to spread the blame around for the impermissible jobs program to several parties, including me.

Though plenty of people in the compliance world had agreed with my initial interpretation that Prop 48 athletes could work during their initial year of enrollment as long as it was not gained by the nebulous special arrangement of "athletics intercession," on advice of Hilliard I was willing to concede that my allowance of Prop 48 student-athletes to work that ESPN game back in 1999 constituted athletic department intercession, and was a violation even though it was open to all Marshall students and we had other athletes and non-athletes working that game for the network. Though I wasn't totally convinced it could be construed as "athletics intercession," and it was a minor secondary violation at best, we were going to say that my misinterpretation on that prop-jobs issue had subsequently led to Pruett and the football program's misinterpretation and misunderstanding of the prop-jobs issue at Marshall Reynolds' business.

Hilliard assured me that despite this admission, I would be portrayed to the NCAA as a person who worked hard to do the right thing, reported violations when found, and took strong corrective measures, in addition to being a top compliance enforcer. He also assured me that this "misinterpretation" would not be depicted as a direct link, but a very weak indirect link to the major violations. Often during the investigation, Hilliard would stroke my ego and say I would make an outstanding- NCAA enforcement representative because of my "great work" on this case.

Softening the blow even more was that I wasn't going to be on an island in terms of culpability. Hilliard also wanted to place blame on the institution for not taking a more proactive and aggressive approach to compliance; the football and to a lesser extent, basketball staffs for not communicating with the compliance office even with clear rules education and documentation available; and most of all, put a lion's share of the blame on the person he called a "rogue booster" … Marshall Reynolds.

While I figured we would be slammed for these violations regardless, I was hopeful that this approach would help Marshall escape the dreaded "lack of institutional control" finding, and thought we might just be saddled with the lesser sanction of "Failure to Monitor." Not a great scenario, but the wider goal was to avoid player suspensions, forfeiture of wins and championships, and other major penalties. Hilliard, with nearly 20 years of enforcement experience as a guide, thought this would be the best way to help us achieve that. At the time I had no reason to doubt him.

I hoped the NCAA would interview my former assistant, David Reed, when they visited in June, and I had even asked them several times to do so because it would have added teeth to my contention that we had a strong jobs monitoring program. Reed had been administering the jobs program I had instituted shortly after arriving at Marshall, and I knew that if the NCAA talked to him, they would see that we were doing our level-best to educate our student-athletes and coaches, and that we were monitoring employment in an organized, effective way that was the equal or better of most institutions I knew of.

But Humphrey and Sexton weren't too interested in my request to interview Reed. They decided to go straight to the horse's mouth, and set up a meeting with Marshall Reynolds.

I was legitimately excited for the interview with Reynolds, because I knew it would get us some firm answers on issues that we had struggled to get a grasp on in recent months, and would also get us closer to the end of this ordeal. Plus, I had never met him nor been able to talk with him, so I was just plain curious about what he would say. I was hopeful that Reynolds would confirm what we had been saying all along, that this was not a special arrangement and like employment was available to other non-athletes.

Reynolds wielded a tremendous amount of authority and fear in the Huntington community, and it was no more evident than on the day of his interview on campus. Everyone in authority in the athletic department and Old Main knew Reynolds was being interviewed that day, and as he walked into Old Main, everyone in the building scattered like cockroaches under a spotlight. I went out into the musty hallway on the second floor of the Old Main administration building to see if I could find him as his interview time was approaching, assuming he would be surrounded by an entourage and several high-level university officials. There was no one in sight. Before locating Reynolds I had gone to the president's office, to Cottrill's office, and called Coach Pruett … no answer, anywhere. Clearly they wanted to avoid his wrath.

Though I had never met Reynolds formally, I knew who he was and had seen several pictures. He was impossible to miss, with a prominent birthmark on his face and generally a large wad of leaf chewing tobacco tucked firmly into his cheek. He certainly didn't look the part of the richest and most powerful person in Huntington, but whatever … he was finally here. I greeted him in the hallway, and told him I was surprised no one else was here to meet him.

"Typical," he laughed, though I could tell he was seething over the fact that no one was there to greet a man who had given the university millions of dollars.

Reynolds' interview was at once both interesting and humorous, and one I will never forget. Unlike the rest of us, he was not intimidated by the NCAA in the least, and answered every question in his salty West Virginia accent, never removing that huge wad of tobacco while spitting huge gobs of dark spittle, after every sentence, into a large Styrofoam cup while the remainder ran down his chin and on to his shirt, which he did not seem to mind. His lack of respect for the investigators and the investigation as a whole was something I enjoyed immensely, given how the NCAA had been treating me. Reynolds actually did well in his interview, echoing everything that had already been outlined in the self-report.

He stated that this was a transient employment type of arrangement that anyone could perform by literally showing up at the door of Chapman Printing and requesting work. He mentioned that there was a consistent stream of day laborers, including other students from Marshall and other local citizens who had worked for him in the past.

As for a direct connection between the football program and the employment arrangement, Reynolds acknowledged that the program had been brought up during a meeting he had with then-coach Jim Donnan and former athletic director Lee Moon in the early 90's. Reynolds said the employment was brought up as an option for prop athletes since it was allegedly available to everyone, but that it was not a special arrangement nor were the athletes paid any different than any other worker. Reynolds claimed he wouldn't know who was an athlete or not, and that he didn't care. These laborers were there to do GI-type flunky work, and were far below the level of those whom he dealt with on a day-to-day basis.

Additionally, Reynolds mentioned that he was responsible for the initial errors in the self-report in regard to the rate of pay. He said he was skirting some West Virginia tax laws by not taking out taxes for independent contractors, a practice, according to him, that was permissible because he paid them out of a non-union shop by the name of McCorkle Machine Shop. This was all completely over my head, but he confirmed that the athletes were paid $100 per day and worked Saturday and Sunday just like anyone else. When asked by the NCAA if he could provide the names of others who worked the jobs for the same rate of pay along with providing accurate pay records for the athletes, he said that he would provide anything they needed.

The interview was fairly short and to the point, but I had the information I needed. The investigators instructed me to discuss any eligibility issues with the NCAA reinstatement staff, but in general we agreed that if the athletes repaid the money and Reynolds provided accurate documents, there should not be any eligibility consequences. I was relieved, and went to work on doing what was necessary to ensure the players did not miss any games.

Just as I had figured, Laura Wurtz from the NCAA Student Athlete Reinstatement staff instructed us to put the players who had worked for Reynolds on a monthly repayment schedule, which was prorated based on how many months of competitive eligibility they had remaining. The money could be paid to a charity of our choice, but had to be tracked very closely, including where the money being repaid came from. The student-athletes would have to sign an affidavit stating they only worked for $100 a day, at a rate of $12.50 per hour, and Reynolds was to supply the paperwork that would confirm this. After we had begun the repayment plan, we could file an appeal questioning whether the prop-jobs arrangement had really constituted "athletics intercession," since it appeared clear that this job was available to all members of the general public. This helped us keep the players on the field, while also delaying the payments as the NCAA sorted out whether these jobs constituted athletics intercession.

If the appeal was upheld - and I thought there was a great chance that it would be - the players wouldn't have to pay back a dime. I was actually feeling pretty confident that we might -come out better than I thought, meaning this whole employment episode may not be a violation at all or at worst a secondary issue. If Reynolds could back up his assertions of rate of pay and other non-athletes working the same job for the same pay, we would be in great shape. I convened a meeting after discussing the reinstatement strategy with Wurtz, happily apprising the assembled group of the likelihood that we would be able to spare the athletes paying any money, along with minimizing the violations. Hilliard agreed with the decision to appeal, as did West, Crane and all of those I briefed, with one notable exception: Bob Pruett.

Pruett threw a wet blanket on my plans by talking down the players affected, saying many were "too damn dumb" to know what they were saying, and that saying the wrong thing during the appeals process could get us into more trouble. Pruett was adamant that we just needed to repay the money, acknowledge the mistake, and move on. He said that the athletes could get jobs during the summer to pay the money back, or their parents could help. I was stunned, and pressed Pruett on why he was giving in.

"I just want this over with, and the players want this over with," Pruett said. "They would rather just pay than go through interviews again during the appeal, and I am afraid they will say the wrong thing."

The consensus I had built on this issue quickly moved to Pruett's side of the table. I was outnumbered, and everyone including Pruett voted for me to move forward with the repayment, accept the interpretation, and ensure that the kids would be able to play in 2000 season. I left the meeting disheartened that the athletes were bearing the brunt of this when it was avoidable, and I knew it was wrong to do this. If the truth was on our side, why not appeal? Pruett grabbed me in the hallway of Old Main and tried to assure me this was the best, most expedient solution. I held my nose and moved forward with the eligibility reinstatement and repayment plans because I was not going to win the argument, so the football and basketball athletes in question could be eligible for the upcoming 2000-2001 season. All they had to do was make monthly payments to a charity to offset what we now deemed as impermissible earnings. Still, I wish I had held my ground on this one and I regret giving in. I would find out many months later why Pruett was so adamant about not appealing.

I finally received the records I needed from Marshall Reynolds shortly before the end of June 2000, and they stated what he said they would. Although they would not be used for an appeal, I needed them to begin the reinstatement process and repayment plans. There were no tax records or 1099 forms, which Reynolds said weren't required of this employment arrangement, but there were check stubs and what appeared to be timesheets. It was enough paperwork to start the process, and I told associate head coach Mark Gale to summon the football players so they could sign the necessary affidavits that would accompany the forms. The players were not to be told why they were assembling, and Gale and Pruett were not to be in the room nor give the players any indication what the meeting was about. This would not be unusual or raise any red flags, as I would meet with smaller groups on the football team regarding various issues from time to time.

To my surprise, Pruett was in the room when I arrived at the stadium to address the players. I politely asked him to leave, but pulled him close and said, "What did you say to them? You were not even supposed to be in here." Pruett whispered, "All I told them, Dave, was you needed to meet with them." Pruett then left, as his presence could be interpreted by the NCAA as influencing their actions on this issue.

Facing a dozen-or-so athletes who are about to be told they have to pay back hundreds, or in some cases, thousands of dollars they appeared to have worked legitimately to earn, was not my idea of fun. I explained the situation before putting the affidavits in front of them, even detailing the decision not to appeal. Surprisingly, no one questioned the repayment arrangement, nor the decision not to appeal. It seemed that the players just wanted to move on, as Pruett had suggested. The forms the players signed were simple and to the point. Each one was the same except for the names, amounts made and owed, and dates worked. Basically what the affidavits said was "I worked for eight hours a day, Saturday and Sunday on these specific dates and was paid $12.50 an hour or $100 a day at McCorkle Machine Shop." No one blinked, nor seemed to doubt the accuracy of the statement on the affidavit. All nodded in the affirmative when I asked if everything was true and correct. No one mentioned to me any inaccuracies or issues with the statements at all.

After they had signed the forms, I had Dave Reed track down Pruett to return to the meeting. I prompted him by stating how personally and professionally sorry I was about the situation. Pruett echoed my comments, and in front of the players, said that ultimately the whole thing was his fault as the head of the football program. I interjected that there was much blame to go around and part of that falls on me. With those mea culpas out of the way, and the business of the meeting done, the players were dismissed. To me, it looked like we were nearing the end of this ugly episode and ready to move forward. The repayment plan, and acquiescing on an appeal, enabled many of the athletes, who should have been ruled ineligible, to play the entire 2000 football season, which culminated in yet another MAC Championship and fourth straight Motor City Bowl Victory.

There has since been confusion, as well as flat-out misstatements from multiple figures (specifically reporter Chuck Landon and local attorney Marc Williams who was retained in 2001 to assist the football athletes in regaining their eligibility) regarding the signing of these forms. To be clear, the athletes signed two statements that were used to assist in regaining eligibility - the first one being before the 2000 season, in which Pruett was present. The players signed the second set of affidavits before the 2001 season in a last ditch effort to preserve their eligibility for that season. No specific amounts were noted on the second set of affidavits and Pruett was not present when the 2001 forms were signed.

Meanwhile, the NCAA was quiet, almost too quiet. Weeks and months went by without any word on the status of the investigation. I would often ask Hilliard what was going on ... surely by now we would have word on a hearing date? But save for the occasional letter to Reynolds requesting information on other non-athletes who worked similar jobs, nothing was happening. We still had no answer, and the media began pressing us for information on a conclusion. Usually, no news is good news, but in this case it was just the calm before the storm.

Chapter 17:

The Eye of the Hurricane

From the summer of 2000 to February of 2001, there was little to no communication between the NCAA and Marshall University on the status of the investigation. The biggest news was that Cris Sexton had decided to leave the NCAA enforcement staff, and that Mark Jones - one of the most prominent and notoriously tough Directors of Enforcement at the time - would be supervising Humphrey, and by extension the Marshall case.

Jones, in a reversal of the usual makeup of investigators, had an athletic background but no formal legal training. He had been a mediocre assistant football coach who had failed to climb much further than the middle of the ladder before becoming an NCAA operative, and I often wondered if this failure as a coach compelled him to go after people so hard during NCAA investigations. His hard-nosed reputation preceded him, most notably in the NCAA's long chase after former Mississippi State head football coach, Jackie Sherrill,[35] but Hilliard had some positive history with Jones. The two had worked together for several years at the NCAA, and had even been roommates at one point. Hilliard said Jones' appointment was a good thing, because Jones liked to finish cases, not let them drag on, and was very experienced. In addition, he thought it would be good to have a clean slate with someone other than Sexton, who clearly had personal problems with me.

Finally, the NCAA announced that they would be returning to conduct additional interviews in June of 2001, almost a year to the day since they last visited campus. This was worrying, because it was fairly obvious they wouldn't come back unless they had additional information. What I thought was almost over was beginning all over again. The letter from the NCAA revealed that they wished to interview me first, and that my presence would not be allowed during any other interviews. The feeling at the NCAA was that I might inhibit the process of interviewing other witnesses, and/or those witnesses might feel pressure to not tell the truth with me present. It was hard not to think this was a personal attack on my integrity, but Hilliard told me not to worry about it, and that it was standard protocol in the gathering of information. Still, after being present for close to 100 interviews, it seemed strange that I was now banned from the proceedings and it made me wonder what was going to happen.

My interview went about as expected. I answered the same questions in regard to my interpretation of the prop-jobs rule for the ESPN game, why I made the decisions I made, and the fact that I hadn't known about nor approved the Marshall Reynolds program. Humphrey pressed me, was very accusatory, but I stood firm on the story we had been giving over and over. There were other questions about the Bruce McAllister/test issue - including several about a copy of the test that had somehow escaped my possession, and the NCAA still seemed intent on humiliating me while trying to pin blame for the violations on me - but nothing new on that front.

Finally, after many hours, Humphrey wanted to discuss a minor women's soccer issue that had already been adjudicated as a secondary violation. I asked her why she even brought this up, as it appeared she just wanted to assail me for self-reporting something to show that I didn't know how to do my job. After being calm for most of the interview, I fired back at Humphrey and Jones. Bringing up another issue that had already been decided as a secondary violation and had nothing to do with the case in chief was just a pathetic attempt by the NCAA to make me look bad, and smacked of piling on.

I had originally decided against reading the closing statement that I'd prepared, but after this personal attack I reconsidered and read it. I lambasted Humphrey for her lack of ethics, and for targeting me when I was working in compliance and essentially helping her investigation. I said that I resented what this investigation had become. We self-reported the violations, took strong corrective measures, and there was no intent to deceive nor seek a competitive advantage. I implored them to close this case so everyone could move on. They had what they needed. My closing statement did not go over very well with Humphrey or Jones, but the Marshall contingent patted me on the back.

I was congratulated by Wilkinson and Cottrill for saying my piece, and the new university president, Dan Angel, joined Cottrill in stating how well I did in the interview. As we sat in Angel's office, Hilliard spoke up, asking in general how I would be protected by the university since it appeared the NCAA was targeting me. Cottrill immediately interceded and stated, as he had numerous times before, "Dave, you are the institution, and if anything happens to you, it happens to the institution. We are one in the same." Hilliard also reiterated that it was his role to defend me since I was the institutional representative. Both would reiterate this many times over the next several months.

Since I wasn't permitted to be a part of the additional interviews, Wilkinson served in my role and would give me updates on the progress. She and Hilliard seemed particularly distressed by Mark Gale's interview. According to them, he was evasive and did not come off as especially credible. He denied any knowledge of props working for Reynolds, when previous interviews of athletes and coaches were uniform in suggesting that not only did he know, he was an active participant in arranging the employment. His answers were contradictory and not persuasive. Wilkinson was intensely concerned about how bad his interview made us look. Little did we know that the worst was yet to come.

On Wednesday of that that week. I was at home after a typical long day in the compliance office. I called Hilliard, who was staying at the Radisson Hotel downtown, for a routine update. Rich was acting aloof, and then finally blurted out, "Things have changed, Dave." My heart sunk. Hilliard went on to say that the NCAA had credible information that the athletes were actually only working for one day, if working at all, for $200 or $25 per hour. In addition, it was apparent that this was a special arrangement for football and men's basketball players only, and that we could not argue that this was a benefit afforded everyone (or, it turns out anyone save for the occasional graduate assistant coach) else, as we had thought and were hanging our hats on. He went on to say that the players had been paid by check, not in cash, and the checks were distributed out of Pruett's office.

I could muster little more than silence on the other end of the phone. Finally I mumbled, "We're dead."

In that moment, it had all become clear. Everything Reynolds said, everything that Pruett said, was a lie to throw the NCAA off the trail, and I was the bag man at the heart of their bait-and-switch. I had defended these people to the NCAA, and was now inextricably linked to them. I was duped, and I knew it. I called Pruett and he was evasive, but stunningly, said he had indeed told the truth, that Reynolds was the one who was lying, and that he had no reason, until now, to doubt him. He admitted to the checks being delivered to his office, but thought it was for two days work, not one. Pruett even said, "Fuck him" in respect to the powerful booster, and vowed to rid him from the program. I doubted Pruett's sincerity, not that it mattered now. I knew my primary concern for the rest of the summer would be the players and their ability to play and attend school with all of this surrounding them.

The rest of the week confirmed my worst fears. The NCAA produced interviews with a former football player, Eugene Mitchell, and a former basketball player, Forrest Kirby, that detailed the arrangement of showing up for one day of work and getting $200 for it. Both mentioned that the work was not hard, and that they often did not work at all.

The NCAA also interviewed former Chapman Printing supervisor Russell May. May, who made less than $10 per hour, was "in charge" of the props, who made two-and-a-half times more than he did. May confirmed their rate of pay, the negligible amount of work the props did, and that they only worked on Saturdays. May had been reluctant to cooperate because he did not want anyone to get in trouble and was worried about backlash from those associated with Marshall since he still lived and worked in the area, but he was very credible and it was difficult to not believe him. When asked why he went along with the program, his response was simple: he did what he was told, and he was not in a position to say no. Plus, he was paid overtime for the Saturday he worked.

Longtime football secretary Edna Justice confirmed that checks had been delivered to the office ever since the prop-jobs program started, and that both Pruett and Donnan were aware of it. The checks were normally delivered by May, and hand-signed by Reynolds.

Yup, we were dead alright.

It was clear that this was a special arrangement for football and men's basketball athletes and there was no arguing the interpretation, and that the repercussions would be severe. I had to go back to Laura Wurtz at the NCAA with my tail between my legs, asking where this put us. She said the new findings meant that all money earned was considered an extra benefit, and depending on the extra amount earned over $100, there would be game suspensions. For example, if someone earned $500 they could potentially be suspended for four games during the upcoming season. I was able to successfully argue that they should only be penalized for the amount above what they could have legitimately earned, which was determined to be $6.50 per hour, but that was the best I could do. While this helped reduce the amounts owed and games suspensions, it was of little solace to me. There were no others that worked these jobs for this rate of pay, and this was a clear effort to circumvent the rules. I shuddered to think how many kids had probably been promised these jobs in recruiting (a clear violation of the rules), and what type of ripple effect the arrangement had on Marshall's success in men's basketball and football since it had been in place.

When confronted, Reynolds tried in vain to stick by his story. He provided some written statements of others who allegedly worked the same job for the same rate of pay, but written statements didn't stand a chance against the mountain of evidence facing us. Reynolds, whose signature was on every check that passed through the Marshall football office, could of course provide no proof - pay stubs, time sheets or anything else - that would back up his claims that non-players were given the same arrangement. In a desperate move, he also tried to pass the buck to his hourly supervisor, Russell May, saying that May had been instructed to work the athletes both days for $100 a day, and that he had acted alone in instructing the athletes not to show up on Sunday, so that May could claim the overtime hours. Again, there was no paper trail to back up the assertions. The explanation was feeble given that there was no proof, implausible, and pretty much useless as we could not find anyone that was even paid $12.50 an hour for these jobs other than Marshall athletes. Even if this was true, there would still be suspensions, and was never going to be believed now that Reynolds had been exposed as a liar.

It was a mess, a very big mess. We had to move forward with trying in vain to save the players eligibility through the NCAA's Student Athlete Reinstatement Process. It was at this time that we asked attorney Marc Williams[36] to represent the players in their reinstatement request with me assisting. This was the time that the players signed the second statement that stated they earned a "daily rate" that was normal for all employees. I knew it was a Hail Mary because we already had statements that were signed under Pruett's direction from the previous summer that said they earned half that amount. Those false statements enabled many players to compete the entire 2000 season as long as they were making payments on the amount attested to in the 2000 statements.

The statements in 2001 were handwritten by the players and signed in the presence of attorney Williams and myself. When I asked the players why they had signed false statements the year before, most said that the total amount was correct-. One player, Sam Goines, later mentioned that Pruett told them to sign the form if they wanted to play during the 2000 season. The hand-written 2001 statements were dictated by Williams and while he correctly asserts he was not in the room when the 2000 statements were signed, he was there in 2001 directing them what to write and then sign. The statements seemed reasonable enough, but I knew it would not work. What was even more disappointing were the statements themselves. Many of the kids could not spell, write a complete sentence, or even seem reasonably coherent, yet here they were in college being exploited by people like Pruett who were after glory and money, while many of these kids weren't even getting the education promised to them. Some of them would leave school, or even graduate, functionally illiterate and that just seemed to be fine with people for some reason. I felt nauseous reading the statements, with emotions ranging from anger to disbelief.

It was on this day more than any other that I began to look at college athletics through a much different lens. It was no longer something that had educational benefit first and foremost, it was simply a business hell bent on making money while exploiting the athletes who actually generate the revenue. I am not completely naive, and in reality I knew this before to some extent, but to have it confirmed in such graphic detail was distressing. I began to wonder whether I had been part of the problem as a coach and administrator during my career, advancing the ruse that college sports were about education first. As much as I fought for that myth, I knew now it was just that — a myth.[37]

Regardless of how we got to this point in late August 2001 and how many statements were signed, false or otherwise, there was no way to avoid player suspensions. The player suspensions handed down by the NCAA would range from one to four games, and the suspensions would have to be made public. Though every angle to seek some relief was explored well into August, we were eventually told in no uncertain terms that 12 football players and two men's basketball players would have to serve suspensions. From a football standpoint, the disaster was exacerbated by the fact that the team was scheduled to open at top-ranked Florida on national TV on Saturday night, September 1, 2001. This was going to be big news anyway, and the link to an SEC powerhouse was only going to fan the flames. Thundering Herd faithful would not be pleased.

But before we alerted the media, we had to break the news to the team. Coach Pruett and I had already met with the specific players who would have to sit out games. We then gathered the team in the multi-purpose room at the stadium and it was left to me to make the mass announcement. It was one of the hardest things I ever had to do. I felt the suspended players had been set up, and that the entire team was being forced to take the punishment for a problem that was well beyond their control.

Once word leaked out to the media, things only got worse. The athletic offices were swarming with reporters waiting for the official word, which would be announced on Thursday afternoon, a little more than 48 hours before kickoff in Gainesville. What I will never forget is that Coach Pruett was the one who gave the official statement. No Lance West, no President Angel, no Ed Grose, no Layton Cottrill. No one who had an official title was anywhere to be found. West had decided to take his family and drive to Florida early prior to the game on Saturday, and I was incredulous when he told me he was going to Florida and not stay in Huntington to handle things. I simply could not believe he would run and hide during the biggest crisis of his tenure as AD. Even Pruett questioned why he was going, but Lance simply did not get it. He was an empty suit with a title, and an abysmal failure as an athletic director - obvious before, but never more evident than this moment. A complete lack of leadership and an exclamation point on how bad the leadership was at Marshall.

I had never seen such an important matter handled by a coach, especially one that involved multiple teams, given that men's basketball was also involved, but there was Coach Pruett on Aug. 30, 2001, standing outside his office getting ready to tell the press what most of them already knew. The promising 2001 season was going to get off to a bad start, and it was going to be public that Marshall broke the rules. I actually felt sorry for Bob having to go out in the hallway to face about a dozen members of the press, so I thought it would be appropriate for me to at least stand by him and act like at least some administrator was pseudo-in charge. I was the highest-ranking administrator at this hastily-arranged press conference, a very dark day for Marshall University. Pruett and I were the only two that faced the music publically.

The next day's headline in the Huntington Herald Dispatch said it all, "Broken Rules Force Herd to Suspend 14." The bold-face, large font headline was meant to catch people's attention, and it certainly did. There was also a large picture on the front page of Coach Pruett talking to the press, and me standing behind him. Inside the paper, there was an editorial blaming the rules violations on "highly paid administrators who did not do their jobs."[38] Now the local media was also pointing the finger at me. They wouldn't be the only ones.

CHAPTER 18:

SEEKING SHELTER

WITH PUBLIC SENTIMENT GROWING against me, I requested a meeting with university president Dan Angel to discuss my job status. Angel's office called back and gave me a date and time for the meeting: Tuesday, September 11, 2001, at 7:00 am. Later that day was a pre-hearing teleconference with the NCAA, to discuss the upcoming hearing before the NCAA Committee on Infractions, to take place 11 days later. It was to be a momentous day, for more reasons than I ever could have imagined.

After going on a long early-morning jog through Huntington's semi-posh Ritter Park neighborhood to think and rehearse my words for the meeting, I arrived outside Angel's office precisely at 7:00 am. After waiting about five minutes, Angel showed up and invited me in. There was a person from the food service office already inside putting out some bagels, fruit, and coffee on the large conference table. Angel asked me to sit down.

We talked in general about family, the progress I was making on my doctorate, books that he wrote, etc. After about 10 minutes of small talk, I decided it was time to speak up. I told Angel that I was becoming intensely concerned about my future, and felt I had no choice but to come straight to him. Angel listened intently as I told him about a large mortgage payment, two small children, and the fact I was taking care of my elderly father. Beyond that, I told Angel I did not want to lose my career or my name over this, because I simply could not have prevented it. In short, though I didn't say it in so many words, I wanted a guarantee that my job was safe.

Angel took a deep breath and reassured me that no one's job was in jeopardy. He said he understood my personal situation, and told me he was impressed with my work ethic and abilities, but most of all he appreciated how vehemently I had defended the institution against the NCAA during the investigation. I nodded in agreement, and told him that my primary concern had always been protecting Marshall.

Angel went on to say that although he wasn't thoroughly pleased with how everything had happened and was managed in athletics, he felt we had a good staff in place to enable the department to grow and prosper. Then he started talking about Marshall Reynolds, and Angel's upbeat mood abruptly changed. The president was clear that the finger of primary responsibility was to be pointed at the booster, and it was clear to me that a major battle of egos had begun to evolve between the two figures. Angel angrily said that he was getting tired of phone calls from alumni, politicians, and prominent local businessmen urging him not to connect Marshall Reynolds to these violations. To which Angel claimed he would ask, "Which Marshall do you care about the most?"

Angel wanted to marginalize Reynolds, to limit his influence within the operation of the university, and the prop-jobs investigation was a way to sell casting him adrift. As Angel continued to reassure me, strongly dissuading me when I brought up resignation or reassignment, I continued to agree with him about Reynolds. I felt the booster knew much more than he ever told me or the NCAA, and knew it could only be a good thing to bring him under control. Our discussion was nearly two hours old when suddenly, Layton Cottrill knocked on the glass door and entered the president's office.

"A plane just hit the World Trade Center, and the news is saying it was a commercial airliner," he said. I remember saying something to the effect that it was probably a Piper Cub or something. It was a natural time to stop the meeting anyway, so we all exchanged goodbyes and I thought little of this plane hitting the Twin Towers. My mind was on the NCAA prehearing conference.

As I made my way back to my office to prepare for the pre-hearing, it was becoming abundantly clear that this would not be a normal day. Along with the rest of the country, I watched in horror as the events of September 11th unfolded. Despite what was going on, the intense emotions, and a general feeling of wanting to go home to be with family, there was one entity that still felt it was above it all. No, the NCAA saw no reason to cancel the pre-hearing teleconference, even with the historical occurrences unfolding before our eyes. It would begin, as planned, at 11 am, less than an hour after United 93 - originally bound for the Capitol Building - crashed in a field in Shanksville, PA, less than 300 miles from where we sat in Marshall's Drinko Room.

My mind and everyone else's mind in the room was swirling. A tower had already collapsed. News was breaking that the Pentagon had been hit, along with another plane crashing near Pittsburgh. Yet here was NCAA investigator Mark Jones on a teleconference, acting as if this pre-hearing stuff was the most important thing in the world. The arrogance of the NCAA never ceased to amaze me.

The prehearing conference was essentially to discuss the items that Marshall and the NCAA agreed upon, and did not agree upon, in advance of the Committee on Infractions reviewing the case.[39] Of the four allegations against Marshall, the one that would require the most debate would be the allegation against me of unethical conduct and violation of the cooperative principle. Amazingly, Crane - who did not respond to direct NCAA questions about her secret source - was not even mentioned, and somehow I was being accused of non-cooperation? The basis for this allegation stemmed from the Bruce McAllister test/study guide case. The short of it was that we had discovered an original copy of the test that the students had been given, and I had been keeping that copy, along with several exact photocopies, in a banker's box in my office prior to the NCAA arriving on campus to review it. But prior to their arrival, the original copy of the test had gone missing. Whether it was lost or stolen remains a mystery to me, but regardless, the test itself had no bearing on a case in which all of the general facts of the matter were agreed upon. Still, LuAnn Humphrey was determined to take me down, and insinuated with the charge of violating the cooperative principle that I had done something untoward by "suppressing" the test. What exactly I could have achieved by this, especially since we had several exact copies of the document, no one including Humphrey has ever explained to me, but there it was.

We were just beginning to discuss this issue when Cottrill was alerted by his secretary that the son of a Marshall professor was likely on one of the planes used by the terrorists as weapons.[40] We had just been given news that a plane had crashed into the Pentagon, and I was becoming more and more distraught, as I knew several people who worked at the complex. Though Jones likely would have pressed on given the choice, it seemed appropriate that we finally stop the pre-hearing and reconvene another day. It was determined that we would finish up the following Tuesday, which would be four days before the actual hearing in front of the COI. This argument would have to wait for another day, which was convenient, because just as me and the rest of the world were trying to process the events of September 11th, my trial in the media and court of public opinion began in earnest.

Since the news had broken of the suspensions, there was nary a word in the local media about Pruett and his culpability over the prop-jobs issue. The urge to blame someone, namely me, was spreading like wildfire throughout the public. It was an easy reach for people who do not understand college athletics to blame the person in charge of compliance, and there is a natural predisposition to blame someone else other than the beloved, successful football coach. The university continued to support me, but the anger towards me in cyberspace was growing, and putting pressure on the administration to make a move. I had never spent much time reading internet forums or visiting chat rooms, but friends were forwarding some of the awful things being said about me. I would be lying if I said it didn't affect me, but I was sure to not read it myself. I just wrote it off to idiots who had blinders on and didn't understand how intercollegiate athletics worked.

Pruett continued to support me, at least to my face, but it turned out he was playing defense by going on offense. I had called him a few days before September 11 to discuss some issues regarding the NCAA pre-hearing conference. I had continually been hearing about things being said about me and in an attempt to make myself feel better, I inquired yet again of Pruett of what he thought my status was. He again assured me that he heard nothing negative about me and that everyone was pleased how hard I fought for Marshall. He then went on to mention that, "A reporter wanted to write a story blaming Lance and I told him that we are all to blame, and he should not write that." I knew immediately what reporter he was talking about: Chuck Landon.

Pruett, as many celebrity coaches do, played much of the local media like fools, and Landon, who then worked for the Charleston Daily Mail, was his most willing pawn. Pruett used Landon to advance his own agenda - pay raises for him and his staff, pretending to be offered other jobs, and floating the idea of he himself becoming AD among the topics that Landon wrote about at Pruett's obvious behest. Landon was a quintessential jock-sniffer who felt empowered by his almost creepy fawning association with Pruett, even if it was only as his lap-dog. Landon knew that not being obedient to his master would not yield the treat he so craved: a direct link to the Marshall football program.

Landon is neither strong nor talented enough to write his own opinions, but he penned an editorial, printed on September 12, 2001, blasting me and Lance West. Obviously, Pruett's "warnings" to Landon had been another lie, since we all knew Landon wouldn't really disobey an order from Pruett. The title of the piece was "Someone Should Pay For MU's Problems,"[41] which was about the only truthful thing about it. Landon's contention was that the prop-jobs program had been both legal and well-monitored under Jim Donnan and Lee Moon, and that West and I somehow missed it when NCAA rules changed, that we consciously, approvingly allowed the program to continue running unchecked. The piece was horrible and inaccurate, typical for Landon's writing and research ability. These jobs had never been permissible under these circumstances, and certainly were not permissible under Donnan.

Nothing Landon wrote could have been further from the truth. Donnan and Moon had instituted the program to gain a competitive advantage , and knew there was no one at Marshall at the time to red-flag their efforts, or who wanted to stop it. Though they were gone from the university, they were telling the press and others that the program was permissible, which was inaccurate, self-serving, and disingenuous. Donnan had been fired at Georgia after the 2000 season for failing to meet on-field expectations, and was in the mix for several jobs, including one at the University of Kentucky, who he was telling that when he was at Marshall, the prop-jobs program was legal. When Kentucky contacted me to inquire further, I told them he was lying, and that the NCAA investigation would prove that. Moon was also on the job market, and neither wanted this to stick to them, so they claimed this was program was permissible when they could point to no NCAA rules to support that ridiculous contention. I wonder if Donnan not getting the Kentucky job was a coincidence.

Landon also failed to mention the multitude of other rules violated by Pruett and his staff, such as the recruiting with the promise of jobs, overpayment and work-not-performed, that were pretty simple to understand and completely understood by the football and men's basketball coaching staffs. He based his contention that West and I were to blame on conversations with three unidentified athletic directors - one of whom may have been Lee Moon trying to save his own skin and flagging career - who were uniform in agreement that the situation ought to be laid at the current athletic department regime's feet. It's interesting that these Athletic Director's did not identify themselves to state facts about how the rules permitted this type of arrangement . Honestly, it wouldn't surprise me if Landon did not talk to anyone. He was the king of the "mystery" or "unidentified" source to back up his claims, especially when his primary if not singular source was Bobby Pruett.

It hardly mattered that Landon's prose was an attack without basis in fact, it was effective because it reinforced the viewpoints of everyone within both the public and administration who wanted to blame someone other than Bob Pruett, who had brought the community and university so much success. In the same way that it's reassuring to believe that global warming is a liberal hoax when the alternative is to worry about the earth soon being under water, any answer that refuted Pruett's culpability had to be the right one.

What was apparent from his veritable commissioning of the piece was that Pruett felt the walls closing in around him. He feared that any connection to NCAA violations would threaten his job, and by extension both his lofty community standing and millions of dollars in deferred payments and annuities he would receive for remaining as coach at Marshall. Beyond that, though Pruett's "aw, shucks" persona and deep Huntington ties may have belied it, he had designs on bigger and better coaching opportunities and would have left Huntington in a heartbeat for any big-time job. NCAA violations on his watch would severely injure Pruett's chances of moving up in the college football world.

Pruett could control pretty much everything in Huntington, but he was scared he could not control this. Pointing the blame at me could give him and the university the out they needed, and preserve his own selfish and altruistic goals. Concerned about the piece, I called Cottrill to vent. He told me not to worry about some "second rate loser reporter," and that I had nothing to worry about as far as my job was concerned. He again stated that the university was behind me, that Hilliard would defend me, and that I was safe.

The next week flew by. The chaos of 9/11, feeling of defeat, and impending war took center stage in everyone's life. Marshall's upcoming football game against TCU was canceled, and most sporting events around the country were either scratched or postponed. The university's issues with the NCAA indeed seemed trivial against this backdrop, but a week after planes hit the Twin Towers and changed America forever, it was time to get back to business with the pre-hearing conference.

The completion of the pre-hearing was uneventful until we made it to the allegation against me. While I had been largely disappointed in Rich Hilliard during the investigation up to this point, he did argue passionately for this sanction to be removed. He said it simply did not make sense to charge me with purposely losing the test when I had previously gone to great efforts to make copies and distribute it, especially when the lost test had no impact on the findings or outcome. LuAnn Humphrey countered that I had violated the cooperative principle by being combative during the investigation, but Hilliard correctly argued that it was not a violation to vigorously defend the institution or oneself, and that having these charges leveled against me would hurt my future career possibilities. Mark Jones interjected, nonsensically, that while I may have been distressed by the allegation, I should not have to worry because, "…you are not at risk." Jones was shouted down, with Hilliard and I both asserting that if someone has an allegation against them, they are by rule, at risk. Rich continued that if I truly was not at risk, then the allegation by rule must be withdrawn. Even though Humphrey and Jones disagreed, the allegation was removed by order of David Price, then Vice President for NCAA Enforcement and Student-Athlete Reinstatement. It was a minor vindication for me. The investigators had not liked how I challenged them and prevented them from running roughshod during the investigation, and the allegation was one of their methods for revenge. They were not going to get it on this occasion.

Now, it was time to prepare for the main event, the hearing before the Committee on Infractions, which would take place on Sept. 22, 2001. At

Hilliard's behest, the Marshall contingent who would be present before the Committee ran through a mock-hearing scenario, so that those who had not been through the process would have a general idea of the logistics. He went over the seating arrangements, the best method to answer questions, and other general strategies. The most enduring memories from this meeting concerned Pruett, who was beginning to get a little testy, and was amping up his "plausible deniability" routine. Though we had been over this dozens of times in the preceding months, Pruett continually said of the prop-jobs arrangement, "Dave, I thought you told me I could do this." Again, I reaffirmed that I had never approved this arrangement, nor would I have. Hilliard and Dan Angel both interjected, reminding Pruett and the assembled group that we all needed to pulling on the same rope and that we stuck to the plan. I was also reassured on two points that I raised in that meeting, issues that concerned me over Pruett's latest denials. One, that no one would throw me under the bus, and two, that I did not need personal counsel as I was an institutional representative.

Another interesting aspect of this mock-hearing practice was the angst directed at Beatrice Crane from many in the room. Though she certainly wasn't responsible for the arrangement cultivated by Marshall Reynolds, Jim Donnan, and Lee Moon and maintained by Bob Pruett and the new regime, there was no disputing that she had left out the raw meat that brought the wolves to the door. She had incorrectly insisted that the NCAA knew about the prop-jobs arrangement, had forced the university to hastily file a report on the matter before we could gather the necessary information, and had needlessly, and heedlessly put Marshall in a position of tremendous weakness against all of the charges against us.

Angel specifically stated that he was disturbed by Crane's actions, and he personally requested that she not be at the hearing in Indianapolis because she could do us further damage. The NCAA was interested in what she had to say, or more accurately, what she didn't have to say. The investigators had expressed concern about Beatrice's story of a "secret source," tipping her off about another "secret source," supposedly from the NCAA, who had tipped that person off about the employment issue. Though we knew by now that the direct source was her friend Rob Fournier from the MAC, who had an ax to grind with me, Crane wasn't willing to give up that information and was leaving herself and the university open to a major violation of NCAA bylaw 10.1(b) - Unethical Conduct and Violation of the Cooperative Principle. Fournier's NCAA source, meanwhile, was fictional, lying or ill-informed.

In the world of NCAA investigations, an unethical conduct charge against Crane and Marshall would be devastating, considering what we were already up against. I had actually wanted to report Crane back in 2000 for not answering questions as directed about her sources, but was prevented from doing so by

Hilliard and Cottrill. It now appeared that this issue could come back to bite us at the hearing. Angel said it was time to find out what really happened, and summoned Crane to his office. I thought she might get fired, and though I didn't relish anyone losing their job, I honestly thought that would be best considering how selfish she had been during this entire process. Cottrill pulled me aside and assured me that if she did not come clean, she was gone. After meeting with Angel, however, she was given a stay of execution. I did have a little vindication because we were not going to allow her to come to the hearing, and she was finally disciplined with a letter of reprimand from Angel for her handling of sensitive information and for failing to follow established procedures.

I finally had a measure of high ground over Beatrice Crane in the eyes of the university brain trust.

The Marshall University delegation arrived in Indianapolis on Friday, September 21, 2001. Some, like Angel and Cottrill, arrived by private plane, courtesy of the West Virginia state government. Others like myself drove four hours from Huntington. In addition to the university higher-ups and Hilliard, our group included Provost Sarah Denman, Dean Larry Froelich, Lance West, Linda Wilkinson, and along with their attorneys, Tim DiPero and Craig Kelley,[42] coaches Bob Pruett and Greg White. The Mid-American Conference sent Commissioner Rick Chryst and Associate Commissioner for Compliance Dell Robinson.[43] We all descended on the law offices of Ice Miller, Hilliard's firm, for another strategy session prior to Saturday's meeting before the NCAA Committee on Infractions.

The strategy session was really nothing more than confirming what we had already admitted to, but that we were going to fight any other charges, especially the dreaded "Lack of Institutional Control" charge, because we felt that Reynolds and the previous administration were the ones who formulated the program, and that we had now enacted procedures for avoiding further problems. As it had all along, the strategy was to parcel out the blame to several parties, including me for what was being deemed an insufficient interpretation of athletics assistance for props. Pruett was going to stick to his story that he thought the arrangement was OK based on what Moon told him, the belief that props were being paid commensurate with like employees, and that I said it was OK that props could work. Reynolds would continue to get the lion's share of blame.

We also wanted to stress that this was obviously a new day at Marshall given our efforts and improvements in compliance. Though we would shoulder blame for the situation, however, we would not fall on our sword and take every spurious allegation the committee would throw at us. Hilliard wanted to make sure we defended our processes, and that we wouldn't allow the committee to blame a decade-old problem on a relatively new regime. Everyone left the strategy session feeling pretty good about that approach, and that confidence and optimism was showing during a dinner held atop one of Indianapolis' tallest skyscrapers, One American Square, which also housed the offices of Ice Miller.

Toward the end of dinner, Angel stood up to give a toast. He became emotional while raising his glass, saying, "Everyone around this table is a good person, who has strived to do the right thing. I know that we will do fine tomorrow, these were not problems of our making, it is a new day for Marshall University and Marshall athletics, and I appreciate everything that everyone here has done for Marshall University." Tim DiPero, White's attorney, raised his hand and said, "Mr. President, If I could be so bold and say that if you repeat that statement tomorrow to the committee, it will have a wonderful, positive impact." Everyone clapped and nodded in agreement.

For a few fleeting moments we were all together, united in defense of Marshall, and determined to demonstrate that we were a university committed to doing the right thing. The past was the past, and in spite of everything, I was determined to be a good soldier who was part of a united front. I wanted to show the Committee that while there were problems, I had led the way in attempting to address and ultimately fix them. Given the smooth, reasoned nature of the similar hearing I had endured while at Weber State six years earlier, I really felt that the committee would understand and praise my efforts. I went to sleep that night back at the hotel feeling reasonably confident that maybe it would all be OK.

It wouldn't.

CHAPTER 19:

THE HEARING

THE MAKEUP OF THE NCAA Committee on Infractions, and the nature of the Committee, is interesting to say the least. While appointment to the COI is considered to be a prestigious one for the university and conference administrators that are named to it, it is a secondary, voluntary position for those who serve. While members get travel and hotel accommodations, and some other perks like Final Four tickets, there is no additional financial compensation. At the same time, committee members have a big stick to swing in NCAA governance matters, and it is indisputably the political power that attracts many of those to seek out such an otherwise thankless assignment. Though many competent professionals have served on the Committee, there's no disputing that it's a magnet for the power-hungry, the ambitious, and those seeking to be noticed by being a part of one of the most public forums in college athletics.

They certainly aren't attracted by the volume of work, which is why many members of the COI treat their actual responsibilities on the Committee as an inconvenient chore to be performed at their own discretion. The individuals who comprise the Committee - athletic directors, conference commissioners, and the like - are already among the busiest people in college sports, and often do not have the time to digest the voluminous amounts of material given to them before a weekend of hearings. These weekends, which occur 3-4 times a year, are full Friday-through-Sunday affairs with workdays that can range from

10-15 hours in length and also include numerous phone conferences and work sessions at other given times during the year.

Consequently, these members do not have the time, nor do they usually make the effort, to really get to know the case. Often, their decisions and rhetoric are based on feelings, pushing responsibility away from the higher-profile individuals to whom they generally relate the best, taking cues from the institution, and many times just attempting to get it done quickly. In the Marshall case, Committee members were presented with three large binders of information, and were seen struggling to skim through the materials while the hearing was ongoing. The lower-profile the case (i.e. those involving smaller, non-BCS schools like Marshall), the less interested the committee seems in doing anything other than achieving a quick resolution and getting the case off their books

Several members of the COI spend a large chunk of the day literally sleeping through hearings. In my previous experience during the Weber State hearing, then-SEC commissioner Roy Kramer spent most of the session comfortably dozing off, occasionally snoring, though no one took any action against what I considered to be a serious breach of responsibility. This activity repeated itself in the Marshall hearing, when Committee member and University of Miami athletic director Paul Dee - who in his defense actually had a sleep disorder but was allowed to serve anyway - napped as critical case details were being discussed. Perhaps more revolting is the fact that some members of the COI have had numerous violations at their own institutions. In the Marshall case, figures from Alabama, Miami, and Nebraska - three universities that had been at the height of corruption in college athletics over the previous decade – were sitting in judgment of us, and of me.

Given this situation, it is not very hard to see why this Committee will many times go after an easy target, and make their minds up without really digesting the facts. Though the COI doesn't get everything it does wrong, the duties of the committee and the structure of the process are barriers to having a fair and complete hearing.

Of course, I was considering none of this as I walked into the hearing with the rest of the Marshall contingent that Saturday morning. It wouldn't take long before the actions of this committee would destroy my faith and belief in the NCAA and what it supposedly stood for, but for now I was radiating positivity.

NCAA Infractions hearings typically take place in a large hotel ballroom that is set up with several tables and chairs in a perfect square. The COI sits at the front, to the right of the committee is the institution and affiliated individuals, to the left is the NCAA enforcement staff, and sprinkled in with that group are other NCAA staffers and investigators, as well as at least one member of the infractions appeals committee. In the back row of tables you usually have more NCAA staffers who are handling the taping of the hearing, conference representatives, and any other individuals who might be at risk but are no longer at the institution in question. For example, had McAllister attended the hearing as requested, he would have sat in this row. In the middle of the square there was a court reporter to transcribe the events of the day.

Hearings start out with introductory and logistical formalities. In our case, Angel introduced the institution and institutional representatives, while David Price from the NCAA introduced the enforcement staff. Then, the COI chair introduced the committee and others in the room.

Our committee for that day included some very prominent athletic administrators, Faculty Athletic Representatives, and two outside individuals. The committee consisted of chair Tom Yeager, Commissioner of the Colonial Athletic Conference; Josephine Potuto, FAR and professor of constitutional law at Nebraska; Paul Dee, Athletic Director at the University of Miami (FL); Gene Marsh, Faculty Athletic Representative and law professor at Alabama; Andrea Myers, AD at Indiana State; James Park, an attorney from Lexington, Kentucky; and Fred Lacey, a retired federal judge and practicing attorney in Newark, New Jersey. Craig Littlepage, the current athletic director at the University of Virginia was on the committee then, but was not able to make the hearing.

We had no shortage of egos on the committee we were facing that day, but it would soon become clear that three in particular - Yeager, Potuto, and Marsh - were in search of a spotlight from which they could exert their authority. I often felt we were watching a performance by these three, rather than an impartially adjudicated hearing, despite the serious potential repercussions for a number of people and a university.

Yeager, the chair, was the self-ordained star of the show. He displayed palpable pomposity and ego, and acted as if he truly enjoyed punishing people even if the punishment did not fit the crime. While Yeager is generally respected throughout college athletics by those who don't know any better, he is a classic case of one who can dish it out but cannot take it in regard to following NCAA rules. According to multiple sources within the NCAA, who refuse to identify themselves due to the power Yeager wields within the association, the CAA commissioner interceded personally on eligibility issues regarding international basketball athletes at various schools in his conference, specifically Virginia Commonwealth University. NCAA staffers said that he commanded such fear at the national office that many higher-ups refused to cross him, thus some would-be-ineligible men's basketball athletes were permitted to play despite protests of some very bright people within the organization. According to those same sources, NCAA Vice-President Kevin

Lennon told staffers in regard to crossing Yeager, "This is not a battle we are going to fight."

To me, Tom Yeager was disappointing as committee chair. He did not seem to have a great grasp on the facts, and appeared to have his mind made up about me before the hearing started, through what little research he may have done in preparation for the case, and he was more interested in how he looked as committee chair.

A very close second in arrogance was Potuto. Again, it was tough to watch someone from Nebraska sit in judgment of others considering the legal and NCAA issues that institution experienced over the years, so much so that I was embarrassed that I had ever wanted to work at such a place some years before. Potuto was the worst embodiment of the above-it-all Nebraska culture. Throughout the hearing the New York City-bred Potuto was gruff, argumentative, and oozed an uncomfortable cockiness despite not having a great grasp on the case. Despite also spending a fair amount of time dozing off or appearing disinterested, she was very resistant to any challenges of her authority.

In his defense, Marsh did manage to stay awake during the hearing, though his presence on the committee was puzzling in more ways than one. His institution had been dealing with NCAA investigations on and off for about 15 years, situations that he couldn't seem to keep Alabama out of despite serving in a position that can influence integrity and compliance with NCAA rules. During this hearing, Marsh was among those who lambasted me many times for allegedly not doing enough to prevent Marshall's violations. Ironically, it would later be discovered that Marsh was missing in action during several phases of the upcoming Alabama infractions case concerning booster Logan Young and the impermissible attempt to lure blue chip prospect Albert Means to the Crimson Tide, yet he was praised by the very same committee for his investigative prowess and abilities.

But before any of this fun, we heard opening statements about the case, facts of the case, and a summary of facts in agreement and dispute. Angel said in his opening statement that while he was unhappy to be there, he had full confidence in the people he brought with him, and that it was a new day for Marshall University. He added that among the violations included in the hearing one was the work of a rogue professor and the employment issue was something that started well before our arrival and coordinated by a local booster who was now disassociated from the program. The enforcement staff then stated their stance which was not different from ours. Our goal was to convince the committee not to sanction us for Lack of Institutional Control, and I thought we might have a chance at that.

The first two allegations to be discussed concerned the employment issue.

Despite my new-found confidence in Hilliard following his successful defense of me at the pre-hearing, he appeared to be unprepared now that the hearing itself had arrived. He began to fumble in his answers and explanations. Hilliard had previously said that he did not want me to talk too much, but it took only took a few minutes for him to direct several questions from the COI in my direction. Again, like a good soldier I answered the questions to the best of my ability and in the form discussed previously with Hilliard.

Even though I had been asked not to speak too much, more and more questions were coming my way very early in the hearing. My comments would be intermingled with Hilliard's, and it was apparent he was not doing a good job of explaining the situation. Things were going from bad to worse and the question I knew was coming was asked by Yeager. Sensing an opening he asked, "Mr. Ridpath, is it true that you did not understand this arrangement constituted institutional aid?" I sat for a second and thought about it, and while I really wanted to give the exact and correct explanation, I had been asked not to do that by the person who represented himself as my attorney. I pressed the button on the microphone and simply said, "No, I did not understand."

Yeager looked like a shark after blood and he looked up and down at his committee with a half-smile and said in a very condescending tone, "Uhh … oh-kaaaay." He then shook his head in mock disbelief. I went for the microphone again and looked at Hilliard, who held up his hand motioning for me to not respond. For all practical purposes, the hearing was over. The COI had their person, and they began to pile on, while the people who said they would defend me were conveniently silent and letting this pressure by the COI on me continue unabated. I was getting frustrated and angry, and I regretted that I had listened to Hilliard and answered Yeager's question that way.

At our first break, Hilliard and Cottrill both said that I was doing well, and not to worry about the committee. They both cautioned me about getting frustrated to which I said, "Then someone better start defending me." They were in the hearing saying nice things about others involved, including Crane, to my astonishment, and they couldn't even throw me a bone by defending me as promised. It would be easy for me to say it was a conspiracy, but that would be giving our assembled "team" too much credit. Hilliard and the rest of the group were simply taking their cues from the committee, and guided the institutional response from there. The path of least resistance. Defending me, whether it was the right thing to do either factually or morally, was only going to antagonize the Committee. I was a zebra being thrown to hungry lions. No defense would be coming my way, even though I had sacrificed my career to steer Marshall University successfully through the investigation. It was depressing, and my anger was only building.

The hearing continued, and it was Pruett and White's turn to duck responsibility, claiming that they did not know that they had to report information to me as part of the compliance process. I was more angry with Pruett, because he at least attended rules education on occasion. Greg White attended exactly one rules education seminar over the course of my four years at Marshall, so in a sense he was telling the truth because he was usually missing in action when it came to rules, not that ignorance is an acceptable defense. For his part, Pruett had known damn well what needed to be done to follow the rules,

and just chose not to do it.

Before lunch, the conversation again turned to Crane and her role in discovering the violation with Pruett in early 2000. While fielding a question from Marsh, I revealed to the committee that I was very distraught at Beatrice and Pruett for failing to come to me immediately when there was an inkling of a potential violation. I added that Beatrice had been verbally warned not to seek outside interpretations, and that all interpretations had to go through a central source, namely me. I also felt the need to explain that there were personal issues between Crane and I that had caused the situation to become volcanic. I told the committee I had never had a chance to explain myself, or to spend time researching if there was even a violation before we blew the whistle on ourselves. It smacked of a setup, and in many ways I never recovered.

Also, during questioning from the COI on the fact that Crane was impermissibly giving out interpretations of rules to coaches behind my back, Gene Marsh had made an eloquent statement about how troubled he would get when people at his own institution would fish for interpretations. Marsh went on to say, for the record, that coaches and others would state, "Tennessee is doing this, Auburn is doing that," to which Marsh replied, "I don't care what other people are doing, I am concerned about Alabama." I have many philosophical differences with Marsh, but he was right on the money on this one, and I found myself nodding in agreement, thinking he was going to assail West or Angel on the lack of control over Crane. Marsh ended by emphatically stating he had "been bitten in the butt" by people seeking alternative interpretations and when it happened it made him "want to pull out a gun and shoot somebody." Pretty dramatic stuff from a COI member. I was initially buoyed by this and stated virtually the same things, reiterating how important it was for an effective compliance program to have a central person for interpretations, and to prevent fishing. I then went on to say that just because another institution was doing something, it didn't make it right, adding, "We make interpretations based upon the best interests of Marshall University, and I don't care what other people are doing." Exactly what Marsh said, but apparently I was not allowed to share the opinion.

This was a sound bite pulled out by the COI, and taken completely out of context in the report to reflect poorly on me. The COI used the statement to make it seem that I would heedlessly make interpretations to give Marshall an advantage, essentially playing fast and loose with the rules. I was saying the exact same thing that Marsh was in a much more refined way (I didn't threaten to kill anyone), yet the COI took my statement as a stand-alone. This was an abomination, as the media had a field day with that quote and because of the secrecy of the process, no one could see what was actually said in the proper context. This was a clear cheap shot to discredit me by the committee, and probably one of the most unprofessional things I have ever seen. It was truly sad to see a committee that touts integrity and fairness to operate in this manner. I knew now, more than ever that this process was as flawed as Jerry Tarkanian said it was all those years ago, and that it targeted certain individuals out of spite.

This committee did not take great care when that quote was put in, and they knew they did not have to answer to anyone and that I could not appeal. Situations like these are one of the main reasons the NCAA so vigorously fights any transparency in their process. They know if hearing transcripts and investigative documents are made public, many of the assertions in the report would be proven to be inaccurate and concocted.

When taken in the proper context, it is clear exactly what I meant, and it was in direct response to Marsh's statement in which he was saying the same thing. While I was still criticizing Crane for not following procedures, Mark Jones interrupted to argue that the violation would have never been discovered but for Crane's effort, because I had said it was OK. Now I was pissed. That was an unwarranted cheap shot by Jones, who knew that had I been presented with any information about the Marshall Reynolds arrangement that I would have checked it out. I was never even given that chance, because I was only able to check out the information after Crane, Pruett and Reynolds had concocted a story to lessen their culpability. This conclusion was lost on the committee, and my statements were going nowhere. Right before lunch, Angel made the last statement, and essentially said he had no problem with the actions of Crane. I was grinding my teeth at this point. Here was the president, who just days ago told me Crane was going to be fired and he agreed with me that her actions damaged the investigation, now agreeing with the stance of the investigators that her actions were apparently commendable. Like Hilliard, Angel was taking his cues from the committee, which was inexplicably in Crane's corner. While it was amazing that the committee did not see the obvious issues with Beatrice, including her refusal to answer questions from the enforcement staff during the investigation, it was even more stunning that no one in the Marshall delegation was defending me or even advising me. I was on an island.

My agitation was on full boil as I stormed out of the ballroom. I followed

West into the hallway and grabbed his arm. "Way to go Lance, you hired a stellar SWA in Crane. Do you even realize the damage she has done!?"

"Dave, just calm down and focus, I need you to focus," West said. I just shook my head in disgust, not believing this weak individual ever made it to the position of athletic director.

Cottrill motioned for me to go outside into the courtyard, and he looked angry. Wilkinson and Denman stopped me before I got outside and reported that Humphrey had approached them and said, "Get Dave to calm down, he is killing you." I just laughed and said, "Then someone better start defending me and helping me out. We all agreed that Beatrice screwed everything up and now we are praising her. Whose side on we on here?!"

Cottrill poked his head inside the door and said, "Dave get out here, now."

I went outside and Hilliard and Cottrill cornered me. Hilliard said I was leading with my chin, and Cottrill lamented that I was not helping him and not helping the institution. I again questioned what we were doing, reminding them that we had completely abandoned the strategy, not to mention that no one was defending me. I added that praising Crane and her efforts contradicted everything we had said previously. My pleas were not heard. Cottrill told me not to speak anymore and I said I was happy to do that, but that Hilliard needed to stop directing questions my way. I also told them that if I was going to be their fall guy, I was going out on my own terms.

"I'll go into the hearing room and resign," I said, "But then I am going to say everything I can to make sure the true story comes out." Cottrill retreated into his rhetoric, and just told me to relax and calm down. Surely he did not want me to go in and damage the flow of the hearing and likely reveal details that he did not want the COI to find out.

Next, Angel came out and asked me to take a short walk with him around the hotel. He was much calmer and more cerebral than Cottrill, but he asked me to use caution. He said that airing dirty laundry was not going to help us, and that was why he felt it was necessary to say what Crane did was OK. He reiterated that my job was safe, but said it was more effective to say less. I hesitantly agreed. I was determined to get through the rest of the day, and was more than happy to not say a word.

I stayed true to my word, and only answered one question, regarding the academic issue, the rest of the day. The hearing was winding down as the hour approached 5:00 pm (actually a very short hearing by NCAA standards). Angel gave an impassioned closing statement that was complimentary of me and others, our efforts, and our commitment to following NCAA rules - especially from this date forward. I felt a temporary sense that maybe I was getting rehabilitated a bit. Angel again got teary-eyed, and stated how embarrassed he was and that this type of situation would not happen again nor would Marshall University be in front of this committee again as long as he was president of the institution.

Jones then commented on issues that the committee never touched upon at the hearing, saying in support of the institution and of me that we self-reported these issues and had taken strong corrective actions. The hearing was adjourned shortly before 5:00 and as everyone exchanged pleasantries, the committee members, specifically Yeager, were very perfunctory with me. Marsh was pleasant and stated that we had problems with boosters similar to the ones he had faced at Alabama. He wished us luck. There appeared to be no remaining animosity towards me from the Marshall contingent, as I suppose I performed better in the afternoon and the academic fraud issue was not as convoluted.

Hilliard and I hugged, and he said that I did well considering how I was attacked. He instructed me to write a note of thanks/apology to Marsh just to smooth things over with the committee. I told him I would, and I got in the driver's seat for the long drive back to Huntington. I waved at the members of the group who were getting into a hotel van for the trip to the airfield. In my mind, it appeared everything ended well, but being abandoned by the institution that I so passionately defended was something that really stuck with me. I had a strange sense of foreboding for the institution and myself, in spite of the feel-good goodbyes at the hotel. We just had to wait for the penalties we knew were coming, and we had to hope they were not that severe. The long drive home gave me time to reflect on how the people for whom I'd gone to bat lied and let me, and Marshall University, down.

PART III

CHAPTER 20:

BREAKING DOWN

I WAS EXHAUSTED THE day after the hearing. I was frazzled over the direction it went, how the committee focused mostly on me and Hilliard had let them, how Pruett did a masterful acting job playing the role of a stereotypical dumb West Virginian, and how the committee bought it all. It was a long drive back from Indianapolis to Huntington, but I was glad to be home. Some of my wife's family was in town from Germany, and they would be occupied all day which gave me some much-needed free time. I headed into my office about mid-morning to continue working on my dissertation. Soon after I arrived, my phone rang. It was Greg White, who was surprised I was in the office on a Sunday. After we made some small talk, Greg remarked how sorry he was at the treatment I received from the NCAA, and that he felt it was unwarranted considering how good of a job I had done for Marshall. White went on to say that he had never been that nervous before and every time he spoke, he felt an apple in his throat. As he and I laughed, he lamented that Beatrice Crane was even allowed to have a job considering how badly she screwed up the entire process. He added that he'd said as much to Angel on the flight back from Indianapolis. I wholeheartedly agreed, of course, telling Greg how much better off we would be without her interference. I thanked Greg for the very timely call and pep talk. I hung up feeling better than I had for quite a while.

I also made a quick call to the MAC office to leave a message with commissioner Rick Chryst to seek his permission to survey senior MAC athletes for my dissertation project on factors that influence the academic persistence and graduation of NCAA Division I athletes. Somewhat surprisingly, Chryst was there. We chatted briefly, and he too was very positive and didn't think that anything I did at hearing was out of line, saying the process was not "a love-in." Chryst pledged to assist me in any way he could with my research and lauded my work at Marshall. Two great phone calls in a row — that had not happened for a while.

My happiness would be short-lived, as I had several emails from none other than Beatrice Crane in my inbox. While some were innocuous enough, one message caught my attention. It was an academic issue concerning a women's softball player. Crane had attached email conversations she had with the head softball coach, Shonda Stanton, that concerned an issue with a specific professor and what should be done. While Beatrice did email Michelle Duncan and me with details of the conversation, I was livid that it had already gone that far. I had numerous problems in the past with Crane getting involved in academic issues, and she and Stanton both knew if there was an academic issue it was to immediately go to Duncan or Linda Wilkinson. Crane did not need to get involved because she always gummed up the process.

It was at this moment that the weight of the investigation and the stress of the previous day's hearing reached a boiling point. I overreacted, sending some scathing emails back to Crane informing her of proper procedure when it comes to academic issues. I was channeling my anger toward her within another issue. In hindsight, I should have waited, taken a breath, and confronted her on Monday, but I didn't and in my rage created more problems for myself. Even though I felt I was right to admonish her, I did not do it in the most professional way.

After finally cleaning out my inbox, I went to work on my dissertation for a few hours and miraculously forgot about the hearing, the department, and about every other frustration I was feeling. Later, I took my wife and her visiting family out to dinner at the new Herd Hall of Fame Café, at the time a new restaurant/sports bar in downtown Huntington with a ton of specific Marshall University memorabilia. As we ordered, I proudly watched a local artist painting a huge Marshall football mural on a wall, knowing I had a part in the success of the program. No matter what had happened, I felt strongly for the university and the athletic program. Despite the hurdles, it was not just a job to me, it was something I truly loved. As I watched, I noticed none other than Coach Pruett standing by the artist chatting with him amiably. While Pruett was admiring the handiwork, I yelled "Coach," and Pruett turned around and smiled when he saw me. He immediately came over and said hello to the family and introduced himself to my relatives from Germany. Pruett was having dinner with a couple of donors following a memorial service for Paul Ambrose, a former Marshall student and son of a well-respected university professor who had been killed when Flight 77 hit the Pentagon on Sept. 11.[44] Pruett and I both talked about how such an event could put the NCAA garbage in perspective. As he left he gave my wife a big hug and said, "You treat this guy good, he had a rough day yesterday but he did great." My wife said she would and even after the events of the day, I felt we would move on as a department.

The next morning as expected, the crap began to hit the fan over my emails from the previous day. Beatrice began to send emails basically ordering me to show up for an interview with a new swimming coach candidate. The email exchanges then became petty and vitriolic on both sides, as we slammed each other for various transgressions and I hit her hard on the NCAA hearing and how I was treated. These exchanges went on periodically for the rest of the morning until finally Beatrice confronted Lance with the long list of exchanges. Yet, in true Lance West fashion, he went to Senior Vice President of Operations, Ed Grose, to show him the emails instead of handling it himself. It was agreed by West and Grose that West would give me a good tongue-lashing but West, Beatrice, and I would meet with Grose in the morning for another "come to Jesus" meeting. This was vintage West. He was just not capable of true leadership, or handling a problem he was frankly paid-well to handle. Many in the department, mocking the fact that West was pursuing a master's degree at the same time he was AD, referred to him as the "highest paid graduate student in America."

The issues with Beatrice and I had been brewing for years, and I had literally been daring Lance to handle it, but he never took charge of the situation because he did not want to upset his power base, nor upset Crane, who was well-connected with the Marshall elite and could damage him if he chose the wrong side. West called me after the meeting with Grose, and demanded that I meet him in his office at 3:00 p.m. I chided him and said I liked his new found aggressiveness. He did not take too kindly to my sarcasm, and again stated that I would be in his office at 3:00. I laughed and hung up.

As I walked over to his office, I knew I had to let him have his time in the sun. This was going to be Lance's chance to slam me, and I really had no recourse but to take it. While I can be temperamental and confrontational when the situation warrants, I knew this was the time to shut up. I made it to West's office a little before 3:00 and said hello as I sat down on one of the leather couches near his desk. He did not acknowledge me for about five minutes as he flipped through paperwork, and I just stared at him, not saying a word. He finally got out of his chair and went to get Beatrice and his secretary, Charlotte, who fielded West's emails since he did not know how to use a computer. We all said hello and then sat down in various places surrounding West's opulent desk.

Lance didn't waste any more time, and began to berate me. He said sternly that my attitude and rhetoric would no longer be tolerated. He then demanded that I apologize to Beatrice and Charlotte, who had I also been curt with in a previous email exchange. While not wanting to do it, I gave what functioned as an apology to both, and explained that my emotions had gotten away from me during a very difficult time. Charlotte began to say something to me, to which I replied, "Charlotte, this is between Lance and I and I don't need your input at this point." Nobody said anything, and Charlotte left the room. Lance tore into me again, and I must admit he was doing pretty well for a person that had never previously demonstrated that ability. He was well-rehearsed and had a nice script in front of him. Grose had prepared him well.

As Lance continued his tirade, I just listened and stared directly at him. I didn't blink, smile, or show emotion except for the occasional "yes sir."

As he continued, Lance started to go way back into the past and detail things I never thought were problems, inferring that I had not been doing a great job in compliance, which was about 180 degrees from his previous sentiments (which were documented) toward me. At that point I spoke up in a calm, but stern matter. I said, "Lance, if these things were problems, why did you not say anything before? My personnel evaluations never detailed these things and I resent you bringing them up. It is all well and good to get admonished for the emails, but now you are pulling things out that are unfair … in fact you are acting like the NCAA Committee on Infractions."

Lance replied, "September 22nd is behind us Dave, and it is time to move on." I agreed, but I asked now if I was going to get the help I needed to do an effective job, to which Lance predictably replied no. As the meeting with West ended he said that Beatrice, he, and I would be meeting with Dr. Grose at 9:00 the next-morning. How chicken-shit of this guy, I thought to myself. I was mildly impressed that he showed a little moxie in our meeting, but in the end he was passing his discipline onto Grose. West left the room, but not before saying that Beatrice and I could not leave until we worked out our problems.

That actually caused both of us to snicker a little and smile at each other. I did not mind meeting with Beatrice, but I was just fried after the weekend and all the garbage going on with Lance, much that I admittedly brought on myself. Beatrice and I talked amicably and I reiterated my apology. I told her that we could work together and get along, but I needed her to tell me the truth about what happened and where she got her intelligence on the prop-job issue. I wanted it step-by-step, and she complied. Beatrice confirmed that it was Coach Pruett who came to her and started talking about the "other issue" the NCAA let us know about. She stated it was Pruett who brought up the props working under Marshall Reynolds, and that I had authorized it. She then admitted to panicking and going off to find the truth because she felt the arrangement was impermissible and given the ESPN scenario, she said she did not want to call me.

"Beatrice that is not your choice and you violated department policy!" I yelled. "You believed Coach Pruett's version of the facts without talking to me, and your actions put me in an indefensible position. I never knew or authorized this jobs program, nor would I have!"

"David," she said meekly, "I am sorry too. I should not have done it that way. I should have come to you first."

While this made me feel good, I was beginning to get keyed up as the emotions of those days came flooding back. I asked over and over if she realized that she was wrong, and told her how she damaged the integrity of the investigation. She agreed. I then asked for her to tell me her version of what happened next. She explained that Coach Pruett was very nervous and wanted to find out for sure whether this jobs program was permissible or not. Beatrice offered to call her former assistant at Louisville, Jennifer Smith, who was, and still is, Associate Athletic Director at Michigan State University.

According to Crane she asked Smith point blank, "Can props work," to which Smith allegedly just laughed at her. Again, according to the rules at the time, props could work, they just had to get the job on their own, get proper wages, etc.. It surprised me that someone as accomplished as Smith would get this wrong too, but her interpretation only added to the raging fire that Crane was stoking.

In this meeting, Crane continued to claim that she then received the unsolicited call from the secret source, who turned out to be Fournier. She went on to say that Fournier knew people at the NCAA and they informed him that the investigation was not really about the academic issue, but about Prop 48 kids working. She also said Pruett was in the office the entire time she made and received the phone calls and interpretations. Pruett consistently denied he knew who the secret source was, but he was the one pushing Crane to call Fournier. This was just one of the many lies Pruett continued to repeat, if Crane was indeed telling the truth. Whether it really happened this way or not doesn't matter, and I will probably never know for certain. To Pruett and Crane, the subject was closed. They had the major violation all figured out and they had the person to blame.

I listened and became emotional. At a point when nothing should have surprised me anymore, the level of deception and secrecy within the department, while a game of chicken was being played with my livelihood, was almost too much too bear. Crane put her hand on my shoulder and told me how much I meant to her, how important our friendship was, and how despite everything, she really enjoyed working with me. Even though I had heard her say things like this before, it made me feel better. Still I asked her how she could choose

Rob Fournier and Coach Pruett over me, and the integrity of the institution, when I was trying to do the right thing. She said nothing.

I was at a crossroads. Should I just acquiesce to everything, get along, do my job, and get out once I got my doctorate? I thought that would be the best plan, and I left West's office determined not to let this situation bring an end to what had been a mostly enjoyable career thus far. I reported to Grose's office the next morning as directed. Grose asked me to start and explain my actions. I put on a pretty good performance by stating the emotion of the week, my issues with Beatrice and Lance, and how everything had just caught up with me. Although it was very difficult for me to do, I praised Lance for his leadership the day before, and I pledged to continue being a good soldier and do the job to the best of my ability, as I apologized profusely. Grose was very complimentary of me, my job thus far, and his distaste for the NCAA process. He said that I was very important to Marshall and then said four words I will never forget, "We need you Dave."

Crane and West both shook their heads in agreement. It was becoming a love-fest. Maybe it was superficial or an out-and-out lie, but I certainly felt as secure as ever coming out of that meeting. Grose suggested I try some personal counseling to get over some of the anger I was feeling over this issue, and he pledged to help me move on. He reiterated his support as I left the office.

I immediately went to the Community College to talk to Wilkinson. She certainly did not approve of my emails, but she understood my feelings toward Crane and the situation as a whole. I almost excitedly told her about Grose's commitment to me, and we both resolved to move forward. She was very happy to hear of his support for me because she knew I had to have him in my corner. As I left Wilkinson's office, I was ready to forget about this distasteful episode and work hard. I'd also resolved to move out of Huntington the following summer.

The remainder of the week was actually pleasant and productive for the first time in months. I met with the swimming coach candidates as Crane wanted, and was performing all my other normal duties. I did get a letter of reprimand from Lance on the email episode, but I expected it and chalked it up to experience, vowing not to let it happen again. Friday of that week was nondescript. We were playing Bowling Green in football the next day, and I was excited to see two of the BGSU coaches I knew casually when they coached at Colorado State, Urban Meyer and Billy Gonzalez.[45] The game would be Marshall's first since the Sept. 11th attacks three weeks earlier.[46] That morning I was checking phone messages, and there was one from Grose, asking me to call him back. I attempted to return the call several times that day but could not get a hold of him. I figured if it was important, he would get back to me.

I went to the game on Saturday, Sept. 29th not knowing that it would be the last athletic event I would work at Marshall, or anywhere for that matter. I always enjoyed the games because I did not have a great amount of responsibility and I could spend time talking with visiting coaches and administrators, in addition to watching the action. Nothing seemed strange to me until after the game, when Lance and Coach Pruett were very standoffish. The entire department staff always met in Lance's luxury box after the games to eat, drink, and be merry. I always looked forward to heading up to the box post-game, and it was a nice way to unwind. I went up as normal, but West and Pruett appeared to be avoiding me. Here I was with a new lease on my job, and I had adjusted my attitude, so I was anxious to get back to normal. The cold shoulder was a little strange, but I didn't think much of it. In hindsight, it should have sent up a big red flag.

West and Pruett already knew what I didn't: I was a dead man walking.

CHAPTER 21:

A NOT-SO-CLEAN BREAK

I WAS SITTING ACROSS from Ed Grose on Monday, Oct. 1st, giving the impression that I was listening intently to everything he was saying. But really, whenever you receive any type of momentous news in your life - a child on the way, the death of a loved one, a breakup - it's impossible to keep your head from spinning enough for the brain to process everything you're hearing.

This was one of those moments, and not in a good way. Grose had just told me I was being reassigned from my spot in the athletic department to the Director of Judicial Programs. I remember Grose telling me I had done a great job, but that the stress of the investigation and personality conflicts had contributed to the decision. This from the man who less than a week before had told me how much the university needed me. I was devastated, confused, and strangely relieved all at the same time.

The relief, apart from the fact that I wasn't going to be dealing with the investigation, with Lance West, or with Beatrice Crane on a daily basis, stemmed from the fact that I wasn't being out-and-out fired. I had a wife and two small children to think about, and was also caring for my elderly father, who had received outstanding medical care in Huntington. Ironically, I would be getting a small raise (though I lost my courtesy car) in becoming Director of Judicial Programs, so the position would be a soft place to land until I could resume my athletics career elsewhere. I would also be able to complete the progress toward my doctorate. It wasn't athletics, but it wasn't the worst scenario. And although the duties of the job would be new to me, the position itself wasn't a complete mystery.

Toward the middle of 2001, I had been venting to Linda Wilkinson about how things were going with the investigation, my job, college athletics in general. During that conversation I mentioned "chucking it all," and doing something else, which was when Linda brought up the vacancy in the Director of Judicial Programs job. I never seriously considered it, but I did pull aside the Dean of Students, Steve Hensley, one day to half-jokingly ask about the position "in case I am made the fall guy." I knew Hensley was close to Grose, and thought it might be worth floating a trial balloon in case they were thinking about doing the worst. My feelings about this were very short-lived, especially after the Sept. 11th meeting with Dan Angel where I was reassured that it was all for one, one for all and I wasn't going anywhere. By the time the hearing took place, I had forgotten all about it.

Now, a little more than a week after we had appeared in Indianapolis, my trial balloon had landed. Reassigning me gave Marshall a way to save face, to get rid of me while simultaneously keeping me under their thumb. As long as I was employed at the university, they surmised, I wasn't going to blow any whistles. I knew what they were doing, but didn't have much choice but to go along. In addition to my family considerations, I was also thinking about my future career in athletics. I was concerned about how my reassignment was going to be portrayed to the NCAA, because I didn't want the promising career I had worked so hard to build to be dead.

I told Grose that my top worry was how this would be characterized to the public, the media, and most importantly the NCAA. Grose immediately spoke up, "Dave, this is a mutual management decision between us. We are not saying anything to anyone, to include the media, because it is a personnel issue."

I told him it was very important for me to hear that because I would like to get back into athletics one day, but I could see the benefit of doing this job for a year or so until I finished my dissertation. Grose reassured me again, saying that my job performance would be praised to the NCAA. While I knew that some would view my removal from the department in a negative light no matter what, I felt reassured by Grose's comments. I also knew that I had done nothing wrong, that the university did too, and that there was no way they could honestly blame me for these violations. As long as the transfer wasn't characterized negatively to the press and most importantly the NCAA, I told Grose, I could live with this transfer.

It was agreed. I would accept the assignment. As Grose and I walked over to the Memorial Student Center, where my new office was located, he was talking fast. He seemed almost excited that this move was happening, obviously not picking up on the fact that I was feeling downright defeated. The rest of the day was spent breaking the news to everyone affected - my wife, my colleagues inside and outside the athletic department, and the coaches.

My voice trembled as I told Michelle Duncan and my assistant, Kevin Klotz, that I had been reassigned. Reality had begun to sink in. I had already told Grose that Klotz had my endorsement for successor, and would repeat that endorsement to everyone who asked what would happen with the position. My voice trembled as I told Kevin and Michelle that I had been reassigned. It was really enjoyable working with them, and I hated to leave them in a bind because now so much would be thrown at them. I thanked them both for their efforts and told Michelle that our work was not in vain - we made this a more ethical athletic department and it was the better for it. Later I convened a meeting to discuss the news with all the hard-working enrollment management office supervisors from the offices of the Registrar, Admissions, Financial Aid, and Dean of Enrollment Management.

Next I decided to call Bob Pruett, because I wanted to hear what he had to say for himself, and to discern if he had anything to do with me transferring. There had not been a major decision made in athletics since I had been there that was not coordinated by Pruett, and I was certain Pruett was behind the reassignment. The telephone conversation confirmed it. When I asked Pruett if he had heard about the transfer, he replied that he had but that it was something "the president wanted to do, and he had no choice but to follow along." As always, he praised me and said what a fine job I did, but Dan Angel was adamant about removing me, and his hands were tied. What a load of garbage. All Pruett had to say was "Ridpath stays" and I would not have been transferred. It is sad to say that a football coach controlled the university, but in this case it was a reality. He decided to squash me like a bug to save his own ass.

My last meeting was in the late afternoon in Lance West's office. I shook Lance's hand and thanked him. It was perfunctory and not genuine on either side. Beatrice was there and she immediately gave me a hug and said, "This will be better for you and I wish you the best of luck." I added that I hoped she and I could be friends again, and again endorsed Kevin for the full-time job. Lance listened, then said that Beatrice would work with Kevin in compliance until a full-time person was hired. The hair on the back of my neck stood on end. I had fought for years to keep Beatrice out of the compliance office, and there was no evidence to demonstrate that she knew any more about the department than Kevin or myself. I knew this development would not be well-received by many of the coaches or the university community, because most despised Beatrice. I didn't say anything. It wasn't my problem anymore.

Soon after, I ran into assistant AD Mike Bianchin, who asked if I heard that the person replacing me would have the title of Associate Athletic Director.

This was nearly as devastating to hear as Grose's news had been hours earlier. I was virtually certain that a ton of money and resources was coming the way of the compliance department and my replacement, and I resented it. No matter how much I begged, I was never given the tools I needed to succeed, always being told that we didn't have the money. A few days later I found out that the new Associate AD for Compliance and Student Services would have a secretary, a full-time assistant at a much higher salary, and money for up to three Graduate Assistants. Compliance was being upgraded in a way that virtually assured the department's success, and of course I was going to look even worse in comparison. It was tough to hear that and not be disappointed after all my efforts of trying to make the department better. Still, this was a common playbook for universities, which would suddenly find the revenue to support a stronger compliance department in the wake of a scandal. Ironically, I had been the beneficiary of this thinking on a smaller scale at Weber State.

Before the day ended, Marshall sports information director Ricky Hazel stopped by to tell me that he was getting calls from the press about my status. I also had a couple phone messages from local media. I thought it would be best to give a statement, and no one in authority told me that I could not. I instructed Ricky to tell everyone that called that I was leaving for personal and professional reasons, that I was burnt out and ready to try new things in higher education since I was due to receive my doctorate in May of 2002, and to stress that this was a voluntary move on my part and not connected to the violations. I said as much to the media I personally talked with, and added that I could not control what people thought about the transfer, but I was at peace with the decision and it had nothing to do with the violations. I spent the next couple of days cleaning out my office and tying up loose ends in compliance in order to ease Kevin's transition.

Before I officially moved, I talked with Linda Wilkinson who passed on the news that the administration was highly peeved that I had talked to the newspaper. That was curious to me, because I had only repeated what Grose had promised. Later in the week, I saw Layton Cottrill, who "suggested" that I not speak with the media. By this time though, I had begun to mentally prepare for my new position, in which I was driven to do a good job despite my lack of qualifications. I was determined to succeed and attempt to let this entire NCAA mess blow over.

After starting as Director of Judicial Programs in mid-October, I actually had a few good days in the job. It was a nice break from what I had endured the previous two years, though in my mind I knew I would soon be seeking another job in athletics.

That strategy, as well as the attempt to move on, was derailed almost as soon as it started. The reality of my transfer was beginning to become clear.

CHAPTER 22:

WHITE LIES

A week into my tenure as Director of Judicial Programs, Kevin Klotz stopped by my office with the compliance graduate assistant at the time, Jamie Spatafore. It was good to see some friendly faces, and I joked around with them to defuse any tension they might be feeling from seeing me in my recently-deposed state.

I noticed, however, that Kevin had a look of sadness on his face. It was as if he wanted to tell me something. When I pressed, Kevin mentioned that he had just returned from a compliance committee meeting. This was a new compliance oversight committee that had been borne from the NCAA investigation as a corrective action, an effort on the part of the university to give the appearance of a changing athletic department culture. Of course, it was all a sham. Beatrice Crane, Lance West, Layton Cottrill and Ed Grose all served on this supposed oversight committee set up to unbelievably "review the decisions of the compliance office." A case of the fox guarding the henhouse if there ever was one. The majority of that committee had culpability in the infractions in the first place and now they were reviewing decisions of the one office that was doing the right thing?

"How did the meeting go?" I asked Kevin.

"OK," he said.

"Just OK? It seems like you have something on your mind."

"I probably shouldn't tell you this," Kevin said sheepishly, "but they have made you a corrective action to the NCAA."

I felt the breath leave my body, and I stared at Kevin in utter disbelief. He was telling me that my removal from the athletic department was being used to show increased compliance to the NCAA, inasmuch saying that I had been an obstacle in doing things by the book, and by extension the infractions would be publically viewed as being my fault. This was a 180-degree turn from what I had agreed to. In spite of all that had happened, I never believed that Marshall would do this to me, especially after Ed Grose had told me explicitly that this would not be the end result. I had been lied to again, and I fell for it.

Kevin could sense my blood boiling, and began to reason with me that my designation as a corrective action was not that big of a deal. I knew this wasn't Kevin talking, but the people who had done this to me. I unleashed on him.

"How can you say this isn't a big deal, Kevin?" I yelled, "They just ruined my fucking career!"

Kevin told me to calm down. He assured me that the university would, in fact, say that that I did a great job as Assistant AD for Compliance, but that my removal from the athletic department had to do with my conduct at the NCAA Infractions hearing in September. I wasn't happy about this, though if Kevin was telling the truth about the stated reason for the corrective action, maybe I would be able to salvage my career. Leaving nothing to chance, I asked Kevin if he could get me a copy of the memo that the university sent to the NCAA. I knew obtaining this document and showing it to me would be of great personal risk to Kevin (even though he was not forbidden to not show it to me), but being the true friend he is, he agreed and got me a copy of the memo the next day.

As advertised, the memo did not say that I had done a bad job in compliance, nor did it say that I approved or even knew of the impermissible jobs program. The statement, written by Rich Hilliard, under the heading of "Additional Corrective Actions" said, "…due to the tenor and tone of the Assistant Athletic Director for compliance at the NCAA COI Hearing on September 22, 2001, he has been removed from his position and transferred to another position at the university. A national search is presently being conducted for his replacement."

So it was true. I was being offered up as a scapegoat because I had stood up for myself and fought for the institution at the COI Hearing. Of course, I had been encouraged to do just that in the days and weeks leading up to our trip to Indianapolis. I was not warned by anyone to be quiet or measured at the NCAA hearing, and though I did fight passionately in the face of the committee's badgering and constant airing of misinformation, defending myself was not a violation, it would have been a major stretch for an objective person to say that my behavior had been out of hand, and I bristled at the implication that it was something unusual. As Rick Chryst said, the hearing process is certainly not a love-in. This corrective action was a cop-out on the part of the university power brokers, who had picked up on the Committee's grudge against me early on in the proceedings, and in turn gave them the sacrifice that it was easy to assess they were looking for, and likely hoping for.

As I was processing this information, Kevin dropped another bomb.

"Dave, Dr. Angel is changing that statement," he said.

"How so?" I responded.

Kevin went on to say that while most of the compliance oversight committee and Hilliard had initially agreed on the "conduct at the hearing" strategy reflected in the memo, Angel, Pruett, and Grose were adamant that the wording be more severe. According to Klotz, Angel said he would make the wording stronger with regard to my removal, because he wanted to demonstrate to the NCAA that he was in charge and committed to following NCAA rules and regulations. Kevin told me that Linda Wilkinson, Layton Cottrill and men's basketball coach Greg White had defended me on this issue, to no avail.

And the hits just kept on coming. The memo I was reading, though heinous in its own right, now represented a best-case scenario. My corrective action was no longer even being characterized as a punishment for my supposed "bad conduct" at the hearing, it was clear the entire blame was being laid at my feet. The institution felt comfortable doing this, and was apparently fine with the fact that I had accepted a job transfer under false pretenses.

At this moment, I knew I needed to get all my ducks in a row for a potential fight, and to get things in place quickly. Before I confirmed that I was indeed being made a corrective action, a process that was going to necessitate me confronting those who had apparently lied to my face, I needed to round up copies of all the documents pertaining to the investigation. I knew that those documents would eventually hold the key to proving that I was a help to the university's compliance cause, not a hindrance, if it came to that in a court of law.

This would be one time during my experience at Marshall when the university's ambivalence towards tightening up compliance procedures would actually work to my benefit. During the investigation, I had asked Layton Cottrill several times to provide me a secure location for all of the NCAA investigative documents, because I felt my office could be a potential target. I even asked again on my last day in the office if he wanted all of the investigative material and he replied, "I have everything I need, I don't need any more of that shit." Cottrill never acted on my request, which meant there were 4-5 banker's boxes of important material still sitting unguarded in my former office. I needed these materials before someone at Marshall became aware that I was on to their plot, and wised up and removed them.

While still in the process of moving out of the office and assisting Kevin in the transition, I asked him for his help in getting me these documents. Knowing that I was being railroaded, he agreed. We even had some fun with the transport of the documents. Since Kevin could not be there when I had time to come across campus to get the materials, and given that I needed him to give me the materials so there could be no questions about impropriety after the fact, I came up with an alternate idea.

Kevin was to take the boxes to what we called the "archive room" in the Cam Henderson Center, adjacent to the Gullickson Hall Fitness Center where I still worked out during my lunch hour. The archive room was essentially a storage closet, a mess of a space that mostly had old sports information department materials and past media articles. It was musty, wet, smelly, and full of the biggest cockroaches you ever saw, but it was a perfect place to "make a drop."

The next day during our workout, Kevin surreptitiously handed off the keys to the archive room. He said he would call me later in the afternoon to tell me when the boxes were there. I would then go pick up the boxes, secure the room, and return the keys to Kevin the next day. I waited for Kevin's call. When the phone rang, I knew it was him from the caller ID. I picked up the phone and answered and all Kevin said was, "The cake is in the oven." Then he hung up. I chuckled at this James Bond-type scenario. I wasn't chuckling when I retrieved those boxes, however. In fact, my heart was beating out of my chest. Even though I could have just as easily taken these boxes in the process of moving, the way we set it up felt pseudo-movie-like. Once I made my "escape," I set out to confirm what Kevin had told me, that I was indeed being made a corrective action.

I started by calling my friend Linda Wilkinson, who was part of this new compliance oversight committee. I thought I would get straight answers from Linda, who had always been my ally, but I was discouraged to find this was no longer the case. She was very evasive, saying, "Dave, I cannot talk to you about these things, and I will only speak in generalities."

I persisted.

"Linda, is there something you need to tell me?"

She refused, and I knew what Kevin was saying was true. Everyone, including Linda, who up to that day had been telling me everything, was turning against me. The next day I called Hilliard, who was also cold and distant, far different from our October 1st call. I came right out and asked if I was being made a corrective action and he confirmed that I was, based on my "conduct" at the hearing. When I asked him to elaborate, Rich offered no specifics, only repeating that I "wasn't helpful at the hearing."

Had Coach Pruett been helpful, I asked, when he lied about his involvement in the jobs program and resultant cover-up? Hilliard gave no response, except to continue to berate my performance at the hearing, saying he wished I had said nothing at all. I reminded him that he had encouraged my efforts to defend the institution throughout the investigation. He had told me he was my attorney as well as the institution's, that it would be "gloves off" at the hearing. I also asked if he remembered that he was the one who directed questions from members of the COI to me in the first place. Hilliard, like Wilkinson, was evasive and stammered throughout the conversation. Finally, Rich gave me something I could use. When I pointed out that nothing was said to me at the hearing to suggest that my being made a corrective action was a possibility, he said that while he agreed with the action, he was not the one who recommended it.

During a meeting on the week of October 1st (likely a phone conversation with Hilliard, although it has been described as a meeting), in which the university was devising a way to respond to a letter from the NCAA requesting information on why the COI should not assess the damning sanction of "lack of institutional control" against Marshall, none other than head football coach Bob Pruett had led the lynch mob against me. Hilliard said that Pruett was adamant in the meeting that I be fired because, "He put Marshall University in jeopardy by his conduct." Pruett may have forgotten to mention his lies, his pervasive involvement in this impermissible program, and most of all his encouragement to me to "fight the NCAA bastards" in this meeting.

Angel clearly came up with the decision to fire me during this discussion. Hilliard added that it was Cottrill and Grose who suggested the transfer and the raise during the meeting, because they were certain that I would fight being fired, and this would make it cleaner and therefore protect the university. They assumed correctly, on that count.

I told Rich that I thought the corrective action was egregious, that the NCAA wouldn't care whether I was a corrective action or whether I was transferred to another department for some other reason. Hilliard emphatically stated he disagreed with my assessment, and it turned out he had reason to. According to Hilliard, multiple members of the COI had informed Rich that they would take it easier on Marshall University if I was fingered as a corrective action. I asked Hilliard if that was true and he replied, "I am shooting you straight on this."[47]

I told him I would appeal the corrective action via the NCAA appellate process, a suggestion that made Hilliard audibly chuckle. He reminded me that there was no such relief available for me, because the NCAA did not assess the corrective action, Marshall did. What was clear to everyone else was now becoming very clear to me. The NCAA could cajole and even force an institution to take action on an employee, but they could then disavow all responsibility by saying it was an institutional decision, thus rendering any appeal null and void.[48] The NCAA can sanction an individual, and sometimes does, but since that action can open them to potential liability and civil litigation, it is easier to "suggest" to institutions what they might do to potentially avoid more damaging sanctions. After talking to Hilliard, I felt I needed to contact Cottrill and at least give him a chance to explain himself. I was hoping he would tell me the truth, but my expectations were naturally pretty low at this point.

I set up the meeting under the guise of talking with him about my new job in judicial affairs.[49] When I arrived in Layton's office, he was cordial as usual and gave me a hearty hello and handshake.

I spent the first few minutes asking him about my new job, things I needed to do and not to do, what to learn, etc. I mean, I was totally in the dark on what was a very important position at the university, one that I could not take lightly. Cottrill spent a good part of the meeting praising the job I had done in athletics, and stating how important I was to the university in this new position. It was surreal to hear a man I once trusted lying through his teeth. This was a prime chance for him to tell me about the corrective action, but he did not. Finally, after assuring him I would do my new job to the best of my ability, I blurted out the question that I really wanted the answer to.

"Layton, how am I going to be characterized in the NCAA investigation," I asked.

He paused, stroked his mustache for a couple seconds as he always did when he was trying to think of a politically correct answer, and took a deep breath. It was clear that he was formulating an answer to pacify me, and I had trapped him. He had to answer the question now, and I just stared at him, knowing I was not going to hear the truth.

"Dave, you are just one of 23 corrective actions," he said as he attempted to soften the blow of the truth.

I feigned astonishment. "Corrective action ... what do you mean? That was never discussed."

Cottrill went on to say that yes, I was indeed a corrective action in the NCAA report, but that it was for my conduct at the hearing, and nothing related to job performance or responsibility for the infractions. This in spite of Kevin confirming that Angel had already changed the "conduct at the hearing" language. Cottrill then went on a little rant saying how much everyone, including himself, was to blame, but that most of the blame was at the feet of Marshall Reynolds. He said of Reynolds, in fact, that Marshall was "clipping his (Reynolds') wings a little bit - and it is about time."

"Your job performance will be praised in every public thing we say, however you didn't help us by your vigorous defense at the hearing," Cottrill said.

I interrupted him to say that I disagreed on that point and reminded him that the university - himself included - always encouraged my firm stance. No one at Marshall had ever given me any protocol as far as conduct prior to the hearing, other than to fight hard for the university. This was looking more and more like a setup to make me the sacrificial lamb, one that was formulated prior to us walking into that room in Indianapolis.

By this point, I didn't quite know what to think. Cottrill, the highest-ranking person I had spoken to on this issue, continued to insist my corrective action was only for my perceived conduct at the hearings, which is what the original memo that Kevin Klotz had shown me suggested.

I was partially willing to give Layton the benefit of the doubt because I really had no choice. Perhaps Angel did not change the memo; maybe the corrective action would be minimized. When I returned to the Memorial Student Center, I called Linda again, and Provost Sarah Denman happened to be there too. I told them about the conversation with Cottrill, and they confirmed that every conversation they had with the powers that be on campus (Grose, Angel, Cottrill, and of course Pruett) alluded to me being a "minor" corrective action regarding my conduct and that the university would take special care to praise my job performance, so as to not ruin the long-term career I still sought in athletic administration.

Linda and Sarah were very encouraging, and while I was suspicious of what was unfolding behind my back, I was still willing to give this new job a shot, finish my doctorate, and eventually move back into athletics. At this point, it was the only realistic course of action. My head would still be on a swivel, but I began to get a sense that perhaps I had made too much of this situation. I could withstand the corrective action, I surmised, as long as Marshall University keeps its promise on how I would be characterized.

Like so many expectations I had of those in authority during my time at Marshall, my hopes in that area would eventually fall short too.

CHAPTER 23:

WEIGHING THE OPTIONS

THE POSITION OF DIRECTOR of Judicial Programs at a university brings with it an immense responsibility. This is the office where sanctions are assessed to students for violation of the university's Student Code of Conduct. While the bulk of the infractions that came across my desk in this position concerned underage drinking, recreational drug use, and violations of university housing contracts, there were times that I found myself involved with adjudicating domestic violence cases, alleged sexual assaults and rapes, stalking, and even attempted murder. I certainly did not want to screw up anything in this job while I plotted my return to another athletic position, but I often wondered why I was put into such an important spot, one that could cause the university immense liability, given that I was nowhere near qualified for it.

The position did have a parallel to athletic compliance in that there were rules, and interpretations of those rules, to be followed. Thankfully, my predecessor Dr. Linda Rowe did a wonderful job of having the office in great shape prior to my arrival, and I was grateful that I could call on Linda for help at any time. She became a great confidante, and warned me to be very careful about whom I talked to when I began to navigate the legal terrain. She specifically warned me about my new boss, Dean of Student Affairs Steve Hensley, who Linda said the university would use to try and get information from me. I followed Linda's advice and played it close to the vest with Steve, while also ensuring that his reports about my performance to the administration in Old Main would be favorable.

While the position of Director of Judicial Affairs is important and even prized by many individuals who desire a career in student affairs, and while there was occasional excitement given the nature of the job, on the whole I found it nothing short of boring - with all due respect to the professionals who enjoy it as a career. It was not my passion, not what I had worked for, and not something I desired to do long-term. The job did have intangible benefits of which I took full advantage. I took longer lunches to do my workouts. I was always home on time because there was never a need to stay late. I never came in early, nor did I have the dedication anymore to give the little extra that had helped me move up so quickly in athletics. Everything could wait, because it was not that important to me to excel for a university that betrayed me, and I just fulfilled the minimum requirements for the job. This was strange as I was always one who pushed myself to excel, but those days were gone … at least for a while.

While it was great to spend more time with my family and have all my weekends free, something was missing in my life. There was a part of me gone. I did not have any passion anymore for what I was doing or for life in general. I couldn't shake the worthless feeling I had as I walked away from the athletic department for the last time, or how low I felt watching the football team play Northern Illinois on television the first Saturday after I had been transferred. I knew I was no longer a part of it and while that hurt, what hurt more was a nagging doubt about my ability to get into the business again. It is difficult to explain because I was making good money, I had a fantastic group of family and friends, and seemingly everything else I needed, but I was growing unhappier by the day. I felt lost and without purpose. My personal life was marked by deep depression and some excessive drinking.

Meanwhile, Marshall president Dan Angel had embarked on a media campaign to prove how clean the athletic department was. In one particular editorial he stated that Marshall athletics was now 99% pure, just like Ivory Soap.[50] He made it clear that anyone who violated NCAA rules would be sent on the first train out of town. Although I knew for a fact the football coach was still doing exactly what Angel said he would not tolerate, the implication was that everything was above-board now that Dave Ridpath, the cancer, was gone.

As much as I tried to move on, there always seemed to be something that brought up the NCAA investigation, whether from whispers of people I encountered in Huntington to a funeral director asking me about it and my role in the violations when I was purchasing a prepaid funeral arrangement for my elderly father. I was becoming paranoid about what people were saying and thinking about me. Since I was there and saw pieces of my former life every day, it became increasingly difficult to move forward.

With my depression mounting, in mid-November 2001 I decided to make a couple calls to friends in the athletic community and get their take on what had happened to me. Most of my contacts were shocked that I was blamed, and expressed displeasure at Marshall and the NCAA because they knew I'd done a solid job at other institutions and Marshall. I called John Johnson, then the athletic director at Weber State University and my former boss, and Doug Fullerton, commissioner of the Big Sky Conference.[51] These are two people who I really respected, who had helped me at various points in my career, and I needed not just a shoulder to cry on, but for them to level with me on what my future prospects in athletics were. I must admit that their words, while helpful, did nothing for my current disposition. Both Johnson and Fullerton were blunt. Essentially the message was the same - a corrective action, regardless of how it is portrayed, is a career-killer, and that I needed to do something to stop it.

Johnson indicated that he would give extreme pause before hiring someone saddled with a corrective action in an NCAA major infractions case because the business is ultra-competitive and it was far easier to hire someone with a "clean slate." I asked John point-blank if he would hire me again and while he said he most likely would, it probably would not just be his decision because other university administrators, specifically university presidents, would most likely balk at hiring someone with the taint of a corrective action and perceived problems in an NCAA investigation. Fullerton, who like Johnson suggested that I contact a lawyer, said that I was being very naïve if I thought a corrective action would be portrayed in a positive way. These were people who collectively had about 30-40 years in college athletic administration and coaching. My heart sank as I assessed their take. I knew now that my athletic career was essentially over unless I did something about it.

It was mid-November, and with the NCAA's final report on the Marshall infractions case due by the end of the year, I knew it was time to give Layton Cottrill a call and offer an ultimatum. I called Cottrill's direct line from home in the evening and said, "Layton, we need to meet as soon as possible. I have some problems with this corrective action arrangement and I am contemplating taking some sort of action." I suspected this would get a quick response, and I was right. There was a message from Cottrill's secretary on my voicemail the next morning instructing me to be at Cottrill's office at 2:00 p.m. So there it was. I would have a chance to plead my case and hopefully change this corrective action.

As I walked across campus, I was uncertain of how I would be received, since Cottrill now knew I was not going to go quietly. All doubts about the tone of the meeting were answered when I knocked on the office door. Not only was Cottrill there, but surprisingly there was Ed Grose sitting at a small conference table. Cottrill said hello and asked me to sit down. Before I could say anything he spoke up. "Dave, I have asked Dr. Grose to be here because I did not like what you said on the phone, and I want to prevent you from doing something stupid, but we are here to hear what you have to say."

I started to speak and stammered a bit, but regained my composure and stated my purpose for calling the meeting. "Layton, Dr. Grose, I initially accepted this transfer with the understanding that it was to give me a break from athletics and the investigation. It was also intimated to me that this transfer would not be characterized negatively, and my job performance would be praised. However, I have reason to believe that this corrective action is going to harm me and my future career aspirations. I have talked to some major players in the industry and they have advised me to not accept the corrective action because it will ruin my career."

Grose and Cottrill were both visibly agitated at my response, and both shifted uncomfortably in their chairs. I kept talking. "In addition, I do not think that conduct at the hearing is a valid thing to even say because one, my conduct was not that outrageous, certainly not to the level of a corrective action, and two, it is not an NCAA violation to vigorously defend yourself or the institution."

To which Grose spoke up forcefully, "Not that bad? What do you mean? You put Marshall University in a negative light!"

"Explain to me how, Dr. Grose," I responded. "How did I put the university in a bad light? I didn't lie, I didn't get these kids jobs, I didn't cover anything up..."

Cottrill broke in and said, "Dave, you didn't help us by your posture, hell you would still be in your job if not for your conduct."

I again spoke up, trying to explain that a vigorous defense is not an NCAA violation. "So just defending myself and the university when attacked ... something you told me you to do, is somehow wrong? What about my career, and the fact I didn't do anything to cause these major violations? I simply cannot sit by and not do something to save it, I have worked too hard."

"A lot of people worked hard, Dave, not just you," Cottrill replied in a condescending voice, as if he had something to do with improving the compliance program. I began to speak up again, but was stopped by Grose, who said, "Young man, if you do anything to attempt to change this corrective action, I assure you that you will be out of Marshall University."

"I knew you would say that," I told him.

His voice rising angrily with each word, Grose said, "Yeah, I'm not just saying it, I am telling you that I will bury you personally and professionally if you do anything to dredge up this investigation."

Cottrill added, "You better think of your family, young man. They are depending on you, and Dr. Grose and I can make it very difficult for you to work in higher education not just in West Virginia … but anywhere."

I knew the conversation was going nowhere. In my mind I was now set on what I was going to do. I was going to sue the pants off these bastards and tell every piece of truth I had that would embarrass the institution. It was sad that the truth would embarrass them, but they left me no choice. It was bound to become an ugly divorce.

As I was preparing to leave the office, I just smiled and said, "I guess that's that." To which Grose replied, "Yes it is, and I don't expect to hear any more from you on this subject or you will be done for." I was playing their little game, and I acted like that was the end of it. They had gotten away with threats and intimidation before, but I knew I had to take a very strategic approach to how I would react, and not blow it at this point and time. In essence I was practicing something I learned in the military. It was time to make a tactical move to the rear, to reassess the battle plan, then strike back when they least expected it.

I thanked them for their time and started to get up to leave, but Grose said he had a couple more things to ask me. I sat back down, and bizarrely, the tone of the meeting changed immediately. It was like old times in a sense. Grose asked about my new position, and encouraged me to motivate my new boss Steve Hensley to do a better job as Dean of Student Affairs since he was not a very hard worker. He then added, "My vision is for you to be Dean of Student Affairs here at Marshall one day, so make sure you finish that doctorate."

I stifled the urge to throw up. Here I was, not good enough to be part of the athletics department as a middle manager, having just been threatened lest I attempt to clear my name, and now I am a future candidate for Dean of Students at the same university? It was unbelievable, but I continued to play along.

"Thanks for your confidence in me sir," I said.

Cottrill jumped in and said they had "big plans" for me at Marshall University, as long as I finished my doctorate and did nothing to, in his words, "fuck things up." This coming from the same man who used to tell me I was his "number one" candidate to be the next athletic director at Marshall University. The shit was getting deep, but I guess this was their attempt to not only me feel better, but to resolve their own guilt over the sham of making me their scapegoat.

Grose went on to say that I should stay away from the athletic department, athletic events, and give myself time to get used to Student Affairs. This would be no problem for me. I had no desire to spend much time at a place that I used to love, yet now caused me so much pain. While I nodded affirmatively, inside I was saying that I did not give a damn about student affairs, my passion is in athletics and I would somehow clear my name.

Grose then asked what I thought about Kevin Klotz as my replacement. It was also mildly humorous to me that I was being asked my opinion on my replacement considering I was apparently not worthy of the position myself. Knowing that Kevin was going to help me in the future should I pursue litigation, I obviously wanted him in that position. I also thought he was the best person for the job. He was the best assistant I ever had, by far, and he was ready to take the reins. I told Grose that I endorsed Kevin, though inside I worried what Kevin might have to deal with considering the vast amount of power Pruett had consolidated. I mentioned to Grose that Kevin told me he was not even a finalist for the job, due mainly to the fact that Beatrice Crane was against him getting it thanks to his relationship with me. Grose replied, "I am going to change that. He is working his ass off and deserves a shot." That statement actually made me feel good because I felt in a small way a positive influence on Kevin and I did not want him to suffer because of any feelings towards me by anyone.

Finally I was permitted to leave what had become a very strange meeting. While I was nauseous over the course of the proceedings, I stood up, shook both men's hands and told them again that I appreciated the opportunity to have the conversation. On my way out the door Cottrill patted me on the back and told me to hang in there, better times were ahead. I wanted to scream. I recall clenching my fists and grinding my teeth at that ridiculous comment. I had to stifle the urge to punch him in the mouth, and part of me still wishes I had. Yes, better days were ahead for them … as long as I played ball, but not for me.

As I walked back to the Memorial Student Center feeling like I needed to take a shower after that meeting, I knew that I was going to take whatever legal steps I could to get the truth out and clear my name. Although I did not want to do this, it was clear that they would not do the one thing I requested and was promised me - that I would not be blamed for the major violations. In fact they were going to do the exact opposite. My decision had been made, albeit reluctantly, though I had yet to accurately gauge the cost.

CHAPTER 24:

THE REPORT

As the weather grew ever-colder in that bleak fall of 2001, and December and the Christmas season grew near, my healing process was moving slowly. I had been out of the athletic department for a couple months now, and was still attempting to feel my way around a new job while trying to ignore the search going on for my replacement across campus. This was tough to do, as Marshall was essentially a small town where information traveled at lightning speed.

I already knew, for instance, that the position was to include a snappy new title - Associate Athletic Director for Compliance and Student Services - which came with it a host of amenities that had been little more than pipe dreams during my tenure. The person Marshall was hiring would get more money, a plush office, more support, and was not going to have to fight for a courtesy car as I did throughout my tenure.

Meanwhile, the sycophantic, lazy media in and around Huntington began reporting on the hire in a way that suggested the university was about to hire some kind of savior. The overriding sentiment was that the university needed someone "experienced" in compliance, so that major infractions would not occur again and all would be well. Comments like this were a direct punch to the gut, especially since I knew no one at the university was going to clarify the actual root of the problems in the athletic department, which had preceded my arrival by at least 10 years. The revisionist history, which said I was the one to blame, was already being written and accepted as fact. It was a tough time to be in Huntington for me.

My friend Michelle Duncan was on the search committee for the new compliance coordinator, and asked me to look over some of the resumes over lunch one day. While this exercise felt a bit like picking a new husband for my wife, I had invested a lot in making that department run efficiently and wanted the university to choose someone who could advance the ball I'd put in play. There were some highly qualified people and promising names on this list, including Kevin Klotz, Jeff O'Malley at the University of Massachusetts, Eric Baumgartner at Clemson, Leland Zeller, a compliance assistant at Washington State, and Brad Bertani from the NCAA office. My former assistant, Dave Reed, had applied, but sensing (probably accurately) that he would not have made the final cut, opted to pull out.

Some of those in the running for the job, including O'Malley and Baumgartner, contacted me directly to learn more about the position and the university. I was careful not to bash Marshall because it was important to me that the positive changes I had implemented continued, but I still had to tell the truth about the culture, the power that Pruett had consolidated, and the inability of the administration to foster a commitment to running an athletic program of integrity. Perhaps it wasn't a coincidence that O'Malley eventually took his name out of the running, and Baumgartner was offered the job but turned it down.[52]

Klotz interviewed for the job too, but hurt his own cause during his final interview, with Dan Angel and Layton Cottrill. Kevin said the first thing out of Angel's mouth during their session was, "Why would you put a guy like Dave Ridpath down as a reference?" Angel then went on to lambast my supposed shortcomings, along with regurgitating the "facts" of the NCAA investigation and essentially blaming it all on me. A little taken aback at first, Kevin spent some time defending me and my body of work, presuming that agreeing with an indictment of me would hurt his chances, since he was working in the same department. While it is a credit to Kevin that he stood up for his principles and told the truth, it was eventually to his detriment. He was not hired for the permanent job.

Like Jeff O'Malley, Brad Bertani had originally taken his name out of the running after Marshall low-balled the salary, but the university somehow came up with the resources to lure him back. Brad was a fellow Ohio University Sport Administration graduate, a person I considered to be a friend. He was well-respected from his work at the NCAA. I told anyone that asked that I liked Brad, and thought he would do a fantastic job. One thing that bothered me a bit about Brad was that he didn't call me to ask questions, though this was probably a good thing. Like the others, he may have never come to Marshall after talking with me. Once Brad was officially hired, it was time for me to swallow a healthy dose of pride. The media reaction labeling Bertani as a white knight who would fix the rogue compliance office was somewhat predictable, but the way Marshall rolled out the red carpet for him seemed designed to injure me further.

In addition to a car and a substantial raise, Brad was given a new office, a secretary, and full moving expenses. I seethed when I learned that he and his family were staying in President Angel's guest house until their home purchase was finalized, and it got worse as I watched many paid moving professionals moving Brad and his family into their new home on the south side of Huntington. It made me reflect on the pittance that I and others got to relocate to Huntington, under the guise of the department having no money and resources to assist.

Simultaneous to the compliance search, another bomb was about to drop. I was well aware that the final NCAA report on the Marshall University major infractions case was due to be released, which is when the penalties and sanctions would also be announced. I worried about how I would be portrayed, but people like Wilkinson and Klotz assured me they did not think it would be so bad. I was cautiously optimistic that they would be right.

I received a phone call on Dec. 18, 2001, from Layton Cottrill's secretary, who informed me that the NCAA report had arrived and would be publicly released the next morning. I appreciated the call, because I had requested an advance copy so I could digest all of the information in advance of the media seeing the report.

When I arrived on the second floor of Old Main to pick up my copy of the report, things took a surreal turn. I could look through the glass doors of the huge expanse of the President's office and see everyone that I used to interact with every day concerning the NCAA investigation - Grose, Cottrill, Denman, West, Pruett, Wilkinson, and Klotz - who were all assembled to discuss the report. Angel was away from the office so was piped in via conference call. Though I had lived through the saga that yielded the report for almost three years, I was not welcome. I was literally on the outside looking in, and it hurt. A couple of my former colleagues saw me walk by, but quickly looked back at the report, refusing to acknowledge me. This was not a good omen.

I walked back to the family minivan, sat in the driver's seat, and began to read the report. It was worse than I could have ever imagined. To say I was disappointed with how I was characterized in the NCAA report would be a gross understatement. While there are some accurate and damaging things said about the university in its report, the lion's share of the blame was placed on me. The entirety of the case against Marshall University consisted of the following: impermissible employment of academic non-qualifiers at a rate four times the prevailing wage, impermissible extra benefits, exceeding grant-in-aid limits in football and men's basketball, a failure to monitor the employment of non-qualifiers, academic fraud, and lack of institutional control.

In a typical NCAA infractions case, an institution offers up its own corrective actions and sanctions, in the hopes that the committee will accept those sanctions and not pile on many more, if any. In keeping with that tradition, Marshall sanctioned itself for the infractions that it conceded occurred, which were essentially all of those alleged, except for the broad-based and damning "lack of institutional control," LOIC in the NCAA shorthand. The university's defense position against the LOIC tag, using Hilliard's strategy, was that the bulk of the violations happened over several years prior to the installation of the new administration, and that those who committed the infractions did not realize that the employment arrangement was impermissible.

Hilliard strategized that underlining my own questioning of the rule, and what actually constituted athletic assistance, should be translated into the fact that we (meaning me) did not know the jobs program was a violation. Remember that it was my questionable interpretation of the rule for the $50, one-night ESPN jobs that was being used as justification for Pruett not knowing the rules in regard to the much more wide-ranging jobs program under Marshall Reynolds, a program which everyone, including the NCAA Committee on Infractions, agreed I had known nothing about. Marshall's stance was to blame the gross overpayment solely on Marshall Reynolds, and to deny promising the athletes jobs during the recruiting process.

I never fully agreed nor felt entirely comfortable with the overall approach as it left me vulnerable and left out details of Pruett's culpability in particular, but I was assured by Hilliard and Cottrill that the blame was being spread around and we would win the day by showing what reforms we had already put in place to ensure this would not happen again. Hilliard told us that this is how the game was played, and I really had no alternative at that stage but to acquiesce and believe that I would be protected.

But my portrayal in the COI report[53] was filled with cheap shots, and painted a portrait of an aloof compliance coordinator who did not know what he was doing. The committee took the opening that came from Hilliard's either poorly- planned or covert strategy, making it seem like I said it was permissible for prop athletes to work, and that I did not monitor the employment program.

The report bounces back and forth between alleging that I knew or did not know what was happening, but let's be clear. I did not know nor did I ever authorize, nor would I have, the Saturday program conducted by Marshall Reynolds. Though my interpretation of "athletic assistance" may have been arguably incorrect for the ESPN issue, it's a fact that I was never asked by Pruett nor his staff if we could assist Prop 48 athletes in securing this employment or any other job. The only thing I stated, prompted from a direct but very general question from Pruett, was that props could work if several steps were carried out before commencing employment, most notably approval from me. In addition, I regularly discussed caveats including not promising employment during recruiting, comparable rates of pay and acquisition of the jobs just like any other employee. The safeguards I had put in place were verified by NCAA interviews with staff and coaches, memos, records of rules education meetings, and the first comprehensive compliance manual Marshall University ever had, yet the NCAA chose to ignore this very tangible evidence in the report. What the committee chose to harp on was the fact that I had answered, as directed by Hilliard, that I did not fully understand the athletics assistance rule.

The COI was quite critical of the compliance program and employment monitoring overall which was laughable. There was no mention of the mess that I had inherited, or any credit for how I improved the compliance program, specifically in regard to student-athlete employment. While acknowledging that I enacted the first comprehensive employment monitoring program, the COI alleged that I ran a "passive" compliance system that had "little to no communication between the compliance office and the football coaches." That they arrived at this conclusion is inexplicable considering we provided memos, records of meetings, rules education seminars, emails, and phone records that proved daily contact with the football office on compliance issues. This included monthly memos with a list of all athletes, including props that were cleared to work. The truth is that despite several layers of checks and balances, the breakdown occurred because Pruett and his staff kept the program under wraps, and felt they had a get out of jail free card because I said, correctly, that props could work under certain conditions.

The system did not break down because of the compliance office. Compliance is a systems-based process that requires several people to perform certain steps or triggers. While the NCAA alleged that I vested too much responsibility in the football staff, all I really asked them to do was to give the athlete permission to work, and to give the coaching staff the ability to refuse to give permission to a particular athlete to work if they were not doing well academically or otherwise. All the coach had to do was check a "yes" or "no" box on a compliance form, that was it. Even a phone call or email would suffice. Is this asking too much of a Division I coach or a staff with dozens of assistants and support staff? Absolutely not, and this practice had been suggested by the NCAA itself over the years to give the coaches "buy in" and to help assist in information flow. The COI made it seem like the coaches were in charge of employment monitoring, and they had a mountain of evidence before them that proved this could not be further from the truth.

Pruett and head men's basketball coach Greg White both denied ever being told that they represented a step in the jobs approval process, and added that they didn't know the rules applied to non-qualifiers. The COI chose to take these answers at face value, in the face of overwhelming evidence to the contrary, including testimony from Dave Reed[54] and other coaches. Additionally, as a former Division I coach, I know that coaches know what their athletes are doing more so than any administrator would, and having coaches involved in the process was even recommended as a "best practice" at NCAA regional compliance seminars. Yet for whatever reason, the COI did not recognize this simple and effective step as evidence of a comprehensive employment monitoring program.

The NCAA acknowledged in the report that these violations had been going on since at least 1993, and that any arrangement like this would have never been permissible, before or after the rule changes for props, because there were a half-dozen NCAA rules being violated. This was not just about prop athletes getting assistance from the athletic department in securing a job, it was about impermissible recruiting inducements, extra benefits, overpayment, willful violations and denials on the part of the football and basketball coaches, and rogue boosters, specifically Marshall T. Reynolds, who felt the rules did not apply to them.

What is clear is that this was a program created to bring elite athletes to the Marshall University football program, who could not get in to higher-profile football schools for academic reasons. The jobs were a way to get them to come to Huntington and survive while they completed the one-year residency required by the NCAA to gain eligibility. The evidence overwhelmingly demonstrated that the players were paid $200 a day/$25 per hour for general janitorial work - if they did any work at all. Pruett and Reynolds claimed former Marshall AD Lee Moon knew of this arrangement, while Moon denied it to the NCAA. Someone is lying in this group.[55]

But the bottom line is that had I been told about the Marshall Reynolds program when I first arrived at Marshall University in 1997, and the full extent of it, I would have shut it down, reported it, and MU would have been on probation during the Moss-Pennington years. And that's exactly why I wasn't told about it by Pruett or anyone else. Pruett has consistently said he felt the program was permissible, and that he did not break rules intentionally. If that was the case, why did the football office tell me about other employment arrangements, and not this one?[56]

The NCAA did correctly assail our investigation and our initial responses to it, because we kept submitting the inaccurate and misleading information that was provided to us by Marshall Reynolds and by following Hilliard's instructions. Despite the fact that I was not permitted to interview Reynolds directly, and did what I was told by a supposed NCAA expert in Hilliard, I was the one specifically criticized for the investigative response, not anyone else. In several places the COI claims that I did not perform due diligence in the investigation and even stated, amazingly, that Pruett asked me directly about non-qualifier wages because he was concerned they were "too high." They said on one hand that I didn't know about the program (true), then published a lie, which came from Pruett, that said he checked it out with me. This information came out of nowhere, was never mentioned in the Sept. 22 hearing and was completely contradictory. But as with everything in the report, there were no checks and balances, nor any rights or avenues for dispute from a person in my situation.

The report was little more than an extension of an industry trend. As the area of compliance oversight solidified over the years, the NCAA enforcement staff and the COI moved even further away from punishing the real rule breakers. In the late 90s and into the 21st century as compliance staffs became bigger and more specialized, the perceived addition of greater oversight gave coaches and boosters more cover, exactly the opposite of what should have been happening. The investigators and decision-making bodies became much less concerned about who broke the rules and why, and more concerned about proving how the compliance office had failed. This is a pretty serious break with the fair, upstanding image of its system that the NCAA likes to herald. The truth is that many have gotten away with breaking rules, while lower-level, expendable people are often given the shaft.

The committee also made cursory reference to my first interview with McAllister, claiming that I was trying to trap him into confessing the academic fraud by using leading questions. I am by no means a professional investigator, but found it pretty ironic that the NCAA was able to use threats, leading questions, and badgering to get the answers they wanted, yet was hammering me for what they said was the same behavior. Even if I used leading questions with McAllister, and I don't believe I did, the evidence proved my instincts were correct.

The report certainly could not have gotten worse for me, until the COI took great pains to commend Crane on her misguided efforts, to include her underhanded activities surrounding the revelation of the ESPN game issue. Remember that she violated university policy by not coming to me first and going outside of established lines to get NCAA interpretations, not to mention discussing this issue with Rob Fournier, Pruett, and Cottrill before me, which gave Pruett enough time to plan a firewall of protection. They also failed to recognize that Beatrice was the interim compliance coordinator for two months prior to my arrival and if the issues in the department were so obvious, why didn't she notice them then? For the COI to overlook these major points and then praise Crane for going behind my back to set me up demonstrated that this committee operates in a vacuum, and was simply trying to find an expedient way to dispose of this case. Crane's efforts were not commendable, far from it.

The summation by the COI was incredibly one-sided and fueled by an opportunistic university that saw me being sacrificed as a chance to save face and protect the ones it deemed more important. The NCAA claims that this does not happen and they cannot be conned, but it happens all the time. The COI could speak up and give sanctions with teeth to inhibit schools from scapegoating the expendable, but it would then cut into the profit-making machine. That is why people like UConn men's basketball coach Jim Calhoun stay in spite of massive evidence of corruption, while assistant coaches get fired - it is just easier for the school, and lower-level employees usually will not fight back, hoping to resurrect their career elsewhere.[57] The NCAA hearing was over for me literally within minutes, when the strategy I was ordered to follow failed. As I tried to dig myself out of a hole, my university, colleagues, and attorney never once rose up in my defense. They saw the score, and they weren't betting on me. I never had a chance.[58]

Marshall offered self-imposed sanctions before the NCAA report, which ironically did not include any punitive measures against me save for a letter of reprimand - which everyone got, and I wrote. Typically, if someone is deemed to be at fault, there are changes made well in advance of a COI hearing to appease the committee. Not only was I not fired, demoted, or removed, I was actually told that I was not at fault or at risk by Mark Jones from the NCAA. The main person we were saddling with blame was going to be Reynolds, and we were supposed to accept our minor faults and move on. The only one who suffered adverse employment action was McAllister. The other self-imposed sanctions included a two-year ban on recruiting non-qualifiers, reductions in the numbers of scholarships in football and men's basketball, creating the position of Assistant Compliance Director, requirement of staff members to attend NCAA regional compliance seminars, and then the big one - disassociating Marshall Reynolds from Marshall University athletics for two years along with assessing him a monetary fine to pay for all legal fees (approaching a million dollars) in relation to this case.[59]

Typically, the NCAA will add on more penalties, so it is kind of a gamble to not sanction yourself too hard and give the COI an opening to pile on. It is up to the institution to wait it out to see what, if any, additional penalties may be assessed. In our case, there was an unusual development, however. Dan Angel received a letter from Tom Yeager dated September 29, 2001 informing the institution that the COI believed that the Lack of Institutional Control penalty would be appropriate in this case. However, the committee was going to give the institution a chance to tell the committee why LOIC should not be assessed.

This letter really is what set my corrective action in motion, along with what I believe were conversations among Hilliard, Cottrill, members of the COI (and most likely Marsh based on phone records that showed conversations between Cottrill and Marsh) and Mark Jones. Hilliard and Cottrill were communicating with Marsh on the Alabama case that Hilliard was also working, and it is inconceivable to think that the Marshall case was not discussed too. At any rate, that letter triggered my demise. In a desperate attempt to save itself and to deflect as much as possible from Reynolds and Pruett, the institution sold me out and made me a corrective action. Regardless of how it was couched initially, I now suffered adverse employment action because of these violations. I would never be able to live it down, and I would never be able to progress in my career. It was over for me and I really did not know what to do about it.

The committee read Marshall's lengthy October 15, 2001 report to determine if there were sufficient criteria to avoid assessing LOIC. This report was mainly targeted at me and my removal, along with stating that the university was going to undergo an extensive national search for my replacement. Hilliard, the primary author of the report, somewhat amazingly went to great lengths to demonstrate how strong the employment program was and used an interview with Dave Reed to amplify those points. In the same interview, Dave went to great pains to praise me, the employment program, and our efforts in compliance. It was nonsensical and laughable to can me, then use the system I created as an example of why there was no institutional control.

Regardless of Marshall's efforts to make the employment program look good, after they'd spent so much time tearing me and my job performance down, the committee didn't buy it. The COI indeed assessed Marshall the "gold standard" of NCAA penalties ... lack of institutional control. They added to MU's self-imposed sanctions by placing the athletic department on four years' probation, reducing the number of scholarships in football and men's basketball for the period of three years, assessing a "show cause" order restricting McAllister's future involvement with NCAA sports, and disassociating Reynolds for five years rather than the requested two. It was done. Marshall University and Pruett felt it was over and they could move on relatively easily, with me still warehoused and under their thumb. Pruett said Marshall would get over this "black eye" and rise up like the team did after the 1970 plane crash. His analogies to that tragedy were inappropriate and pathetic.

NCAA public infractions reports are typically written by one member of the COI, then distributed to the other members for review. The committee will then meet to discuss via either conference call or in-person meeting. As I had learned previously during the infractions process, COI meetings were largely about taking the path of least resistance, glossing over details, end expediting the matter as quickly as possible. This meant there was very little chance that the report was going to be measurably changed from its original state, putting the onus on the main writer to set the tone. In this case, to my detriment, that writer was Josephine Potuto, the NCAA Faculty Representative from the University of Nebraska and an endowed chair at the university's law school, who I had clashed with perhaps more than any other member of the COI.

The truth was that even if I had a great relationship with Potuto and the COI, I still would have been the most convenient scapegoat because of my position and the fact that other people at Marshall were railroading the committee to the conclusion that I was the problem. But my conflicts with the committee, and especially Potuto, had made their job a lot easier in respect to throwing me under the bus and backing it up a couple of dozen times.

As I read the report, I knew that there was probably no way that I would ever work in athletics again and I began to cry, it was really over now and it seemed like there was little I could do about it.

After I composed myself, though, I decided that instead of crumbling, I would strengthen my resolve to fight what any objective person would have to admit was a criminally unjust situation. The notion of fighting back against two behemoths - Marshall University and the NCAA - was going to be a David vs. Goliath scenario that would test my resolve even further.

But the alternative to fighting back was not one I was willing to face.

CHAPTER 25:

IGNITING THE FLAME

I ALWAYS THOUGHT PEOPLE who sued were whiners looking for an easy way out and easy money. That's a natural assumption to make, before something unjust happens to you. I had tried every angle to settle my dispute with Marshall amicably, and with little collateral damage, but the university refused. Our legal justice system is designed to help settle disputes, and settling my dispute was not going to happen at the NCAA or within the walls of Marshall University.

I surmised that I had no choice but to sue, and though this was very much a personal battle, I knew I was fighting for others who had faced my situation as well. The scapegoating that was derailing careers left and right in college athletics had become an epidemic, and someone needed to stand up and fight for what was right. Whether I'd ever intended to fill it or not, or wanted my family subjected to the torment that would undoubtedly ensue, this role now fell to me. I had to take my chances in this forum as all other efforts failed.

Suing Marshall required a great many calls to, and conversations with, lawyers. And that was before as much as one document was drafted or one motion was filed in my case.

Over the next seven years, from the time I began considering litigation against Marshall and the NCAA, to the time the final entanglement was unknotted in 2009, I was pretty sure I could go toe-to-toe in legal knowledge with any recent law school graduate. Such was the education I received on the vagaries of the law.

A boyhood friend of mine who was living in the Washington DC area, Bryan Otte, suggested I call a friend of his, Jeremy Schulman, a prominent attorney for the prestigious DC law firm Paul Weiss and Associates. Schulman didn't take my case, but gave me a helpful piece of advice when he told me I would need to file suit within a year of the NCAA report to lessen the risk of the statute of limitations running out.

My next call was to my former boss and the Ohio University wrestling coach, Harry Houska, who I knew had coached a couple of wrestlers that went on to be lawyers. Harry referred me to one of his former All-American wrestlers, Bob Tscholl out of Canton, OH, who I was acquainted with but did not know well. Though he wasn't sure if the matter fell fully within his area of expertise, Tscholl, and his fellow lawyer and brother, John, offered me some direction for the blue-light special (by legal standards) price of $5000.[60]

Early on, Bob and John told me I did not have a case against the NCAA, both because of the numerous legal shields they would throw up and the lack of economic feasibility in taking on a monster of that size. As I suspected, the NCAA could avoid dealing with the matter because it was not them but Marshall who had assigned the corrective action and removed me from the athletic department.

The burden would have been on us to prove that the NCAA inflicted the damage to my career, but the NCAA could just claim they didn't do anything that was directly actionable. Essentially, the NCAA can say something along the lines of, "I didn't tell your wife to divorce you, I just wrote a report saying you were cheating on her." The good news was that I had several strong causes of action against Marshall and certain individuals. As they continued to explore the legal options, the Scholl's began by sending Dan Angel a strongly-worded letter detailing my legal claims and demands prior to my threatened lawsuit.

The legal claims were breach of contract, fraudulent misrepresentation, tortuous interference with a contract, and a violation of liberty interest. The relief I was seeking was removal of the corrective action from the NCAA report, a guarantee to stay on as Director of Judicial Programs until I found suitable employment, and positive efforts and recommendations by Marshall to assist me in my job search. There was no request for any monetary damages whatsoever, proof positive that this matter was about principle and the preservation of my reputation and career, nothing else. It was also spelled out that any attempt to retaliate against me for sending this letter would be met with legal action. The removal of the corrective action, a veritable scarlet letter that stood in the way of me rehabilitating my career in athletics, was the most important issue for me.

All claims in the letter were federal claims, as Bob and John felt I would have little chance at getting a fair trial if I was facing an elected judge in West

Virginia. We closed the letter by stating it was our wish to avoid the courtroom, a media circus, and to settle this matter in an amicable fashion. The letter was faxed to Angel from Bob Tscholl's Canton office on August 14, 2002. It was empowering to know that the ball was rolling and I changed the paradigm.

Bob called me less than a week later and informed me that he just received a letter from Cottrill, stating that he had asked to have legal counsel appointed in this case. It appeared there would not be a quick fix, but this was fairly typical of large agencies like universities. Our new contact would be the Charleston Law Firm of Bailey and Wyant, and their lead attorney, Chuck Bailey.

When the Scholl's met with Bailey in the fall of 2002 via a conference call, he laid out Marshall's position very simply: I should be thankful I was not fired, I deserved to be fired, I put the university in jeopardy, and there would be no entertaining of changing the record or the corrective action or in Bailey's words, "removing a sanction imposed on it by the NCAA." An interesting statement, and a telling slip. The NCAA maintained that they had nothing to do with my corrective action, but here was the lead lawyer from Marshall confirming exactly what I thought. He added that I could stay in my current job indefinitely, and that Marshall would assist me with "fairly neutral" recommendations should I decide to pursue employment elsewhere.

This was unacceptable, of course, meaning litigation was imminent. Bob and John put together the first complaint, which I would eventually file in district court in the Southern District of West Virginia. I was nearing the end of the line with the Tscholls, who told me I would need an attorney from West Virginia to advance the ball further, but I was grateful for all of the critical help they gave me early on in the process, especially in drafting the first complaint. That initial letter and complaint draft was the basis for almost every legal document that we would put together in the next few years of litigation. Since the one-year anniversary of the release of the NCAA report was approaching, they also recommended I file the initial complaint *pro se* (without a lawyer) to preserve the claims and not violate the statute of limitations. I made sure that I did just that, and accomplished it just a few days ahead of the deadline. The lawsuit began making news nationwide, and after suffering at the hands of the public and media myself, I must admit I was enjoying watching people squirm a bit. The publicity increased the anger toward me by many in the Marshall community and fan base around Huntington, but I was feeling more and more empowered each day. There is nothing more fulfilling than standing up for your rights and fighting back against corruption. Now, it was time to get back on the phone and start talking to lawyers again, a practice at which I was becoming fairly proficient. Before hiring a West Virginia-based attorney, I decided I needed an NCAA expert attorney that could navigate and understand the enforcement and infractions process.

While on that search, I had heard about a new faculty group, calling themselves The Drake Group, which was dedicated to the goal of reforming intercollegiate athletics. One of the members of the group, Linda Bensel-Meyers, was a well-known name to me as she had been in the news on a near-daily basis for several months concerning allegations of academic fraud and the football team at the University of Tennessee. Bensel-Meyers, a former Professor of English at UT, discovered improper tutoring, academic clustering, and plagiarism of assignments for large numbers of football athletes. When she brought these areas to the attention of her higher-ups - including university president J. Wade Gilley, ironically the former president at Marshall - the response was to not do anything nor make waves. After getting nowhere with her superiors, Bensel-Meyers went to the press and detailed the types of improprieties UT football players were getting. It didn't take long for a scandal to break, and the ensuing furor led the SEC and the NCAA to Knoxville to investigate, but neither entity could find any evidence of academic fraud despite the mountain of evidence Linda had provided.

Linda was out on an island, even the faculty at UT virtually abandoned her. Her crusade cost her professionally and personally - she went through a divorce and even her children failed to unify behind her - but she fought on. The Drake Group did come to Linda's aid, helping to organize meetings on the Knoxville campus and raising money for Linda's legal defense as Tennessee threatened to sue her for releasing academic records to the press.[61]

I suspected after reading about her case that if there was someone that would be sympathetic to me and my upcoming legal fight, it would be Linda. She responded to an email I sent, and pledged to assist me in any way she could. She mentioned that she was going to see members of TDG, including founder Jon Ericson, in Los Angeles in a few days where she was speaking in front of the Faculty Athletic Representatives Association (FARA) concerning her ongoing situation with Tennessee. My brother Brett, who lived in L.A., was kind enough to meet with Linda and Jon on my behalf, discuss my options and see if The Drake Group could help.

Ericson, who said up front that the group only got involved in issues of academic integrity, was sympathetic and referred Brett to a friend, a Des Moines-based attorney named Jerry Crawford, who might want to assist. I actually knew Crawford and his reputation already, as he had represented basketball coach Ron Abegglen in the Weber State case I had dealt with all those years ago. I respected Crawford, who I knew was a great attorney, and was ecstatic when word came back that he was interested in assisting in my legal efforts. Jerry would be bringing with him a colleague, J.D. Hartung, who had also assisted on the Weber case and seemed like a sharp arrow. J.D. would take the day-to-day lead on correspondence and negotiations in my case.

Jerry felt that this was a classic case of the NCAA and an institution following a simple playbook, in which they followed a systematic plan to set up a predetermined scapegoat so the institution could save the ones they felt were not expendable. Meanwhile, I still needed to find a West Virginia attorney, which was becoming quite a challenge given Marshall's standing in the community. This is not unusual, and a common problem for those who want to enter in litigation with a university or large corporation. While many West Virginia-based attorneys were sympathetic, they were fearful of fighting the institution. One name kept coming up, however, when lawyers would refer me to others that might be interested: Jason Huber.

Huber was a Marshall alumnus whose time on the Huntington campus as a student activist had seen him involved in anti-war and gay rights protests. After attending law school at West Virginia University, Huber had become a well-known civil rights attorney. Before I even had a chance to contact Huber directly, he called the Tscholls, who passed on to me that he was interested. Huber was part of a firm in Charleston by the name of Forman and Huber, which while small, had become known for standing up for civil rights issues and fighting for the little guy. This was handy, because there was probably no littler guy than me. Jerry and J.D. were encouraged by Jason's interest, and it felt like a plan was coming together.

When I arrived at the modest offices of Forman and Huber, I walked in and asked a simply dressed person with a goatee and his long hair in a ponytail if he could tell me where I could find Jason Huber. The man looked back at me and said, "You are looking at him." Jason certainly did not look the part of the well-dressed, button-downed attorney, but was a well-qualified advocate for my case and had no problem going after the sacred cow that was his alma mater, Marshall University. He was a most valuable part of the legal team, which was in place at last.

The attempt to sue a state agency is one that is fraught with roadblocks, and the fact that I was combining federal and state claims elicited another layer of red tape. As a state organization with immunity, Marshall's first act was to file a motion to dismiss the case. The motion was easily defeated in federal court in early 2003, with nearly all of the claims made in the suit allowed to stand, but that motion was hardly the only trick up the university's sleeve.

If Marshall couldn't get rid of me quickly, the university and its lawyers surmised, they would attempt to outlast me physically, emotionally, and financially. The downside to being in federal court versus state court is that the process takes longer, and provides many opportunities for delays and additional motions. This process was to Marshall's advantage. While I was essentially diving for change behind the couch to keep my suit afloat, Marshall and its co-defendant employees were being subsidized entirely by the West Virginia

State Board of Risk Management. Rich Hilliard's defense, meanwhile, was being paid for by his firm, Ice Miller.

Over the next few months it was clear that Marshall was in no mood to negotiate. Losing the motion to dismiss only strengthened their resolve. My lawyers said to buckle up for a long ride, at which point I took it upon myself to begin rounding up witnesses, at the direction of my attorneys. I contacted several current and former players, telling them explicitly that I was just gathering information and that they didn't have to answer of my questions. Almost all were glad to help to me, and many expressed that they felt terrible about what happened to me. Those I talked to certainly had some interesting details to share on the employment issue.

Most of the former props told me they were actively recruited with the promise of $200 jobs, and that they were explicitly warned not to report these jobs to the compliance office and to "keep it in the family." Even the least worldly members of this group said they knew they were supposed to report the jobs to compliance, but followed the directives of the coaching staff so as not to upset their status on the team or playing time.

One former player, Sam Goines, added that he and several other prop athletes were also given jobs at a local used car dealership, Fish and Bates Motors, for which they were paid $100 cash and told not to report it. Others discussed working for a local meat processing plant, called Logan's Meat Packing. (This was later confirmed by other players and coaches.) We never determined what wages they received or what was happening at the other businesses, but the fact that I had no record of it and athletes were working there was a problem that screamed of potential impropriety and a pattern of circumventing the rules.

Any deep seated doubts I may have harbored about Bob Pruett's culpability in this case were wiped away during this round of interviews. I had ex-players telling me they were hired by Pruett for work done at his house, such as mowing the grass or parking cars for booster events. What's more, he was funneling them money for the NCAA repayment plan, the very plan set into motion because of the illegality of the prop-jobs he had helped broker under Marshall Reynolds.

Goines was very specific on Pruett's involvement, telling me that Pruett would invite players over to his house under the guise of work, then fire up the grill, feed them, and give them a couple hundred bucks each to use as funds to pay the eligibility penalty. According to multiple players I talked to, Pruett would laugh and remind them, "to make sure everyone knows you were working for that money."

It was all pretty astonishing, yet at this point, somehow not.

Of course, it wasn't long before the brass at Marshall were made aware of my interviews. One of the players, Curtis Jones, who had talked to me and provided some helpful information, went to Pruett and told him about the interview in order to cover his bases. Though I wouldn't have chosen for Pruett to find out what I was doing in this manner, it was perfectly understandable that Jones went to his coach.

What was far less expected was that my former assistant, Dave Reed, would turn on me and disclose to the top brass at Marshall that I was securing witnesses.

David G. Reed II, or "Boog" as he liked to be called, was a former Marshall student who bled green and white. He enjoyed his time as an undergrad immensely, so much so that he found himself kicked out of school due to academic deficiencies. Soon after finishing his undergraduate studies at what is now Mountain State University, near his hometown of Beckley, West Virginia, Dave called my office in search of a job. This was early in my tenure as compliance coordinator, and I happened to be in need of a graduate assistant who could help out with the monumental task of overhauling the department.

I took pity on Dave, a former Marine reservist who had seen the error of his past ways and was ready to buckle down, get a master's degree, and move on to what he hoped would be a career in the sports industry. He contacted me because he had done research, and saw compliance as an avenue to get into college sports administration. I was impressed with his conviction, his willingness to admit his own mistakes and learn from them, and I also felt that I heard a little of myself in that phone call. Here was someone who needed the same type of break that I had gotten at Weber State some years back.

I decided to give him a chance. Dave worked hard for me during his time as GA, and we hit it off both personally and professionally. I put him in charge of running the Marshall University Student-Athlete Employment program, a very important area considering NCAA rules were being modified to allow scholarship athletes to work, and it needed full attention. Dave was a major factor in both getting that program off the ground and monitoring it. After his stint was over at Marshall, Dave secured a full-time compliance position at the University of Cincinnati, and I was proud and happy that he had come so far so fast.

But not long after he went to Cincinnati, in the fall of 1999, Reed called me in tears. He had been fired at UC over a bizarre incident that left me embarrassed for having recommended him, and his own fledgling career in shambles. Dave explained that he was trying to avoid paying Ohio state taxes, and on advice from another Cincinnati staff member purchased a post office box across the Ohio River in Covington, Kentucky. Dave was told that all he had to do was mail a letter from that PO Box address in Kentucky to himself in Cincinnati and he would be a permanent Kentucky resident. Whether this is true or legal, I have no idea, but Dave did send that letter to himself.

Unfortunately for Dave, he made a very stupid error in doing so. He used Cincinnati athletic letterhead and a departmental envelope to mail the letter to himself at his athletic department address. He also wrote "my job sucks" on the letter inside the envelope. When it arrived, an astute employee was curious about why Reed would send a letter to himself, opened and presented it to UC athletic director Bob Goin, and Dave's direct supervisor, associate AD Brian Mand. Goin and Mand fired Reed in a matter of minutes.

Dave had messed up and knew it, but I told him to hang in there, go across town to Xavier University, and volunteer in the athletic department so his skills could remain current. Soon after, I decided to replace my new GA, who wasn't working out, and bring Dave back as a full-time assistant. This was a risky move given what he had done, coupled with the fact that we were by then in the midst of an NCAA investigation. But I still believed in him, and the fact I had resuscitated his career made me feel good.

Dave eventually landed a great position at the University of Pittsburgh, and during both the investigation and its immediate aftermath, could not have been more supportive of me. He actively told anyone who listened that I was getting screwed, and went as far as to inquire about jobs on my behalf. He was among those who encouraged me to sue Marshall, and pledged to help me as a witness or in any other capacity I needed. During the investigation he also provided key information to Hilliard that bolstered my repeated contention that the program was in place, communicated, monitored, and the coaches were simply not following it. Amazingly, despite my requests, the NCAA never interviewed Reed, though his interview with Hilliard could have been a cornerstone of our defense. I always feared that Hilliard did not use it because it put the onus where it should be, right at the feet of Pruett. Because of my relationship with Reed and his allegiance, I continued to discuss my plan in filing suit with him, to the extent of tipping him off that I was planning on talking to a group of current and former players. But just as I was getting ready to file suit in late 2002, it seemed that Dave was starting to get cold feet. He became distant, no longer wanted to talk to the press or anyone on my behalf, and started to tell me that I did not have a prayer in my lawsuit and could never beat Marshall in the state of West Virginia. It was a strange about-face from a person who I thought was a loyal friend. I began to suspect that Dave had been playing me, and providing information to prominent athletic department figures at Marshall. I'm not sure who got to him, but my feeling has always been that the department turned him by giving him an indication that he would be able to one day return to his beloved Marshall, if he separated himself from me.

When I confronted him, he claimed that working at Marshall was not important to him, but he would not turn it down if offered. He claimed we were like brothers and he would still do anything for me because he owed me. So I asked him to talk to writer Robert Lipsyte, who was preparing a piece on the case for the New York Times, even if it was off the record. It was a test, and I knew he wouldn't pass it. He refused to talk to Lipsyte. I went nuts. In a series of e-mails that would unfortunately become public later, I let my one-time protégé have it.

"Your choice is friendship or no friendship," I wrote. "Remember Marshall University does not give a [expletive] about you and you will probably never get a job here. I can almost guarantee it. Remember who saved your sorry fat ass when you were down. It is time for you to step up to the plate."

"[I]f you try to protect your sorry ass, useless, piece of [expletive] alma mater that you couldn't even graduate from then you will hear from me," I continued.

The threats were to no avail, nor did I really think they would be. At a horribly weak moment, I also relayed cheap shots to Reed about his father and sister that I dare not repeat here, and were about personal things that Dave confided to me. It would cause me great shame when the emails were released by Reed and printed in newspaper accounts.

"You have not heard the last from me, but our friendship is dead," I finished. "Don't ever come within 10 feet of me you worthless fat [expletive]. You and Marshall deserve each other, but I will always be there as a thorn, trust me."

Clearly, Reed's betrayal was difficult for me to swallow. Does that justify my behavior or choice of words? Not in the least. But just as I had with Beatrice Crane all those months ago, I had been boxed into a corner, conspired against yet again by those with unscrupulous intent, and reacted to the situation. I did say those things and I have to own up to it. Everything I had worked for was crumbling and now a key witness and supposed loyal friend was turning, but regardless of the circumstances, I could have handled it better.

My penance was two-fold. One, those emails would be made public, and I remain mortified about my behavior in that correspondence, even if it was provoked. Two, I was pretty certain that Reed was now funneling information to the higher-ups at Marshall, a situation that would soon have me facing down Ed Grose in a tension-filled meeting. Also, Reed would eventually be hired by Marshall just as he had hoped. Somewhat surprisingly, he was hired as Associate Athletic Director for Internal Operations, replacing Bianchin who decided to leave the business. Much like when Bianchin got the job, Reed wasn't qualified for it either. It made me think Reed was being brought in to be controlled, rather than on qualifications. Reed got what he wanted, though whether your character and integrity are an appropriate price to pay for the job of one's dreams is a subject worthy of debate. Not long after my heated exchange with Dave Reed, I learned that Grose was furious about my efforts to secure witnesses, and I was summoned to his office for a face-to-face.

Jason Huber suggested that I surreptitiously tape-record the meeting, lest any threats were made against me or my employment. I wanted Jason there with me, but he thought it would be the wrong approach. I felt like I was in an episode of Mission Impossible as I stopped in the bathroom outside Grose's office to switch my mini-recorder - which was duct-taped carefully to my right calf - into record mode.

When I arrived, tape recorder on, Grose immediately lit into me for allegedly threatening and harassing enrolled football players in an effort to gain information to advance my case. I corrected him that many of the players were not enrolled, but in reality, it didn't matter as I had the constitutional right to talk with them about their involvement in my case. I told him the truth that I never threatened or harassed anyone, and all information was provided voluntarily. Many of those I spoke to would later sign affidavits acknowledging as much.

Grose interjected forcefully. "You still work here. You have to follow the rules that I set, and if I say don't talk to anyone at Marshall about the case, then you can't do it."

I knew he was bluffing, but I said, "Dr. Grose, I am not going to walk outside this room and go talk to anyone because I do what I am told, but I will confer with my lawyer to decide what I will do in the future."

He casually threatened my employment several times and then openly asked why I was even still there if I did not like Marshall University anymore. I answered, simply and directly, that I had nowhere else to go and I had tried to leave. I reminded Grose that he was one of the reasons I was trapped at Marshall in the first place. The look on his face when I said that was priceless. He did not like that I was fighting back, and his frustration began to show. I found out that powerful people are not so powerful when you fight back.

He then blurted out an accusation of me pertaining to a Marshall football player, Toriano Brown, who had played in the team's opening game against Appalachian State despite the fact that the university knew he was ineligible. I had learned of this fact, and reported the information anonymously to the NCAA, mostly to show that Dan Angel's rhetoric about the athletic department being squeaky-clean was completely bogus. My phone call set off a shit storm, but I hadn't told anyone about it except for Dave Reed, before his betrayal.

Now, here was Grose confronting me with the information, and it took less than a nanosecond to realize that Reed was his source. I just smiled when Grose brought up the Brown incident. Nothing was solved at that meeting except a very uneasy détente.

The awkwardness of working at a place against which I had filed a very public lawsuit was palpable. I certainly was a pariah at Marshall, which made going to work challenging. I continued to apply for jobs, though nothing was happening, and I was able to complete the requirements for my Doctor of Education degree in May of 2002. It was a very big moment for me and my family, and it was nice to focus on something positive for a while. I walked across the commencement stage in the Huntington Civic Arena and directly stared Dan Angel in the face and shook his hand forcefully.[62] I then said, "Thanks Dan," knowing he hated being called that by subordinates. I knew that regardless of what happened with the case, this educational accomplishment would give me a new direction I could pursue since a career in athletics was likely over. I began to apply for assistant professor positions.

In August of 2003, while I was on vacation in Colorado and attending my 20th high school reunion, it appeared that we had some real movement on the case. We had decided a few weeks earlier to voluntarily withdraw our initial complaint without prejudice, meaning we could re-file it, which was the intent unless Marshall wanted to negotiate some kind of agreement to end this thing. The purpose for the withdrawal was so that we could add some new defendants, including Layton Cottrill and Dan Angel, to it. Cottrill and Angel had both said through counsel that they wanted scorched-earth litigation if they were ever added to the lawsuit, but we believed they needed to be added, along with Grose, to make the case stronger. Our stated intention to re-file prompted some action.

Jason and J.D. let me know that a local attorney and Marshall trustee, Menis Ketchum,[63] had called and offered to act as an intermediary to solve these issues and hopefully mitigate any need to re-file the complaint. We took this as a good sign. Ketchum, who is now a West Virginia Supreme Court Justice, definitely had the ability to force people to the table. Almost simultaneous to Ketchum's call, Jason was contacted by Alton Lewis, a prominent New Orleans attorney who was representing none other than Marshall Reynolds. Lewis was worried that we would be adding his client to the suit. Jason told him that Reynolds would likely not be named as a co-defendant, but he would definitely be called as a witness.

Lewis mentioned something else of particular interest - Reynolds was considering suing the NCAA over his own penalties incurred in the infraction report, and the threat was serious enough to warrant an almost unprecedented type of meeting between Reynolds and the NCAA investigators, led by David Price.

I was dumbfounded by both Reynolds' posturing and the fact that the NCAA would legitimize his claims by discussing them. This was almost unheard of. It was beyond obvious that Reynolds knew the extent of the jobs program and misled the NCAA, and there was little chance of him disproving the allegations in court. All of which was unbelievable and revolting, but it was fairly easy to figure out what was going on if you followed the money and looked at the people who really control what is going on in college athletics. Reynolds was a major university benefactor, and was withholding money unless Marshall fought vigorously on his behalf to get the penalties against him removed. In the summer of 2004, Angel even wrote a letter on Reynolds' behalf, most likely at the point of a bayonet, to have his penalties reconsidered. LuAnn Humphrey made a return visit in the fall of 2004 to Huntington to interview Reynolds, as well as Russell May, to see if there was anything to Reynolds' claims that he did not overpay the athletes, and other non-athletes received like pay and benefits. It's amazing that the institution and even the NCAA national office would kowtow to a person like Reynolds. His hands were all over this, and neither group would give me the time of day or another interview. They basically said "case closed." Just another part of the system that makes one want to take a shower. Thankfully the NCAA turned Reynolds down, and shortly thereafter, in December of 2004, Dan Angel resigned as Marshall president. I guess money talks. It was clear that the future of Dan Angel at Marshall was tied to Reynolds being exonerated and once he was not, Angel was shown the door.

Ketchum, meanwhile, knew this case could be damaging to the institution and as a trustee, had an interest in it going away. Marshall's defense attorneys had less urgency - they were being paid handsomely and billable hours were a hot commodity to them - but Ketchum's presence suggested the university might be willing to play ball via a settlement. Ketchum went as far as to tell Jason and J.D. that he was "calling the shots" now, and not anyone else.

Ketchum basically asked Jason and J.D. what it would take to make me go away. It was simple, they told him. I wanted the university to go through the NCAA to have the corrective action removed; all misleading statements in the NCAA report refuted via a national press release, which would say that I agreed to a transfer for personal reasons only; a guarantee that I could keep my current job until I found suitable employment; no retaliation against me for any reason connected to the lawsuit; positive written and verbal recommendations for any and all job inquiries; and a reasonable monetary amount to compensate me for legal fees. Other than the money, it was exactly what I had asked for in the first letter that the Tscholls sent Marshall.

Over the course of the next few hours, I was on and off the phone at least a dozen times to discuss the offer, and the reaction of Ketchum and Marshall to it. Crawford also offered to call new athletic director Bob Marcum (Lance West, mercifully, had been moved to a position within alumni affairs), an old acquaintance of his when Marcum was the AD at Iowa State, and urge him to work his connections to move the case toward settlement. I was feeling pretty good, especially after Jason told me that Ketchum felt everything I asked for was doable and negotiable, and he thought he could get the monetary damages up to $50,000. Since 50K was not enough to even cover my bills, we countered with an admittedly high figure of $350,000, expecting Ketchum to meet us somewhere in the middle. Honestly, I would have taken $75,000 as long as the other demands were met, but Marshall never gave me the opportunity. Ketchum immediately turned down the $350K request, saying that it was out of line, and instructing us to serve the new complaint while refusing to negotiate further.

We were surprised that he bypassed negotiating down, and became convinced that he wasn't really able to come up with the non-monetary stipulations we were requesting. Perhaps others in the Marshall inner circle balked at settling, and were using the money as an excuse. If money really was the factor, it turned out to be a bad play for Marshall. While I never got $350,000, the money Marshall would spend on their defense and my eventual settlement far eclipsed what they would have been able to get away with in 2003. The complaint was re-filed the next day and the process would begin anew. I was as far away from the end of this thing as ever.

CHAPTER 26:

UPPING THE ANTE

THOUGH THINGS REMAINED AWKWARD for me at Marshall, I hadn't suffered any immediate, direct retaliation on campus for the lawsuit. My assumption was that the university knew that any act that even hinted at getting back at me would prompt action from my lawyers, and that no one on campus would be that stupid. I was wrong. They were that stupid.

It was in the summer of 2003 that the chair of the Exercise and Sports Science (ESSR) department, Dr. Jeff Chandler, contacted me via phone and said he needed to come to my office to discuss the upcoming fall class I was teaching, Seminar in Intercollegiate Athletics. I had taught this class before, it was very popular amongst the graduate students, and Chandler himself had written me a glowing evaluation the previous spring. I figured Jeff's visit had something to do with enrollment numbers for the class or something.

When he arrived, though, Chandler looked incredibly nervous, was short of breath, and was sweating profusely. He said there was a problem with my class, and with my teaching in ESSR as a whole. When I inquired, he said there had been several student complaints about my teaching style, because I was saying "inappropriate things" about my lawsuit in this class. I knew that wasn't true and so did he. While I had weaved in my own experiences, given that it was a college athletics course, my evaluations from him and the students had been excellent. Plus, I had taught the class in question another time since the filing of the lawsuit with no complaints whatsoever including stellar evaluations from Chandler and his predecessor, Bob Barnett.

I knew immediately that this was retaliation, an unwarranted attack on my integrity and academic freedom, and that the same university that ruined my athletic career was now trying to derail what little chance I could have at an academic career. I was incredulous that athletic interests were now directly interfering in academics, something that should not be allowed in academia, and was flat out unconstitutional.

"Who put you up to this, Jeff?" I asked. I knew he was too weak to do this on his own, and he had just written me a great teaching evaluation a few weeks before.

He took a deep breath and said, "This was my decision, and there are several other things that have disturbed me." When I pressed, he brought up something ridiculous about my having used another employee's phone without permission, and that my assignments and tests - which had been fine before - were inappropriate. This was getting deep, very deep, and I made it clear that I would fight my removal from the department. He just smiled and said that since I was an "at will" employee that I had no right to the position. I told him we would see.

After Chandler slunk away, I immediately called Jason and J.D. They both agreed that this was a not-very-subtle smokescreen for retaliation, and that in spite of this being a bad thing for my career, it ultimately might strengthen our case. We would add the termination of my adjunct position to the complaint, charging that it was retaliation and a violation of my first amendment rights. We also began the state grievance process to be reinstated to the position, and compensated for the class that was taken away from me. Though I would never teach at Marshall again, the grievance process would go on for several months and through four levels of review, in turn giving us a great deal of information to use in the civil case. In trying to hamstring me, the university had actually enhanced my artillery.[64]

By the spring of 2004, my case against Marshall was at a standstill due to the various motions and appeals in place, which meant my life and career were at a standstill too. I was taking medication for depression, going through major emotional upheaval while dealing with the case and being on a campus where I was not wanted nor respected. I felt imprisoned at Marshall, with a job I didn't want and few prospects in either athletics or academics thanks to the way I was unceremoniously removed from both arenas. My life and psyche at that time were the exact reason people were fearful of fighting the athletics machine. If this was happening at little old Marshall, imagine what it was like at Tennessee for Linda Bensel Meyers? The respect I have for those who have attempted to fight back is immense, because I can think of few things personally and professionally more difficult.

The thought that the case could drag on for another five years, and that I would remain stuck in Huntington, was unbearable. I was staring the age of 40 in the face, with a job I hated in a field for which I had no passion. I wanted more than 40 hours a week and a paycheck, I had worked too damn hard to settle for that.

As I contemplated my future, a call came in the spring of '04 that saved me. On the line was Dr. Carla Smith, an assistant professor at Mississippi State University, who informed me that I was a finalist for an Assistant Professor of Sport Management position at MSU. I nearly swallowed the phone, not least due to the fact that I didn't even remember applying for the position. I had applied for so many jobs in the preceding months in my desperation to get away from Marshall that it was hard to keep track, especially since no one was calling back. She asked if I had some time to come to Starkville during the next couple of weeks for an interview. It was an exhilarating feeling. I had a chance. I went home and told my wife, who was excited at the possibility because she knew how bad being at Marshall was for me mentally.

Meanwhile, as I was feverishly preparing for my MSU interview, I got a call from my old friend Juliene Simpson.[65] Juliene, the former women's basketball coach at Marshall, was a staunch supporter of my efforts to rectify the NCAA situation and re-start my career. She had moved on from Marshall to East Stroudsburg University, a Division II school nestled in the Pocono Mountains of Pennsylvania. She was on the search committee for the school's vacant athletic director position, and asked whether I would be interested in an interview. The dual job opportunities were another lesson in feast or famine.

While I was excited about my new prospects, I was a bit worried at the same time, that finding employment would hurt my case against Marshall. After all, we were alleging that the corrective action had injured my career - getting an AD job at an NCAA school would not exactly reinforce that contention, but it was worth the risk.

Not to worry though, because it became clear during my interview at East Stroudsburg that the circumstances of my dismissal at Marshall were very much coloring perceptions. This is another big reason that many lower-level administrators and coaches will not fight back, because the athletic world is so small and fighting back is usually detrimental to any job prospects. So is being associated with NCAA rule violations, even if you were not responsible.

According to Juliene, longtime East Stroudsburg head football coach Denny Douds had asked her why "we were interviewing the biggest NCAA violator for athletic director." I don't know if Douds spoke directly to Pruett, so I can only speculate, but the football fraternity is small and word travels fast.

But I really knew I was dead when I talked to the president of the university, Robert Dillman, formerly the president at Fairmont State in West Virginia, who mentioned to me that he knew Grose and Cottrill well. Considering what

I was up against, it was amazing I even got an interview, but this situation showed in graphic detail what I would have to deal with on every job interview for any athletic position I applied for the rest of my career. Needless to say, East Stroudsburg never called back.

The interview at Mississippi State went much better. I was surprised at how much I liked the campus and community. Starkville had always been rated among the worst SEC towns in fan polls, but I think that's unfair. I felt very welcome when I came to campus, and something just told me, this was where I needed to go, this was the next step. The job was an Assistant Professor of Sport Management in the Department of Kinesiology. While I would be taking a pay cut, it seemed like a great time to make a break and move on to something new. I still needed to clear my name, but a new career at Mississippi State provided an opportunity to regroup mentally, one that I was very thankful for.

Even under the circumstances, it was tough to leave Huntington. Despite all that had happened, this had been my home for over seven years, the place where my children were born and where my family had made friends and shared many good times. It was sad that it was ending this way, but it was also an opportunity for me to turn a big setback into a big comeback. I could not wait to get to Mississippi and get started.

Moving a family of four is never easy, and ours was complicated further by having to move my dad into assisted living in Starkville. But we all came through the transition fine, moving into faculty and staff housing right off campus and immersing ourselves in the Starkville and Mississippi State communities. We felt at home practically right away, thanks to the warm and wonderful people of Starkville and MSU. I really began to love it there.

I was also inspired and emboldened by my new position. I primarily taught graduate classes and while I was not the most experienced teacher, I found a talent that I did not know I had. The whole experience was a breath of fresh air, and the best thing about it was that I was permitted to speak my mind and incorporate the injustices in college athletics into my teaching.

It might have seemed, walking into the intense juggernaut that was SEC athletics that I was venturing into hostile territory but I found that I was mostly embraced for having the courage to speak out on issues like academic integrity in college sports. The oddity of a professor in the SEC who would dare speak out against something that was such a part of the fabric of life in the south and the SEC made me very attractive to the media. This was a golden opportunity to leverage the press both as a vehicle to get the word out on intercollegiate athletic sports reform, and also keep my case against Marshall alive. I had become an active member in the Drake Group, and later its executive director after being nominated by noted author, reformist, and then-Indiana University

Professor of English, Murray Sperber. Soon into my tenure at MSU, whether it was about TDG's efforts, my own research, or to opine on the latest scandal in college athletics, I found myself speaking to a reporter or appearing on a radio show almost daily.

I was also getting contacted by people who had similar experiences with the NCAA, those who like me had been mistreated by the process. I was asked to be an expert witness in the prominent case brought against the NCAA by former Alabama assistant football coaches Ronnie Cottrell and Ivy Williams, who felt they were cast in a negative light and had future job opportunities ruined by the way they had been portrayed in an infractions case. The case stemmed from the improper recruitment of Memphis-area prospect Albert Means and alleged payments made by Alabama booster Logan Young to Means' high school coach Lynn Lang. Cottrell was accused of accepting an improper loan from Young and lying about it (a loan which, amazingly, was approved and notarized in the University of Alabama compliance office), while Williams was accused of being involved in the recruiting scam.

Cottrell and Williams had been "defended" before the NCAA Committee on Infractions by none other than Rich Hilliard, who told both of the Alabama coaches that he was their attorney and would defend them as university employees. Yeah, we had some common ground. I was happy at this opportunity to assist Ronnie and Ivy, and hopefully expose many issues and problems with the enforcement and infractions process.[66] Once I became involved in the Alabama case, my own media exposure increased in spades. I continued to assert myself as a critic of the NCAA in my research, the media, and outside consulting, and was regularly writing editorials and providing interviews in the national and international media.

As a result of my heightened profile, I was asked to appear in front of a congressional subcommittee in Washington, D.C. to discuss due process and the NCAA. The Alabama coaches' attorneys were working every possible angle to break the apparent lack of due process at play for figures involved in the NCAA enforcement and infractions process. One of the ways they were putting pressure on the NCAA to address the absence of due process was to attempt to expose it through the legislative branch of the government, and had secured the endorsement of Alabama congressman Spencer Bachus to help look into the matter.

Historically, the NCAA has not made significant changes to its autocratic processes without intervention from government or courts . For example, the NCAA's television monopoly was not broken until the landmark Supreme Court case that pitted the Universities of Georgia and Oklahoma against the NCAA in 1983. Before the case, the NCAA maintained the right to broadcast just one NCAA game per Saturday, but the Supreme Court's decision afforded colleges and athletic conferences the power to negotiate their own television deals. The decision would forever alter the face of college football, and college sports in general.[67]

In another instance, the NCAA fought the publishing of graduation rates until Congress, led by Maryland congressman and former All-American basketball star Tom McMillen, stepped in to force the issue. More recently, the case that pitted former UNLV coach Jerry Tarkanian against the NCAA spurred a blue ribbon committee, at the behest of Congress, that was commissioned to do an external review of the NCAA's enforcement and infractions process in 1991. This committee listed 10 realistic steps that the NCAA should take to strengthen the fairness of the process, soon after which the NCAA adopted several seemingly common-sense measures. Before this committee made its recommendations there was no appeals process, interviews were not tape-recorded, individuals were not permitted to have counsel or representation during NCAA interviews, and there were no outside members of the COI. All are now requirements.

While the changes were necessary, my case and that of the Alabama coaches were proof that the NCAA still had a ways to go. In order to achieve due process, the NCAA still needed open hearings, impartial juries, and the right to cross-examine witnesses to include identification of all witnesses. In my case in particular, an open hearing would have prevented things being taken out of context, mischaracterizations, and frankly the outright lies that were published in the report. The NCAA as expected balked at these changes.

As I was assisting Congressman Bachus and his staffers on preparing for the September 2004 hearing in Washington, it was determined by Bachus and his staff that my in-person testimony might be beneficial.[68] When they asked me to appear, even on short notice, I jumped at the chance. It didn't hurt that one of the witnesses testifying on behalf of the NCAA would be Josephine Potuto, who had so injured my career with her scathing, wildly inaccurate report and comments during the hearing. The opportunity to face down Potuto was one I relished, and had waited a long time for.

I did not sleep a wink the night before the hearing from anticipation and nervousness. I pulled an all-nighter in order to finish my five-minute opening statement. The next morning, as I emerged from the Metro Station near Capitol Hill, I was struck by the scene of the iconic Capitol Building, with its famous rotunda. It was hard to compute that I would soon be testifying in that building. I had knots in my stomach as my contingent walked into a hearing room I had seen on TV countless times in my life.

Prior to the hearing, I exchanged pleasantries with a number of members of the NCAA entourage, even though we would be in an adversarial situation here. Kevin Lennon, the Vice President for Membership Services at the NCAA and a fellow Ohio University sports administration graduate, approached me to say hello. David Price came by as well. These were all good people, even if I thought they were wrong in drinking the NCAA Kool-Aid on matters that were unjust. Not surprisingly, Potuto did not come by, nor did then NCAA President Myles Brand.

All of the commotion riled up Congressman Bachus, who was concerned that the NCAA figures were trying to intimidate me and influence my testimony. I told him there was nothing to worry about.

The committee I was appearing before was the House Sub-Committee on the Constitution, chaired by Steve Chabot (R-Ohio) and a part of the House Committee on the Judiciary. Due process issues fall under the interpretation of the Constitution, and since Bachus was on this committee, it was where the discussion ended up. As I made my way to the hearing table, I saw Potuto, who was in no mood to be friendly. She seemed put off by having to be there, and would soon share a kind of "how dare you question us" attitude toward the whole proceeding.

After Chabot's opening statement, and out-of-place comments from minority members of the committee which amounted to rants against the Bush administration, Bachus took the stage. He stated that the hearing was about the NCAA's refusal to adopt common-sense recommendations of due process that the Lee Commission had put forth following the Tarkanian case, likening the current process to the star chambers of medieval times. While arguing that "sunshine was the best disinfectant," Bachus implored the NCAA to adopt open hearings and discontinue the practice of using witnesses that cannot be cross-examined to test the validity of their claims.

Potuto, who was there to protect the status quo, countered that the NCAA would not be able to properly conduct its investigations if certain informants were revealed, witnesses were cross-examined, or if the hearings were held in public. To me that was precisely the problem. The NCAA could scapegoat certain people, conduct poor investigations and reach conclusions without any checks and balances.

When it was my turn to speak, I supported Bachus' statements and added that part of due process is getting a fair hearing and being presented with charges. Being told you are not at risk, and participating in the investigation only to find out you are the one holding the proverbial bag, doesn't exhibit the semblance of fairness that the NCAA attempts to portray. I also called out Potuto, vehemently disagreeing with her statement that the NCAA enforcement, infractions, and eligibility reinstatement process was not in need of repair.

After the opening statements, the real fireworks started. Already aggravated by my statement, Potuto was in no mood to be questioned by members of the committee. Most of their questions were directed at her, and she became very defensive, directly stating in a feeble effort to counter my claims that I was not "up to my compliance responsibilities in the Marshall case" and that she stood by the NCAA report that she herself authored. She knew that the December 21, 2001 Marshall University Infractions Report was not worth the paper it was printed on, but Chabot stopped me from countering her cheap shot. Which was all the better, because she was doing a fine job digging her own grave.

Potuto lost the committee with her grating personality, holier-than-thou presentation, and needlessly defensive answers to simple questions. I found her woeful performance extremely ironic, given that she had authored a report flogging me for my performance at the NCAA hearing. I was convinced from that moment that there is karma in the universe.

At the conclusion of the hearing, the NCAA staffers scattered, while I, along with former Colorado wide receiver Jeremy Bloom, spent some time talking to members of the committee. (Bloom's testimony stemmed from the NCAA's decision to bar him from playing football after accepting endorsement money as part of his Olympic skiing career). The committee members joked that the hearing was a rarity, because they had reached true bi-partisanship - all agreed that Josephine Potuto was a terrible witness who actually confirmed many negative stereotypes about the NCAA. As we dined with Bachus in the House Dining Room, other members of the committee approached to tell us how arrogant Potuto was, and how bad she made the NCAA look.

The hearing was really more theater than anything else, but it did aid in pushing the NCAA into finally doing away with secret witnesses when it reviewed its own procedures a couple of years later. Although Ronnie Cottrell eventually had his 30 million dollar jury verdict thrown out by an activist judge in Tuscaloosa, the case succeeded in bringing a little more transparency to the process.[69]

From a personal standpoint, my appearance enabled me to tap more media sources and keep my case against Marshall in the news.

The end was growing nearer.

Chapter 27:

Endgame

THOUGH MY CASE AGAINST Marshall seemed to be moving at a glacial pace as we reached the spring of 2006, things were continuing to happen for me professionally. I was accomplishing much in the way of teaching and research at Mississippi State, and remained in demand as a speaker and media guest. My family was settled and happy in Starkville, and things appeared stable. Then, opportunity knocked again.

An old friend and fellow Ohio University Sports Administration alum named Jim Kahler was hired in early 2006 as the executive director of the newly-established Center for Sports Administration at Ohio University. With other graduate programs beginning to catch up to the Ohio brand, the university hired Kahler in order to solidify the program as the industry leader once again. Kahler had previously been the Senior Vice President for Sales and Marketing for the Cleveland Cavaliers for over 10 years, and more recently had built the Sports Business Management Program at Arizona State University into one of the best in the country.

I was a big proponent of Jim getting hired, as were many Ohio U. alumni. Once he was in place in Athens, I began calling Jim, and lobbied him and others for a job. My family loved Starkville, but Jacqueline and I sensed an opportunity to make this our last move, and to give our kids a place they could call home permanently. Professionally, this would be a chance to work in the country's elite program again, and an ancillary benefit would be that I could be closer to Huntington and have the ability to manage my case much better.

Probably after folks at Ohio tired of me asking them all of the time about returning, I was able to secure an assistant professor position at Ohio starting in the fall of 2006. However circuitous and bizarre the route had been, it felt good to be going back.

Just before we were set to begin looking at houses in Athens in May of 2006, word came down that the 4th Circuit Federal Court of Appeals had finally determined that our case could go to trial. It had been 15 months since the Court had heard arguments in the motion to dismiss the trial, and my lawyers and I had been understandably lulled to sleep by the delay in what was ultimately a landslide decision in our favor. Marshall hastily submitted their last layer of federal appeal, an en banc hearing in front of the entire 12 judge panel of the 4th circuit, which was denied, and in the summer of 2006 it was time to get a scheduling order and start the litigation phase of the case.

Once this happened, we heard from attorneys for Hilliard, who were ready to settle with me out of fear that they would lose once the case reached trial. We eventually settled at the relatively low price of $25,000, but keeping Hilliard - a former attorney with plenty of resources - as part of the suit threatened to bog us down. As part of the agreement we also requested the opportunity to have a lengthy discussion with Hilliard to gather information. In addition, former NCAA investigator Mark Jones had moved to Ice Miller, and we wanted him to be part of the conversation too. By 2006, Hilliard was a disbarred, disgraced attorney, a shell of the well-respected lawyer who I had put so much faith in when the NCAA investigation was simmering back in 1999.[70]

Looking back, it appears that part of the reason Rich did such a poor job on our case was that he was immersed in Alabama's, although it's not as if he did a bang-up job in Tuscaloosa either. Popular Alabama radio host, Paul Finebaum, said that if ESPN did a SportsCentury show on the worst sports lawyers of all time, Hilliard would have the honor sewn up. He was eventually removed as lead counsel for Alabama's appearance in front of the NCAA Infractions Appeals Committee, and due to the public bashing, the cases for Rich and Ice Miller began to dwindle.

Hilliard was still hired to represent Rick Neuheisel, who was then head football coach at the University of Washington, when he went before the COI concerning recruiting improprieties when he was head coach at the University of Colorado. Later, Hilliard was hired by Quin Snyder, former men's basketball coach at the University of Missouri, to represent him in a major infractions case that concerned impermissible recruiting allegations, suspect junior college academic issues with certain recruits, and extra benefits. Snyder gave Hilliard an initial $15,000 retainer for representation, which Hilliard neither deposited nor recorded with his firm. It turned out that Hilliard used the $15,000 to pay off gambling debts, and later lied to his firm superiors about his transgressions.

He was fired from Ice Miller and disbarred. Whether Hilliard can repair his legal career or not, it's clear he will no longer be participating in the lucrative business of defending institutions and individuals in NCAA major infractions cases, and that is a very good thing. At his meeting with my lawyers, Rich showed little contrition or accountability for his pathetic defense, claiming that I brought everything on myself. Interestingly, he even tried to blame the violations on me, and accused me of losing the test in the Bruce McAllister case on purpose. I chuckled when I heard that. Pathetic, but predictable.

Jones was a little less negative toward me. He did say that I was too defensive at the hearing, but also said he knew "this wasn't Ridpath's fault," and that he felt they "never got to the bottom of the jobs program or the academic fraud allegations." Jones also added that he felt Pruett knew much more about the academic fraud allegations than he revealed to the NCAA. My lawyers left that meeting feeling both Hilliard and Jones would be pretty good witnesses for us, if it came to that. The Marshall contingent was incredulous over the Hilliard settlement, which seemingly weakened their case, and their attorney, Chuck Bailey, even threatened to sue Hilliard on behalf of the university. He eventually relented.

While we were getting nearer to trial in the spring of 2007, my brilliant West Virginia-based attorney, Jason Huber, told me he had bad news. He had just been offered a prestigious two-year fellowship at the University of Chicago Law School, and he simply had to take it. While it tore me up for him to leave, he had worked his ass off for five years, and who was I to deny him the opportunity? Jason passed me off to one of his close friends and attorney colleagues, Jon Matthews, who would move forward with the case at an exciting time, just as discovery and depositions were beginning.

During discovery, as Pruett's attorneys sifted through the office-full of boxes that I had compiled concerning the case, they came across a draft of this very book and found the passage that discussed Kevin Klotz and I getting the documents from my office a couple of years before. Pruett's lawyers claimed that this constituted theft, and gave them grounds to delay the proceedings. It wasn't theft, of course, since the documents never left campus, I had been the custodian of those documents, and when I tried to secure them by pressing Cottrill to put them at a secure location, he had refused. We also disclosed that we had these very documents as required, but they thought they had an opening to get the case dismissed.

Still, the situation stretched that case into another year, as Marshall attempted to get it dismissed. It was becoming clear in our opinion that winning the case would be difficult for Marshall based on the evidence, so they threw an immense amount of weight behind their latest motions and ancillary issues. In these motions they argued that I was a common thief who should be prosecuted for taking the documents, and also being in possession of attorney-client documents that I was not authorized to see. On top of that, my legal team was also threatened with sanctions and imprisonment. It was not quite a Hail Mary, but they felt it was something they had to try.

After months of fighting this out through paperwork, it became a push. The court did not dismiss the case, but determined that of all the thousands of pages of documents in my possession, I had to return 300 or so that were deemed to be attorney-client privileged. This was really not a big deal at all and we gladly returned those documents, as they were not as important as the remaining thousands of pages. With that delay having fizzled, we were moving toward depositions, and I was finally going to get some people to talk under oath. It had taken a long time, but we were now on a scheduling order, and trial was set to commence in October 2008.

As a sidelight, Bob Pruett - who had abruptly "retired" as head coach at Marshall in the spring of 2004 and had scarcely been heard from since - surprisingly accepted the defensive coordinator job at the University of Virginia in time for the 2008 season. I knew that he had been looking at jobs, as multiple ADs and friends in the business called me to check out his credentials, most notably Temple and Kentucky, but more importantly, his involvement in NCAA violations. Morally, I had to tell the truth.

In one conversation I had with a university regarding Pruett, I was told that he alleged that this "jobs program" was once legal, certified by the NCAA, and that it was compliance (meaning me) that missed the change to the "new rule." It was amazing that a university out there would be willing to believe that recruiting academically marginal athletes with the promise of jobs requiring little or no work, paying $200 a day, with the proviso that they couldn't tell anyone about it as required by the NCAA, was somehow permissible yet mishandled by the compliance office. Donnan also made the same assertions to University of Kentucky officials when he was in the running for that job, saying that this was at some point legal and Marshall was following NCAA rules under his watch. I laughed when I was first told this by the University of Kentucky, as this is simply not the case. While I bash the NCAA Public Infractions Report often, the Committee on Infractions makes it crystal clear that at a minimum, arranging employment for athletes is and always has been a violation, it was never permissible. In addition to the overpayment and recruiting issues, the concealment of this from the compliance office was also going on under Donnan, well before Pruett's arrival. Once I explained to several colleagues the actual situation, most backed off of Pruett. It surprised me a good school like Virginia would even take a flier on Pruett, but they were persuaded by Cavalier head coach and longtime Pruett ally Al Groh to take the chance.

This impacted the case because almost immediately, Pruett filed for a continuance, claiming he could not appear in court during football season, spring football, or recruiting periods. He was asking for more than a year delay so he could enjoy his new coaching job, at the expense of me and everyone else involved in the case. We told the defense we would not accept a continuance, and that UVA had plenty of coaches to keep things going if Pruett was indisposed. We also liked the idea of having the trial during football season for extra publicity. Predictably, the court turned down Pruett's request. It looked like he might actually have to be in court during football season.

Like Pruett, more and more people involved in the case were moving on to new positions away from Marshall. This certainly made it challenging once we arrived at the deposition phase to round everyone up, but time marches on and people moving on is not unusual. After much discussion we decided at a minimum we wanted to subpoena Pruett, Cottrill, Grose, Reynolds, Angel, and Dave Reed.

We also had two experts to help give credence to our position: Kathy Noble, a former member of the NCAA Infractions Appeals Committee and Associate Commissioner of the Big Sky Conference, and Dr. Jon Gerdy, a Drake Group member who worked for the NCAA in Legislative Services, and later was the Associate Commissioner of the SEC for compliance and internal affairs.

As expected, I was the first one deposed in March 2008. Even though I had been deposed as an expert a couple times, and was also deposed as a fact witness in the NCAA restricted earnings coach case in the 1990's,[71] I must say I was nervous to have to face questions about this case. I had waited for many years, and now the day was here … litigation was starting. Depositions are interesting in that the person being deposed is somewhat out on an island because any question can be asked and there is very little your lawyer can do except raise an objection that will have to be decided later. Not much is off limits, and the deposed must answer the question.

The defense was represented during all of the depositions by Vaughn Sizemore for the university defendants, and Ed Kowal for Pruett. Both are fairly competent attorneys and clearly I had irritated them enough over the years that they wanted to get a piece of me and harass me during the deposition. My attorneys warned me of this, so I was prepared. Their strategy was to simply rattle me and with the deposition being videotaped, they wanted to memorialize any time that I might get frustrated or lose my temper. I was focused on not letting that happen. My deposition lasted over the bulk of three days, for about 18 hours of actual testimony. While Sizemore and Kowal did their best to rattle me, the fact that I maintained my composure made them more aggressive in their questioning.

Kowal, who is grossly overweight and a heavy smoker, looked like he was about to keel over whenever he got worked up. It almost became theater in itself, but we also had them on film acting like fools so in the end it likely would have benefitted us. I just refused to be intimidated, and stuck to the truth. While I made mistakes in my job, nothing I did contributed to the major violations found by the NCAA, and I was blamed for the transgressions to protect others. I was the convenient fall guy. That was my consistent message, and I never wavered from it.

We also acquired affidavits from three people - former Marshall assistant strength and conditioning coach Mike Jenkins, and former players and Proposition 48 athletes, Sam Goines and Charlie Tynes. All three stated that the jobs program was available for the props only and certain assistant coaches. While Jenkins never worked at any of Reynolds' businesses, he confirmed that his former graduate assistant, Jacob Belmont and then-graduate assistant football coach and later Assistant Athletic Director Mike Bianchin, did work there, along with there being other places that prop athletes worked, specifically a local meat packing plant and used car dealership that had never been mentioned to the NCAA. Jenkins added he believed that Pruett had full knowledge of the McAllister academic fraud scheme, revealing that Pruett had mentioned in a football staff meeting that "Dani Derricott was guaranteed to get an A in McAllister's class" when he was questioned about the possibility of Derricott being academically ineligible for the 1999 season. Goines and Tynes were particularly helpful in stating that they were recruited with the promise of $200 a day jobs (a definite NCAA violation), and that they were told to not speak about these jobs outside the football family. Both also added that they signed the initial false affidavits per instructions from Pruett before my arrival at the meeting to discuss. This information was huge, and rattled the defense since these were major NCAA violations.

As we entered the summer of 2008, more and more depositions were happening. We deposed Cottrill, Grose and Pruett, all of whom stuck to their script. Cottrill and Grose said that I was not very good at my job, in spite of being in the position for more than four years and getting consistently high praise and positive evaluations, gave unreliable information which caused the violations, and that my conduct was poor at the hearing. They categorically denied threatening me, and both stated that I should consider myself lucky I was not fired outright. Pruett said that while he felt I was good overall at my job, he claimed that I was fully aware of the jobs program and that I alone chose not to track it. He also said that he would bring forth witnesses to support his contention. I know these witnesses never really ever existed, though I heard he had some friendly former football coaches ready to go to bat (and lie) for him.

This is another tactic used by high profile coaches, who will pressure assistant coaches to lie and protect their bosses to insulate their own career and reputation. Several assistants, including former Baylor men's basketball assistant Abar Rouse, have gone against this normal protocol and sacrificed their careers for doing the right thing and not protecting their coach. Rouse was pressured by former Baylor head coach Dave Bliss into going along with a fabricated story that basketball player Patrick Dennehy, then missing and later found to have been murdered by teammate Carlton Dotson, was a drug dealer. A university committee and police investigating the disappearance had begun probing the nature of tuition payments being made by Dennehy during the year between his transfer from New Mexico and the season he would become eligible at Baylor, payments which it turned out were being paid by Bliss. Rouse, who was threatened with being fired if he failed to go along with the story, surreptitiously taped a conversation with Bliss detailing the scheme as a way to protect himself, blowing the lid off the scandal and eventually leading to the firing of Bliss and major NCAA violations for Baylor. In doing so, however, Rouse irreparably damaged his career, as he was considered a "snitch" by many in the world of college basketball. The trajectory that Rouse's career followed doesn't exactly serve as an inspiration to those coaches who would blow the whistle on their bosses, whether they're morally doing the right thing or not.

Meanwhile for me, the October 2008 trial date was approaching and we needed to travel to get some of the remaining depositions. In the span of about two weeks I was in Huntington, San Francisco, Indianapolis, Charleston, WV, Philadelphia, and back to Charleston for depositions of various people.

We deposed Marshall Reynolds in Huntington, and he seemed agitated that a low-level person like me could actually make a rich man like him come to a deposition. Even under oath, Reynolds was all over the map and inconsistent. He spent a good amount of time berating Dan Angel, criticizing his leadership abilities to the extent of saying, at one point, "Dan Angel is not capable of organizing a two-car funeral." I'll admit that was a great line.

Reynolds denied ever doing anything wrong, and said he was only providing these jobs at the university's request. He emphatically stated that these jobs were open to more than athletes, despite never even providing even one name of a non-athlete, that the kids were paid "non-union scale" wage of $9.73 per hour (an amount I was hearing for the first time, and was inaccurate), despite no documented evidence of this, and that all of these hires were supposed to work Saturday and Sunday but did not because supervisor Russell May was trying to scam the company by claiming overtime on Sundays when he was not there. It was a desperate, silly claim by Reynolds. No athlete ever testified to working on a Sunday, nor being asked to. A comprehensive review of May's pay and tax records confirmed he never claimed hours for any Sunday during the time he worked there. The pay records of the athletes showed in every case that the players were paid $200 per day for one day of work, and no taxes were taken out of the gross pay.

In the end, one was left with the impression that Reynolds was a bad liar, clueless, or worse yet, just felt untouchable because of his money and power. Maybe it was a combination of all three. In any event, Reynolds was a great witness for us.

From there, we took the time to depose Dan Angel, who was now the president of tiny Golden Gate University in downtown San Francisco. It was a far cry from the pompous, arrogant president I knew in Huntington. He almost seemed ashamed to have landed at what looked like a glorified community college and commuter school with high school-looking lockers in the hallways. It was a long fall for a man who must have felt on top of the world while in Huntington. Angel also seemed irritated that I alone was able to take away one day of his schedule for a deposition. As expected, he was incredibly harsh on me, belittling my job performance and conduct at the hearing during his deposition. You could also tell he resented the fact that this situation, and his disassociating Reynolds from the athletic department, caused his downfall at Marshall. He was clearly uncomfortable discussing the efforts to get Reynolds reinstated, because it was now certain that it was done under extreme pressure from other major contributors and politicians who said that he needed to fix this problem. He acted like he could not remember the name of Bob Marcum, the AD he hired to replace West, and he denied ever discussing this case with former Conference USA commissioner Mike Slive when Marshall was seeking entry into Conference USA, despite the nature of the meeting being discussed and confirmed in local media and athletic department meetings that I was a part of.[72]

In many ways it was sad to see what had become of Dan Angel. He had visions of going to bigger and better places, and Bob Pruett and others had a major hand in getting him out of town, just like they did me. In some ways he and I had were kindred spirits, though he saw me as part of the reason he was no longer at Marshall, instead of realizing the early alliance he made with Pruett in an effort to bolster his own popularity and presidency actually doomed it from the start.

Our first expert, Kathy Noble, was her brilliant self in her testimony. She deftly fielded all of the questions and expertly backed up our claims. Sizemore and Kowal tried to derail her by bringing up issues I had with Beatrice and others to which Kathy stated that she would not agree nor support things that I allegedly did, but she knew me well and worked with me such that she never saw anything that resembled inappropriate behavior. She went on to say that she would have to look at the situation, but in some of the cases my reactions might be considered reasonable since my livelihood and my family were at risk.

Next it was on to Indianapolis to depose former NCAA investigator Luann Humphrey and Marshall's expert, former NCAA Committee on Infractions chair and University of Oklahoma law school president David Swank. Surprisingly, Humphrey was very cordial when she saw me that morning, and more friendly than I remembered her. She even pulled me aside to mention she was sorry about everything that had transpired and said she appreciated how nice I was to her after the 2001 hearing to her. Humphrey's deposition was good for us in that we were able to confirm that she had numerous doubts about the findings in the investigation, to include verifying she wrote an email to David Price and Mark Jones during the 2003 attempt to remove Reynolds' penalty as, "everything in this case points to a cover-up, and people were trying like hell to throw us off track from the beginning and we may never know the real story."[73] She steered away from placing any blame on me, saying it was for the institution to decide, although she certainly was not a fan of my aggressiveness toward her during the investigation.

When given the affidavits from the Prop players to review, Humphrey seemed curious but not surprised. She stated later to me in the hallway during a break in the deposition that she was not surprised at all by this new information. I replied, "Now, what are you going to do with it?" She just smiled and walked away. Sad, because the NCAA should be reinvestigating this matter now based on the new evidence, but has not, in contradiction of its own rules on unethical conduct, which is not covered by any statute of limitations. The truth is that they do not want to have to admit the inadequacies of the process, and that the Marshall investigation and findings were basically a sham.

David Swank did not add much to hurt us despite his deserved stellar reputation, though he did try to focus on the employment legislation being simple, testifying that it was an incredible oversight on my part not to "know" this - even though I actually did know it. But his contention came unglued when my attorney, J.D. Hartung, had Swank try to walk through the myriad of rules one must use to come to this conclusion, because there is not a direct rule that does not permit athletic assistance in securing jobs for prop athletes nor is "assistance" ever defined clearly in the manual. While it was clear that the arrangements Marshall was punished for were violations, they were made more obvious by the clearly stated violations of recruiting inducements and overpayment for work performed. What constitutes assistance is a matter of interpretation and varies widely. In other words, if Reynolds was telling the truth and these kids got jobs like anyone else and were paid a commensurate wage, there would have been no violation if we had been tracking it.

Swank couldn't really explain how it was that, in spite of rules education and interpretations of the rules that included a monitoring component, that the coaches simply ignored it. He couldn't explain why the coaches promised these jobs during recruiting, and failed to report their existence despite being mandated to do so. Swank even stated in his deposition that the coaches had an obligation to report all employment activities to the compliance office, in direct contradiction of the COI who assailed me for relying on information provided by coaches - an interesting and flawed conclusion by that committee. One strategy of the defense was to acknowledge that saying Prop 48 athletes could work was essentially true, but that I had failed by not spending time on the caveat issues like reporting, recruiting, wages earned, etc. That was false, and we had documentation to prove that I had explained the caveat issues to coaches. Swank could not explain nor excuse that oversight by the coaches. In front of a jury, this kind of stuff was gold. Any worries I had about Swank being a defense expert were gone after that day.

The next few days brought a deposition with Gerdy in Philadelphia, who also provided great expert testimony on NCAA rules and compliance, and with Kevin Klotz, who Marshall's lawyers simply wanted to hammer for helping me move the documents. Kevin held up well, and on redirect questioning he was able to confirm everything I had been claiming, also adding that he spoke to Dave Reed on many occasions and Reed could confirm the strength of both the employment program for athletes and the compliance program as a whole. Kevin closed with an important statement, saying that he had worked in compliance previously at Maryland, Ohio, and Akron, that Marshall's program was the best he had been a part of, and that he utilized many of the policies and procedures learned from me in his current program at Akron. It made me feel good that Kevin stood up for me and the compliance program. His loyalty and honesty will never be forgotten.

The October trial date was inching closer, but in keeping with the theme, nothing could be that easy. Sizemore, one of Marshall's attorneys, was scheduled for a kidney transplant near the trial date. Judge Chambers decided to delay the trial until January because of extraordinary circumstances. Then, it turned out that we would need an additional delay until March, as my attorney Jon Matthews departed to take a position with the ACLU office in Connecticut. The burden of who would be the West Virginia attorney was an open question, and it ultimately fell to Huber's longtime partner and mentor, Roger Forman, by default. Initially Forman was skeptical about being able to help on such short notice, but we managed to eventually persuade him to jump in with both feet. It turned out to be a tremendous benefit. Roger did yeoman's work in getting up to speed in the case, and was as passionate as anyone about me and the case.

While we were still preparing for a summary judgment hearing, pretrial issues, and trial, it was time to resurrect the case in the media and get some publicity going to put some pressure on the other side. CBSSports.com reporter Dennis Dodd, who had interviewed me on several occasions and with whom I had struck up a professional relationship, had begun to express interest in the case. Dodd felt this was a big story for several reasons. He could not understand how Pruett was able to be hired by Virginia without the school doing a complete vetting process, and wondered what vetting process there was, if any. We both surmised that Pruett told UVA that this lawsuit was not a problem, and that I was just a disgruntled employee making trouble.

My lawyers and I gave Dodd the green light to break the story in early August 2008, and it gained steam even quicker than I had hoped. It was huge news and was picked up by all the major outlets. Most of the stories detailed how lawsuit documents claimed Pruett knew of NCAA violations at Marshall. Fall football camp was beginning at Virginia, and the story put Pruett on the hot seat as he and head coach Al Groh found themselves answering more questions about the lawsuit than about the team's prospects.[74]

Marshall and Pruett wasted little time in getting their own message out. In their summary judgment motion they stated that I was removed for my "mediocre job performance," and in response to the lack of institutional control charge brought forth against Marshall by the NCAA. Many articles came out saying how Marshall fired back at my claims and they certainly did, but it was nothing that we would be prevented from attacking in court or in our resistance to their summary judgment. Everything they said was what we expected. Summary judgment is the last chance for the defense to get a case dismissed in whole or in part before trial is a definite go.

The delay also gave us time to do additional depositions before Judge Chambers would rule on the summary judgment motions. We scheduled additional evidentiary depositions with Goines and Jenkins to support their affidavits, so the evidence would be admissible without them coming from out of state for trial. Both Goines and Jenkins agreed to come to West Virginia just before Christmas 2008 to put their statements under oath and on videotape.

Tynes became a reluctant witness, and even provided interviews to the media claiming he did not know what he was signing when confronted with the affidavit.[75] He also disputed the very claims that he confirmed on the affidavit. It was a public setback, but even though Charlie decided to jump ship, we knew that he could be called as a witness in trial and he would have to explain why he signed the affidavit. To be clear, Charlie Tynes signed the affidavit of his own free will. It was mailed to him with a return UPS envelope. He did not have to sign it, but he did voluntarily and to my knowledge, no one else was present. We had numerous conversations with him and his parents who all confirmed everything we thought. The props were recruited with the promise of these jobs, they were told to be quiet about the circumstances, etc. I think at the end of the day, it became real to Charlie and he panicked once he heard his name in the media. He is from West Virginia, and I think the local scrutiny became overwhelming for him. While his reversal publically made Marshall supporters feel good, it was a mere inconvenience to us, as we knew we could still call him to trial and get to the real story.

Both Jenkins and Goines were strong in the depositions they gave in December of 2008. Jenkins specifically detailed the spelling out of steps for employment in rules education classes along with having forms and documentation. Jenkins also stated for the record that he believed Pruett was fully aware of the academic fraud in McAllister's classes, and even encouraged it.

As strong as Jenkins was, Goines hit it out of the park. He was specific and rich in detail on how Pruett and then-assistant coach Kevin Kelly,[76] during a home recruiting visit, promised him a $200 dollar a day job during his Prop 48 year in residence, if he would agree to come to Marshall. Goines had opportunities to go to prep school and/or junior college to get his academics in order so he could go to one of the many BCS schools that were recruiting him, but he testified under oath that the promise of a job was the clincher to persuade him to come to Marshall over all other options.

Goines also spoke of how the jobs program was managed upon his arrival. He revealed that he was told by Ralph May that this job was to be kept in the family, and no one needed to know how much the players made because they were props. Goines added that he could not recall any employment monitoring prior to my arrival midway through his prop year in 1997-98, but once I arrived he remembered specifically a process being put in place. He said he was told by May not to worry about reporting the job, even though I mentioned it during several different meetings with the football team. With regard to the affidavits that were signed in the summer of 2000, Goines confirmed that he and others questioned the statement's validity to Pruett, with regard to them saying they made only $100 a day and $12.50 per hour. Goines stated, as I suspected all along, that Pruett instructed them, in my absence, to sign anything I gave them or that they would not be able to play during the upcoming season. Goines went on to add that he and the others were afraid to not sign the statements based on that information, but they knew that the statements were false. Goines so flustered the defense attorneys that they started asking him silly questions, like why he did not pay taxes on his earnings. It was so desperate, and irrelevant, that it was hard for me not to laugh. I cannot remember too many days during this ordeal where I felt better about the case falling my way.

The next few weeks had us waiting for Judge Chambers' decision on the summary judgment, which could come at any time. We also had a court-ordered settlement conference scheduled, and though we knew it was unlikely Marshall would settle, we put our demands on the table. We had thrown out numbers before on a settlement before, but this was the first official conference so we wanted to be pretty close to exact of what our minimum demands would be. We hammered out what I thought would be a pretty good demand and at least give them something to chew on for the next few weeks. We essentially asked for the same things we had wanted all along, with an adjustment made for the monetary settlement given that I was dealing with seven years of legal fees:

- Removal of the corrective action from the NCAA report, along with clarifying my role in the NCAA investigation including that I was not responsible for any major violations.

- That I maintain publication rights to this story, and that the university and Pruett take no steps to prevent publication of this story.

- A cash settlement of $350,000.

In exchange, I would offer a pledge that I would not actively pursue reopening of the Marshall case in accordance with NCAA Bylaw 32.6.3, which allows cases to be reinvestigated beyond the four-year statute of limitations. Frankly, I should not have had to even bring it up as the NCAA had enough information to reopen the case, but I knew they would not without prodding because it would reveal their investigation and the process as flawed and in need of overhaul.

The gauntlet was essentially thrown down, and the reaction from the opposing attorneys was somewhat surprising. There was no disgust, laughing, rolling of the eyes or anything that would suggest we asked for something outlandish. The body language spoke volumes. It appeared to me that there was pressure coming from somewhere to bring this case to an end. The specter of a renewed investigation, and more sanctions raised by Dodd in his articles, was having the exact effect we wanted. They wanted to settle this case, I just knew it.

I felt we put forth a very reasonable offer, and it seemed like it was one they were considering, even with the case not yet definitively going to trial. It was December, and the clock was ticking toward our pretrial hearing scheduled for January 20th, 2009. What would turn out to be a pivotal and historic day for the United States of America, with the inauguration of Barack Obama as president, also turned out to be quite a day for this case.

While "Team Ridpath" was driving from Charleston to Huntington for the hearing, Bailey called to let us know that two insurance adjustors, current Marshall president Stephen Kopp, and members of the Board of Governors would be at the hearing. This gave us some hope that we might at least discuss settlement, but they would not do it until the judge ruled on dismissal of the case. The main purpose of the pretrial hearing was to get a ruling on summary judgment, but also to rule on several motions, filed primarily by the defense. The defense filed 18 motions to limit evidence, and when taken as a whole, they were motions to essentially gut our legal theories of the case. The motions ranged from suppressing the testimony of Gerdy and Noble, to a lengthy motion detailing why I would never have been able to become an athletic director even in the best of circumstances. Some of the motions, like the latter, were semi-humorous, and I wondered about the man-hours it took to write some of these. We were successful in resisting almost all of these motions. Overall, the case was intact, our theories looked strong, and we were well-positioned for trial. It was a very good day, and things were pointing positively in our direction. Our statement during the hearing was consistent - "the defendants cheated knowingly and willingly to gain a competitive advantage in direct violation of NCAA rules."

These statements seemed to go over well with Judge Chambers, and of course not so well with the defense. Kowal threatened to bring in "several" witnesses that would testify that not only did I know about the jobs program and all it entailed, that I approved it with the full knowledge it was a violation. While I was trying not to laugh out loud at such an absurd comment, I also realized that this was a desperate ploy.

We had a brief recess after Chambers ruled on some of the motions and Hartung approached Kowal in the hallway and shot back, "You are actually going to bring in witnesses and say your client did not cheat ... when he cheated? He cheated Ed, and you know it!" Kowal responded by saying, "My client has made some mistakes." Hartung said again, "He cheated Ed!" I was fired up at how JD called out Kowal and stood up for what was right. Kowal simply could not respond and JD, Roger and I retreated down the hallway to avoid further confrontation.

As we entered the courtroom later in the afternoon, the mood had shifted dramatically. The defense looked not only irritated, but in my opinion, beaten down by the direction of the hearing. Judge Chambers closed the day by saying he would have rulings on the few pending motions and anything regarding the summary judgment motions soon, but he asked both parties to go to separate rooms, so he could talk to each individually. It was almost 6:00 pm, and all of us, including the lawyers, were unsure of what was going on.

Chambers spoke to us first, and said he was going to the Marshall contingent to ask if they wanted to start immediate settlement discussions. When he departed, I said I thought it unlikely they would want to do that before an official summary judgment decision. Forman spoke up and said,

"They know they will not win summary judgment based on what happened today." Hartung agreed. While it would be great to be wrong, I was certain that the case was going to continue to drag on.

Chambers returned about 10 minutes later, to tell us that the defense was indeed willing to continue the discussions in Kowal's offices a couple blocks away from the courthouse. We obviously had no problem with this development, and were mildly surprised to find out that they were willing to talk.

We arrived at the conference room located in the Campbell Woods law firm to find the entire defense team, seated along with the two insurance adjusters from the State of West Virginia, around the large conference table. It was clear that the finish line was near.

Bailey took charge of the meeting and revealed that a couple of weeks earlier, the people authorized to give him the green light to enter serious settlement negotiations for this case said to explore the possibility. He then railed on me directly, saying things like, "it could have been much sooner but for my activities with the media," and the worry that, "I may crow over any settlement as a victory." This was a silly statement, but par for the course.

I bit my tongue and just listened, letting Roger and J.D. speak for me. Roger spoke up and said that there was no use discussing what may or may not have happened, where do we stand now? Bailey went through the earlier settlement demand of 350K, removal of the corrective action from the NCAA report to include a letter clarifying my non-role in NCAA major violations, and maintaining publication rights to this entire story. We did not discuss me pursuing additional action through the NCAA infractions process, and it appeared to be an issue they were not concerned with. Bailey again reiterated that publication rights were a non-issue since Marshall is a public entity and volumes of information about the NCAA case and civil case are available by simple web searches, and he focused right on the corrective action and asked me directly what I wanted.

I spoke up this time and said, "Exactly what I have been asking for eight years, which is Marshall University taking affirmative steps to clarify my role in the investigation and requesting removal of the correction action from the public NCAA report." I added, "If the NCAA chooses not to remove the corrective action on their own, then it is not your problem and we will take action against the NCAA. This was the only thing I wanted eight years ago, not my job back or anything else, and it is the single most important issue to me."

Bailey, not surprisingly, seemed befuddled by my statement, to which Hartung spoke up and explained it in very plain English. "We will assist you in writing a letter clarifying exactly what we want and that is mutually agreeable to all parties. Then we will worry about the NCAA, not you." Bailey seemed to finally understand. Forman chimed in and said, "The state adjustors are here, it is late, and we probably need to discuss a monetary number."

Bailey agreed and politely asked me and my attorneys to adjourn to an adjacent room so the discussion could begin. As I got up, I locked eyes with Cottrill, who just seemed disgusted by the sight of me. Here was this powerful man who so brazenly threatened me years ago, who assisted in disposing of my career like an old newspaper, now sitting in what appeared to be utter disbelief that I was able to command this type of meeting and discussion. Someone had fought back very hard, and it affected him. He looked beaten. I stared at him, and smiled. It did not take him too long to avert his eyes.

Forman, Hartung, and I entered a small conference room and after about 10 minutes, Kowal entered and asked if I could leave the room and sit in the hallway. He said it was nothing personal, but he felt discussions would go better and he was going to act as a shuttle between rooms. My attorneys agreed, and I had no problem with it. What transpired over the next 90 minutes or so was interesting. I sat in the hallway near a main reception desk thumbing through the various magazines and talking to my wife on my cell phone. I had a clear view of both doors to each room and I would see Kowal walk back and forth between the two rooms, then one or both of my attorneys would go to the big conference room and return, usually closely followed by Bailey and/or Kowal. Something was going on, and after 90 minutes of this, J.D. motioned for me to come to the small conference room. The news wasn't great, which considering the history of the case was no surprise.

"They have only offered 50K as a settlement," J.D. said, and Kowal is sticking with his intention to bring in witnesses who will state you knew about and approved the jobs program. I began to chuckle and said, "This is getting good, who in the hell can he bring that would spout that drivel?" J.D. said that Kowal intended to bring in three former assistant coaches under Pruett. The coaches were Gunter Brewer, who was at Oklahoma State, Kevin Kelly, the head coach at Georgetown, and Jay Hopson, then at the University of Michigan. Hearing these three names made me almost laugh hysterically and I blurted, "Please let him bring these guys to trial and we will eat them alive, especially in the case of Kelly, who was the one who promised Goines the job in the first place." I was a bit surprised that we were in settlement talks and Kowal was still pulling this crap out of the air. Why were we even attempting to settle if he had this great plan?

Roger then interjected, "Dave, he also says that this potential trial will hurt you and your career at Ohio University." Again I laughed. This was becoming better than Comedy Central. Ohio University had fully backed me on the case and knew of all the implications when they hired me. I had not hidden anything and it had never been an issue, in fact by all indications they were rooting for me. I speculated this might be something thrown out by Marshall's new President, Steven Kopp, who used to be at Ohio U.[77] and perhaps felt he could call folks there to influence my promotion and tenure. Both J.D. and Roger thought it would be the height of stupidity to actually interfere with my employment at Ohio University, but we did not put it past them. But in the end, we surmised that it was little more than a bluff. Their image would have been injured by a trial, not mine, and they still thought I was stupid enough to believe differently.

After I laughed off their ever-so-slightly raised offer of $75,000 later in the evening, J.D. said, "What is the minimum number you need to pay everything [your legal fees] and break even?"

After some number crunching, the minimum number, without me pocketing a buck, was $177,000 and that did not include the close to $100,000 I had already spent and largely paid back. More activity ensued, and slightly before 9:00 pm they countered our latest offer of 300K with $100,000. The negotiations were not nearing an imminent conclusion - we would not blink first.

Sometime in the next 48 hours, after I had returned to Ohio and the various lawyers had scattered, the Marshall contingent got the message. Our resolve was rock-solid, and we were prepared to go to trial, where I was certain we would wipe the floor with them. You still never know with a jury trial, but it was a risk we were willing to take. We also accelerated things by requesting a deposition of Reed, who was now working at the University of Miami. We also contacted all three schools where the former assistant football coaches were working to inform them that we were going to depose them also. Former Georgetown athletic director Bernard Muir (now at Delaware) and then Michigan head football coach Rich Rodriguez were very concerned that their coaches might be involved in an issue they wanted no part of. We also informed them that we strongly believed that their testimony would not be credible, perhaps even viewed as perjury. We wanted to give them a chance to speak, but clearly the schools wanted no part of it. We were not going to slow down and we were positioning ourselves for trial.

We also interviewed Russell May. May was very eloquent and credible, as he had always been. It was also clear that this mess had affected him deeply. I always felt for Russell as he was another who did the right thing and got shafted. He told the truth and was a loyal worker who did exactly what he was told - supervise the football players for one day. He knew what they were getting paid and that he was making much less even with overtime, but he just simply did what he was asked. May felt that as an employee he had no room to speak up, even though in his mind he felt it was "kinda peculiar" what the players were getting paid.

May reiterated that the program was only for Saturday and that many of the players barely did any work. There was never a non-athlete that worked under this arrangement other than the occasional graduate assistant coach. He himself delivered the paychecks to Coach Pruett or his assistant, Edna Justice. He also added how devastating this had been to him and his family to include threatening phone calls and lost friendships. I certainly empathized with Russell, given my own trials and tribulations, and I appreciated his consistent testimony throughout. He said that he would gladly go to trial, but he hoped that this would "soon be over." We agreed, and told him that his testimony would assist us in getting thing finished.

On January 22nd, two days after we had first come to the table, I was back in Athens and received a call from Forman, who said there was a pretty good offer in play. The monetary offer was for 200K, and full payment of the bill for Swank (whose $7000 fee we were on the hook for), a mutually agreeable letter to the NCAA clarifying my role in the investigation, that would not directly ask for removal of the corrective action, but would ask the NCAA to consider it.

On Marshall's side, the agreement was to include a provision that I would not "crow" about winning the case and say I beat Marshall. That was not too much of a concern, as in many ways, the case was really a push. In total, including the Hilliard settlement, I received $232,000 which barely covered my bills and nowhere near compensated me for the pain and anguish my family and I went through, or the injury to my career. At the end of the day, I took the deal because it accomplished the main things that I desired. It was not a victory or a loss, and though it did bring a sense of relief that it was finally over, there was nothing to crow about, just a sense of relief.

My role was clarified in the investigation to state that I was not responsible for major violations at Marshall University. We were agreeable to hammering out a mutually agreeable settlement agreement, clarification letter to the NCAA, and not pursue this case further in the court system or the NCAA. We made a handshake agreement, and told the defense we were going to notify the media while abiding by the terms of the "no crow" agreement. The defense didn't object, and we put out a generic release about the settlement without the monetary amount noted, just calling it a monetary agreement, along with mentioning the letter of clarification to the NCAA. When the story broke, Bailey acknowledged to the media that an agreement had been reached in principle and the final details were being ironed out.

This did open up some interview requests for me, and with Roger and J.D.'s blessing I gave several interviews in print and on radio. Since there was not a non-disclosure agreement, I felt I owed the media interviews, considering how many reporters stuck with this story and refused to let it die. Knowing that I would be asked about Pruett lying and cheating, and his role in covering up the scandal, I had asked my attorneys what I should and should not say. We all agreed that the settlement did not change our stance in the original complaint and while Marshall and the defendants accept no responsibility, and I released them from any and all legal claims, it doesn't change what I believe nor what the evidence shows. So in all interviews I was allowed to state that I was scapegoated to protect Pruett and Reynolds, that Pruett provided false and misleading information to the NCAA, and Marshall knowingly and willingly cheated to gain a competitive advantage for its football and men's basketball teams.[78]

One particular interview raised the ire of Bailey and the defense. It was with popular West Virginia media personality Hoppy Kercheval. Hoppy is an excellent newsman, and does not shy away from the tough questions. I opened the interview by stating what the settlement was about and that both parties were satisfied. Hoppy asked me point blank if Pruett lied to the NCAA and I answered truthfully… "absolutely."

Hearing this, the defense claimed that this constituted crowing about the settlement, and they were considering withdrawing the settlement offer. We of course reacted in kind, reminding Bailey and the defense team that nothing I had said to the media post-agreement went against the no-crow clause, which only applied to the settlement agreement, and that there was not a non-disclosure agreement. It was apparent that the Marshall side thought this would be the end of it, that no media would be interested, and that there would be no book. This was a misjudgment on their part, and naïve. I am certain that Bailey and others were getting heat about making such an agreement, but they had to live up to it and not change or interpret it as they saw fit.

Several phone calls and letters went back and forth during February 2009, with both sides accusing each other of violating the settlement agreement. Bailey went as far to write lengthy letters to my counsel, claiming that my saying I was not responsible for major violations at Marshall University was untrue. He wrote that I was responsible for the ESPN game violation, and that the NCAA stated numerous things I did wrong in the public infractions report. Here we were again arguing the same petty points. I was responsible for secondary, minor violations at Marshall, and the NCAA report, as it pertained to me, had been largely discredited.

Bailey also took exception to me stating that Pruett lied, and threatened to counter-sue me if I kept on saying it. We responded by saying we were ready to go to court or ask Judge Chambers to enforce the settlement agreement. We were extremely confident that he would do just that, and if not we still liked our chances in court. After fighting it out again over the same issues, Bailey notified us in March 2009 that he had received authorization to proceed with the settlement but he warned, "Ridpath better stop talking to the press and if he says Pruett lied again, I will sue him."

To that, we just instructed them to move forward with the agreement, and not to worry about what I had to say because it had been consistent for eight years, and was also true. I fully stand and will continue to stand by those statements, and have the evidence to back them up. I doubt Marshall University or Coach Pruett would want to go down this road again.

Epilogue

Marshall University's athletic program, in particular its once-proud football program, has fallen hard since those football glory days of the 1990's, and much has changed - for better or for worse - since my days in the athletic department. The university made what by all appearances was an ill-advised move to Conference USA in 2003, and also hired veteran athletic director, Huntington native, and Marshall alumnus Bob "Kayo" Marcum to help shepherd them through the transition. Marcum, who had previously presided over a department at the University of Massachusetts that had reached an NCAA Final Four in men's basketball (an appearance eventually vacated due to violations), in addition to winning an FCS National Championship in football during his tenure, was brought in to help get Marshall out of the MAC and into a better league.

While many, including Marcum, had their sights set on the Big East during the massive conference realignment of 2002, Marshall settled for a watered-down C-USA. Instead of being in the regionally practical MAC, where they were playing schools in nearby Ohio, Michigan, Illinois and Indiana, they joined a league with a footprint that stretches from the North Carolina coast to the Texas/Mexico border, to central Florida and New Orleans. Obviously, being in C-USA has dramatically increased the travel and athletic infrastructure budget of the school, while sapping it of some budding regional rivalries.

Exacerbating the problem was that Marshall's football program was already on a downturn in the MAC when it left for "greener" pastures. The four-year probation that came with the NCAA investigation, and resultant loss of scholarships, was a big blow for a team that failed to win a conference title during its final four seasons in the MAC. There should be little question that the inability to bring in a large number of highly-talented, but academically challenged Proposition 48 athletes took its toll on a program that had by now distanced itself from Marshall Reynolds. The props had offered a competitive advantage for Marshall for more than a decade, and now the playing field was leveled.

Bob Pruett saw the writing on the wall, and by 2004, could foresee lean years coming. His reputation as an outstanding coach had dwindled once the Prop 48 pipeline had dried up. Pruett had also been brazenly posturing to make West Virginia a regular fixture on the schedule as well, and as this came closer to reality, the world could see that WVU was light-years ahead of Marshall. This was not likely to reflect well on Pruett.

So what did he do? He ran, resigning the day before spring practice 2004,[79] leaving his assistant coaches wondering if they would have jobs, and an entire team in limbo. I learned through my remaining contacts at Marshall that Pruett had been posturing for administrative changes, to include bringing academic advisement for football back under his control, facility and staff improvements, and other amenities that few level-headed administrators were going to bend over backwards to give a coach who was not winning anymore and lacked the political capital he once had. But Pruett demanded action, threatening to resign, and the administration led by interim President Mike Farrell, called his bluff.

His stint at Virginia lasted only one year, after which he retired again to Huntington, apparently for good. His departure from UVA was curiously close to the date of my lawsuit settlement, and I've been told by some reliable sources close to the Virginia program that my lawsuit and the subsequent media coverage were factors in Pruett leaving after only one season on the job. He remains a big man about town on Huntington, and still maintains a restaurant partnership with Marshall Reynolds.

Pruett was succeeded at Marshall by Mark Snyder, a former star safety for the Thundering Herd in the 80's who had previously been defensive coordinator at Ohio State. Snyder, in my opinion, clearly tried to run the program with integrity, but the harsh reality is that without cutting the corners that Pruett, Donnan, and frankly a large number of successful coaches throughout college football had (and continues to), it was going to be difficult to succeed at a high level. Snyder was 22-37 in five years as head coach at Marshall, resigning after his best season, a 6-6 campaign of 2009 that included a win, under interim coach Rick Minter, over none other than Ohio University in the Little Caesar's Pizza Bowl in Detroit.[80]

In December 2009, the team hired John "Doc" Holliday, a longtime assistant at WVU, to try to restore the Marshall program to its former greatness, yet he went just 5-7 in his first season of 2010 and 7-6 (with a bowl win) in 2011.

Snyder accepted a defensive coordinator position at South Florida under his old friend, Skip Holtz. He now coaches at Texas A&M University.

Other players in this story have retired, including Ed Grose. Layton Cottrill is still at the university as General Counsel, although his role as Chief of Staff has been taken away. Lance West is the Vice President for Development of the Marshall University Foundation, a fundraising job that he is frankly much better cut out for than any type of leadership role in athletics.

Beatrice Crane also remains at the university in her roles as Associate AD and Senior Women's Administrator, and has amazingly survived three changes of athletic director. I never thought she would last this long, but she married, and had children with, a local attorney so perhaps she has modified her attitude a bit in order to keep her job and remain in Huntington.

Once he got his law license renewed after being disbarred, Rich Hilliard turned up briefly working for the Arena Football League, though his current whereabouts are unknown.[81]

Of my former protégés in the compliance department, Dave Reed is at the University of Miami, and our friendship has been destroyed based on his actions. Reed has become part of the media spotlight of ills in college athletics as Miami became embroiled in a prostitution and extra benefit scandal driven by an imprisoned booster, Nevin Shapiro. Shapiro physically attacked Reed in President Donna Shalala's box at the 2007 Orange Bowl, accusing him of preventing Miami's ability of being competitive in football. In spite of Reed seeming to be doing his job, Shapiro remained in good standing with Miami until he was imprisoned in 2010.[82] Kevin Klotz is still plugging away as Associate AD for Compliance at Houston after a long, successful stint at the University of Akron where ironically he worked alongside my old Weber State boss Chad Gerrety, who is still selling sponsorships for the Akron athletic department as a General Manager for IMG College.

My lawyers are still fighting the good fight, doing their jobs and giving us little guys a chance. I can never thank Jason Huber, J.D. Hartung, Roger Forman, Jon Matthews, Bob and John Tscholl, Jeremy Schulman, Jerry Crawford, my brother Brett, and most of all, my family for sticking with me through a process that I know I did not make it easy at times.

A longtime acquaintance and fellow Ohio University Sports Administration Graduate, Mike Hamrick, was hired as Athletic Director at Marshall University with much fanfare in July 2009, after Bob Marcum's retirement. Mike is an experienced athletic director, with three Division I AD jobs on his resume, and getting him to come to his alma mater of Marshall from UNLV was in my view a major coup for the university.

Hamrick loves Marshall, Huntington, and is passionate about the Thundering Herd - let there be no doubt about that. He is a West Virginia native whose transition, by all appearances, has been seamless. In his introductory press conference, he took on the previous NCAA issues head-on and said that the athletic department under his leadership would be one of integrity, and would follow NCAA rules. I was particularly struck by his statement that his Marshall University degree was important to him, and he was not going to let anything tarnish that. I wondered what Bob Pruett, who was sitting in the press conference room at the time, thought of those words.

In the past, Marshall degrees have been tarnished by a willful culture of cheating in the athletic department, and by the allowing of influences outside of the department and university to control key issues - something all too often seen in intercollegiate athletics. In reality, Pruett has already tarnished Hamrick's degree, along with those of more than 100,000 others, including myself, who have come through Marshall's academic programs. I truly believe that Mike Hamrick does not want history to repeat itself, and that he will not accept a department that breaks NCAA rules as others before him have. I hope the rest of those who claim to love the university will follow suit, because the integrity of the institution depends on it.

I wish Mike Hamrick, and the Marshall University of the present and future, nothing but the best with the hope they will do it the right way and not find themselves in a position they have been in far too many times before.

Postscript: What Can be done to fix College Sports??

I remember the first college sporting event I attended. It was the 1975 Air Force-Navy played in Colorado Springs, Colorado. It was an electric atmosphere, and one I will never forget. The fighter jet fly-bys, the procession of the corps of cadets from each institution, and the singing of the school songs, by both teams, at the end of a hard-fought game helped ignite my love of college sports. It soon became my passion, and eventually, literally became my life. While I was not good enough to continue my checkered athletic competitive career, I was intent on being a part of my number one passion in one way or another.

Through determination and hard work I was able to find my way into a profession that I and countless others have dreamed about being a part of. It is very easy to get sucked in to the romance of college sports, and even easier once you get on the inside. It is one thing being a fan of your school, but it is another when you have an investment in working with coaches, staff, athletes and fans of an institution on a daily basis, even if you did not graduate from there.

You truly become part of the family, and part of the machine. You want to believe that what you are doing is part of the greater good, and a vital part of the mission of higher education. In spite of all the high-profile hoopla surrounding college sports, I and many others who work or have worked in the business always believed we were doing the right thing. By doing the right thing, I mean that I believed intercollegiate athletics, at the Division I level or any other, were at their core about education and giving people an opportunity at a college degree. I drank that Kool-Aid willingly, and looked upon anyone who thought the system was flawed as being off their rocker or misinformed. I mean, how could college sports be wrong when so much of what they provided - including a ton of money and exposure for the institution - was right?

What changed my thinking is spelled out pretty clearly in the preceding pages. In the end, I was wronged by the business of college athletics, and the injustice was enough to remove my blinders and I certainly look at it through a much different lens than I used to. Still, while some might think this is a case of a disgruntled person being upset at being kicked out of the club and lashing out as a result, it is much more than that. I do not deny that my feelings were hurt, and I was devastated that a career I dreamed about and worked so hard to attain was snuffed out through very little fault of my own. But the way I was ground up in the machinery of college athletics could have happened to anyone that was in the same position. And that person would have been left to blame the machine as well, because it's one that isn't working properly.

By the day of the COI hearing, I already knew that the NCAA was not what it advertised, and was not an organization committed to education, integrity and doing the right thing within the concept of fair play. It was about presenting a facade that those things were at the core of its mission, and that it cared about preserving them. But if the NCAA can participate in the process of allowing an institution to throw a person like me aside, for the purpose of protecting a corrupt football coach, rich booster, and backstabbing athletic department just so it can continue playing games to entertain the public under the false pretense of education, then something is tragically wrong. While the manner in which I came to this realization was personally sad for me, I found that many people have come to the same largely correct conclusions.

I never really set out to become a reformer (I prefer this term as opposed to critic because rather than just criticize, I try to offer solutions with my rhetoric), and even when confronted with the opportunity to play that role, I was unsure if that was a direction I wanted to go. I had the more pressing responsibility of the lawsuit and navigating the strange legal terrain that it demanded, and was really was not in a position to speak out on the ills of college sports when I was dealing with my own problems.

When I first met with the Drake Group in Chicago in April of 2003, my goals were largely self-serving. My initial purpose was to go to the meeting and drum up support for my lawsuit in the form of a "group edict" against the NCAA and its unfairness in its enforcement and infractions process. While the group understood and sympathized with my plight, it was not a mission of TDG to go after the NCAA and its policies per se. As a faculty group, the mission of TDG was to insure academic integrity on individual campuses, something that faculty can actually control.

Although I would have loved to leave Chicago with an official statement of disgust by TDG in my hands, all was not lost. We did have a reporter from GQ Magazine at the meeting who was interested in reporting on my case, and I also met new friends and others who would become my support system and confidantes for years to come.

It was truly remarkable to meet people like Allen Sack, a professor at the University of New Haven, author of several books, and former All-American football player at Notre Dame; Bill Dowling, a professor at Rutgers who was the faculty voice behind the noted "Rutgers 1000" movement to restrain commercialized expansion of college sports there, and of course Linda Bensel-Meyers, a faculty member who had her own legitimate issues with the NCAA and the way she was treated by the University of Tennessee. There were many others, like Ellen Staurowsky, Bruce Svare, Jon Ericson, John Gerdy and Murray Sperber who I would meet at subsequent meetings, and who were all supportive and have become dear friends. It was these people who encouraged me to become a faculty member, and to use my experience in college sports as a base of knowledge in teaching and research.

In addition to encouraging me in a new career, these people helped give me a new life, as an active participant in correcting a system that desperately needs it. One message became abundantly clear during my initial introduction to The Drake Group. While there are many things wrong with college sports, too many to mention, and it might seem more logical to focus on sexy issues like commercialism, coaching salaries, conference realignment, institutional subsidies for athletics, etc., those stories miss one key element. The point lost in many intercollegiate athletic reform conversations is the most important one…education.

The Drake Group convinced me that it is better for a group to focus on one thing that can be changed without relying on movement from the slow-moving glacier that is the NCAA, or even the institution. The first step in reform has to be at the core of what higher education is all about. While it took me a while to buy into this, I am now even more convinced that the other issues in college athletics will never be fixed until we reformat the relationship between higher education and college sport. We cannot let the allure of college sports swallow up the institution and destroy the bedrock mission of higher education.

Once I was fully indoctrinated into the TDG and its mission, it was time to speak publicly and begin to educate people on the realities of intercollegiate athletics and most importantly, what can be done to reform the industry before it kills itself. Although I also launched a separate and very important crusade against the unfairness and inequities of the NCAA enforcement and infractions system, along with highlighting other issues in college sports, one of my main thrusts of reform has been on the academic side with The Drake Group. Once I became a tenure-track faculty member at Mississippi State, my opinion became valued and sought-after by the mainstream press, giving me a very stable forum to discuss all the different arms of the debate.

I have encountered resistance, of course, from those who don't wish to believe. I realize it is hard for people to hear negative things about their institutions or the sports and teams they love, but facts are stubborn things. I see college sports differently than I did back in 1975 - when I would have thought the 2010 version of myself was crazy - and it is a view that others need to explore to reform this enterprise.

On the NCAA enforcement process, I have spoken to media and in front of a congressional subcommittee regarding the NCAA enforcement and infractions process, and have made several suggestions that can make the process better and more fair. If we continually strive for fairness on the field of play, we should strive for the same off the field of play. I am not for abolishing the process of NCAA jurisprudence, and there is no doubt that it is better than it was 20 years ago, but reform is still needed and there is a long way to go.[83] Over the years, other reformers have made many common-sense suggestions that the NCAA membership refuses to adopt. I have put together eight suggestions that can reform this process so it can operate in the manner it was intended.

The suggestions I make are in line with the 1991 Lee Commission, and are echoed by noted sports law professor and dean of the Indiana University School of Law, Gary Roberts. My suggestions include:[84]

1. Create an independent, fully-trained and compensated, and engaged NCAA Committee On Infractions, as well as an Appeals Committee of athletic, faculty, and public officials with an independent administrative staff. No one currently at a member institution should ever serve on either committee, and conflicts of interest must be monitored closely and eliminated. As Roberts's states, the current method using volunteers that come solely from the NCAA system is inappropriate. His idea of professional jurists is an excellent one, and should be immediately enacted. This is also one of the most important recommendations from the Lee Report.

2. Create an independent oversight/ethics board to review processes and assess grievances, specifically to govern oversight and training of the Enforcement and Student-Athlete Reinstatement staff. This board could respond to the frequent complaints of inappropriate behavior, vendettas, and questionable investigative tactics by NCAA investigators and the COI. As I stated at the hearing in Washington, DC, I strongly disagree with Potuto's contention that the investigative staff and COI are "separate and independent" from one another. The investigators have a cozy relationship with the COI, and work directly with the Administrator of the COI, who works in the same national office. It is ludicrous to think that the committee would question the tactics of investigators that they interact with all of the time, and they certainly did not question them in the Marshall case.

3. Ban the use of secret witnesses. Everyone must have a right to face their accuser and talk to all witnesses.

4. Explore ways to give the NCAA enforcement staff subpoena power, to hold subjects and witnesses in the investigation accountable for what they say under oath. In the current process there is no real penalty for lying, especially when an institution wants to protect an individual. It will also hold the NCAA accountable for their actions. This is a matter of public policy and can be done through Congress.

5. Adopt procedural and evidentiary rules that are constitutional, to include the disclosing of all information, witness statements, and other evidence in the true spirit of cooperation. The cooperative simply does not exist now. It is cooperate and acquiesce…or else. As I learned, if you challenge anything or put up a vigorous defense, an individual or institution is in danger of being sanctioned for not cooperating. Hardly in line with U.S. Constitutional values.

6. Make all hearings open to the public and media, to include public disclosure of hearing transcripts. If the NCAA feels what they are doing is right, and that their system isn't an ultra-secretive, cloak-and-dagger process, then why not add a little "sunshine" that can verify that contention? Transparency is the ultimate disinfectant. Potuto's contention that public hearings would damage the process and hurt individuals is simply a smokescreen to protect the "on-the-cheap, get-it-done" unfair process that exists now. In simple terms the secrecy of the process is its biggest flaw because while the NCAA feels confidentiality is necessary for effective and unbiased enforcement, it is also inevitable that the prerogative of secrecy will be used to hide the misdeeds of those determined to protect their own interests or who are deemed to be too important and valuable to the money making machine.

7. Have the intestinal fortitude to sanction those who deserve to be sanctioned. Eliminate the commonly-accepted practice of institutional scapegoating, in which politically expendable individuals are offered up to give the appearance that something has been done to correct the problem. Subpoena power can release the enforcement staff from relying so much on the institution for information, which is often sanitized and manipulated to protect the powerful before it reaches their desk.

8. If an individual is made a corrective action by an institution regarding NCAA violations by the institution involved, new procedures should be

enacted allowing that individual the right to appeal IF the NCAA accepts the sanction as the institution's own.[85] There can no longer be a convenient place for the COI or institution to place a scapegoat, where the NCAA can deny culpability in a sanction even though it has accepted, or in my case essentially recommended it.

If college sports is going to have a judicial system, it simply needs to be run better, and it can be. If the NCAA fails to adopt measures like this, there is really no need for a process at all, just let the institutions govern themselves as they did before the enforcement process was birthed in the 1950's. As it stands now, they're being allowed to govern themselves to a considerable extent anyway. In reality, there is not much difference in what was going on in college sports in the first part of the 20th century as opposed to now. The 1929 Carnegie Report detailed improper recruiting of academically unqualified students, academic improprieties in enrollment of athletes, athletes not attending class or being given certain grades, boosters funneling money to players and coaches, and even a veiled reference to fears of commercialism. Eighty years on, and NCAA athletics still face all of these same issues. The more things change, they more they stay the same.[86]

Apart from the NCAA, the academic relationship with intercollegiate athletics must be strengthened, a mission that The Drake Group has undertaken. To its credit, the NCAA has made some in-roads in this area. The initial eligibility standards enacted in the 1980's did have a positive impact on the academic profiles of incoming athletes. It became rare to see a college athlete who could not read or write, thankfully, although that was a situation that happened at Marshall during my tenure.

What cannot be called a success is a program that the NCAA introduced with great fanfare. Under the leadership of its since-deceased president Dr. Myles Brand, the body enacted the Academic Progress Rate (APR), which is little more than a public relations ploy by the NCAA to lull the public into thinking that athletes are truly being educated, should they meet a certain standard.

The APR is calculated by allocating points for eligibility and retention — the two factors that research identifies as the best indicators of graduation. Each player on a given roster earns a maximum of two points per term, one for being academically eligible and one for staying with the institution. A team's APR amounts to the total points on a team's roster at a given time, divided by the total points possible. Since this results in a decimal number, the Committee on Academic Progress (CAP) decided to multiply it by 1,000 for ease of reference.

Thus, a raw APR score of .925 translates into 925, which is the standard that the NCAA requires. A number below 925 can result in the loss of scholarships or a ban from postseason play for that team. The APR is designed to measure semester-by-semester academic progress, and is separate from the Graduation Success Rate (GSR), which only aims to measure the actual percentage of student-athletes who graduate, thus omitting students who would have graduated but left school early for non-academic reasons such as a professional sports career. This number is now currently at 950, but the same problems remain.

The APR sounds like a laudable plan, but in addition to being overcomplicated, it completely misses the point while almost inspiring institutions to fail in educating their student-athletes. With the APR in place, it has become far more likely for schools to direct athletes into certain majors, with specific faculty, to ensure eligibility under the guidelines of the APR at the expense of a true college education. It's all about coming in at over that number, as opposed to ensuring athletes will regularly attend class, have time to study, or pursue a course of study that interests them. The APR just offers more incentive for schools to emphasize the latter part of the term "student-athlete." In this day and age of commercialized college sports, the first part of the term has in many cases become a forgotten entity. [87]

The Drake Group has put together an effective plan to bring back academic primacy to intercollegiate athletics. This plan will have no effect on the competitive nature of college sports, but once it is enacted we can all take solace in the fact that we are watching actual college students playing college sports. Focusing on this aspect can also create a better environment to solve the other myriad problems in college athletics mentioned ad nauseam every day in the newspapers around the world.

I believe in this plan as the first, best step to return college sports back to what they were designed to be, an extracurricular activity for college students and as an impetus to get an education. TDG's plan - which has been vetted by renowned scholars, former athletes, coaches, and administrators - is one that will work and actually start changing the game for the better in all phases, not just academic integrity. The beauty of a plan like this is that it can be enacted at the institutional and/or conference level. It does not require NCAA approval, and puts academic issues back under the purview of the faculty, as they should be.

The Drake Group plan is proposed in three phases of academic transparency, academic priority, and academic-based participation. The plan, which is posted at www.thedrakegroup.org is as follows:[88]

The Drake Group (TDG) urges Faculty Senates and other bodies concerned with academic the ever-widening gap between athletics and education. Our approach is in three phases. TDG firmly believes that enacting the proposals listed below will dramatically improve the academic integrity of college campuses and return control of the classroom back to the faculty.

Phase I: Academic Transparency. Ensure that universities provide accountability of trustees, administrators and faculty by public transparency of such things as a student's academic major, academic advisor, courses listed by academic major, general education requirements, electives, course grade point average (GPA) and instructor - without revealing the names of individual students. In addition, TDG requests that average SAT and ACT scores for revenue producing sports teams be reported along with those of athletes in non-revenue sports, and scholarship students in the symphony orchestra, band, and other extra-curricular activities. Similar comparisons should be made regarding independent studies taken, grade changes by professors, and classes missed because of extracurricular demands.

Rationale: The goal of TDG with regard to academic transparency is to seek to ensure that all college athletes are afforded the full and equal opportunity to earn an education. Athletes devote long hours to their sport - up to 44 hours a week in a sport like football - and are often admitted to college by criteria lower than the average for the student body as evidenced by empirical studies done by the Knight Commission and even the NCAA. The Drake Group simply wants to ensure that athletes are afforded the opportunity to earn a college education as promised to them when they accept an academic scholarship and/or agree to participate on a team. Academic transparency is the first step toward creating an atmosphere on college campuses that encourages personal and intellectual growth for all students, and demands excellence and professional integrity from all faculty charged with teaching. We call on colleges and universities to disclose the courses, including the name of the instructor and course GPA of members of student groups such as athletic teams, and other cohort groups, sufficient in number to protect the privacy of individual students and that which is allowable under FERPA since individuals will not be identified. The format will list the courses by grade received. Public disclosure ensures accountability by Governing Boards, Presidents, Academic Administrators and faculty for the academic integrity of the institution. Transparency, then, is directed at institutional, not student behavior, and provides for a necessary condition to address allegations of academic impropriety in college athletics.

Phase II: Academic Priority. Require students to maintain a cumulative GPA of 2.0 each semester to continue participation in intercollegiate athletics.

Rationale: Students whose cumulative grade point average falls below 2.0 in any given semester need to give immediate attention to academic performance. Some will argue that this is an unfair standard because the standard for student academic eligibility on some campuses may be less than a cumulative 2.0 GPA in a specified semester. Given the often low graduation rates for athletes, most notably in the revenue-producing sports, and the acknowledged stressors on the lives of athletes, this measure would provide a safety net for those athletes who are most academically at risk.

Make the location and control of academic counseling and support services for athletes the same as for all students.

Rationale: The NCAA's stated basic purpose is to maintain intercollegiate athletics as an integral part of the educational program and the athlete as an integral part of the student body. This proposal further reinforces the notion that athletes are students and should be integrated into the general student body. Separate athletic counseling centers have been spawned by the separation and control of the athlete - a philosophy TDG rejects. Academic counseling should be rooted in a genuine concern for assisting athletes in the pursuit of their education, not a short-sighted goal of keeping them athletically eligible. This goal cannot be accomplished in a setting that is compromised by pressure to produce winning athletic teams. Faculty Senates can and should act to ensure equal access to education for all students.

Establish university policies that will ensure that athletic contests and practices do not conflict with scheduled classes.

Rationale: To protect the athletes' right to have equal access to educational opportunities, faculty need to enforce the policy that class attendance should take priority over athletic participation. Whenever there are scheduling conflicts between sports and course requirements, faculty members and administrative staff members, have a professional responsibility to enforce attendance policies that support quality instruction. In some instances, the problem arises because faculty, rather than athletic personnel, does not demand that students attend class. Faculty Senates can, and should, require faculty to establish attendance policies that treat all students equally.

Phase III: Academic-Based Participation. Replace one-year renewable scholarships with need-based financial aid (or) with multi-year athletic scholarships that extend to graduation (five year maximum).

Rationale: As long as coaches and athletics directors use factors related to athletics to determine whether financial aid will be renewed, athletes are under considerable pressure to make sports their main priority during enrollment. This highlights the inherent hypocrisy in the term "athletic scholarship," a term that should relate to educational opportunities. To ensure that education remains the priority, renewal of athletic scholarships should be unrelated to athletic performance or athletic scholarships themselves replaced with educational grants awarded on the basis of financial need. In either case, universities should be committed to athletes as students whose value to the university exceeds their role in athletics. The Big Ten Conference, Knight Foundation, and several coaches including Dean Smith, Terry Holland, Bill Curry, and John Wooden have listed the creation of multi-year scholarships among possible reform measures they could support.

Require one year in residency before an athlete can participate in intercollegiate sport. This rule would apply to transfer students as well as to first year students.

Rationale: Keeping first year students and transfer students out of varsity competition until they have completed one year of residency would assist them in transitioning into college life without added pressure and time commitment inherent in athletic participation. A one-year residency rule would also discourage coaches from recruiting high school and junior college players as a quick fix to turn around a losing program. Many coaches, including Dean Smith, Terry Holland, Bill Curry, and the late John Wooden have listed a return to a one-year residency requirement among possible reform measures they could support.

Part of the strategy of TDG is to lobby the US Government to get involved to analyze whether Division I sports are still educational and non-profit in nature. It's tough to maintain that they are when the primary focus is winning and revenue-generation, and coaches and administrators are making millions of dollars a year.

The recent athletic conference game of musical chairs, designed primarily to garner more television and sponsorship money, might just be the catalyst to get the government involved due to potential antitrust issues and the ever-widening gulf between academia and athletics. College sports enjoy a non-profit tax exemption that also needs to be reviewed, as a way to wrestle control back from well-heeled boosters. Currently, boosters get an 80% tax deduction for athletic donations, as they are couched as educational donations. This means boosters like Phil Knight at Oregon and T. Boone Pickens at Oklahoma State have a very convenient tax shelter and a pulpit that carries with it too much control over athletic issues, such as hiring and firing of coaches and athletic directors.[89] Marshall Reynolds is not at the level of these two gentlemen, but his control over Marshall athletics was similar, and oftentimes just as powerful. Curbing the ability of boosters to shelter their money, which in turns gives many of them the feeling that they run the department, will go a long way to curbing the excesses of college sports.

Typically, the NCAA has not reacted to change unless the government gets involved, such as when they made the initial changes to enforcement and infractions in 1991. Government intervention makes the NCAA and its institutions jump, and we are at a point where government intervention must happen. Just like with Major League Baseball, which was threatened with a loss of its limited anti-trust exemption by Congress in order to force action from the league in the wake of its steroid scandal, Congress can dangle the tax exemption as a carrot to force changes in enforcement and academic integrity.

It would be very easy to tell the NCAA to adopt academic transparency (similar to the congressional demand for public graduation rate information, ironically fought vigorously by the NCAA in the early 90's)[90] or face a loss of its tax exemption. I also believe that stemming the flow of dollars via the removal of the tax exemption would force institutions to be better managers of resources, and to cease and desist on the never ending arms race currently in play in college sports. Any of the other Drake proposals could be enacted in the same way. Politically, it may not seem the best use of government's time, money, or energy to worry itself about the business of college sports, but that might not deter Washington. Many congressional leaders are already stung by conference realignment and how it has affected schools in their states, and many want to review the purpose of college sports within higher education in more depth.

Are these suggestions for reform in academics and NCAA justice the panacea? Far from it, but they will go a long way to ensuring that college athletics entail college students playing amateur sports. These proposals will change the game, and the paradigm, for the better. What is unacceptable is doing nothing, as the current financial model is unsustainable and continuing to spend money at a greater rate affects everything else, including academics.

If we do nothing, then we might as well just get rid of the façade, and admit that we have college teams made up of some athletes who go to school because they want to, and others that just play. Why not just formalize an already-existing system of academic fraud and greed? I still believe, maybe still naively, that college sports can fit within higher education, but the paradigm must change. Those that cannot play by the rules must be punished and punished severely, but more than anything college athletes must have the ability to be actual, matriculating students who can take the major of their choice. We need to become as concerned about the next 50 years of someone's life as we are about their 4-5 years as a college-athlete. It is the athlete, the primary stakeholder that has influenced my change in attitude. I am not lobbying for pay-for-play or anything like that, but I am lobbying for a better chance at an education and using that focus to create a system that is better in all phases such as enforcement, commercialism, and integrity. This type of change can prevent situations like the one I encountered at Marshall University from happening again.

While my passion for intercollegiate athletics has naturally waned somewhat and I look at it through a much clearer window, I do still love it. There are many days that I think about my days working in the business with some semblance of fondness. At this point I don't think I could ever resume my pursuit of a chance to become an athletic director considering the state of the industry, but the passion is still there, even if the window I look at the business through has changed. Sadly there are many people in college sports, many good people, who have the same passion but have found themselves co-opted by the lure of money and greed. Many do it intentionally and cross over to "dark side" if you will, others are simply naive enough to believe that the good outweighs the bad.

Most ardent supporters of college athletics will often point to the benefits of intercollegiate athletics to an institution such as increased marketing, enrollment enhancement, fundraising, and money for academics. While there are many good things about college sports and there are some intangible benefits to an institution that sponsors athletics, the majority of credible research is clear - there is little-to-no sustained benefit to these ancillary areas, and if there are benefits they are usually short-lived or do not return sufficiently on investment due to increased spending in college sports. The money made is just more grist for the mill.[91]

In other words, the many positives advertised by the still-deluded have an opposite effect much of the time. For schools like Ohio University and other teams in the Mid-American Conference, it is a losing battle trying to keep up with schools that have a broader infrastructure and can turn a profit sponsoring intercollegiate athletics. Institutions in Ohio U. or Marshall's category, often called mid-majors, are where the problems will come to a head. These institutions are subsidizing athletics largely with student fees and other institutional subsidies, and eventually the bubble will burst, likely sooner rather than later. It is simple economics, and there will be a market correction in college sports just like there was in the housing and financial markets.

Unless we do something to right the ship before it gets to that point, and put our greed in check, college athletics will morph into something unrecognizable. Perhaps the scorched earth-option is best, so we can start from scratch and do things the right way. That's probably a pipe dream, but I do know that if we do not enact changes soon to reform the enterprise, it will hang itself. That will be a sad day for all, though hardly unexpected to some of us.

An August 2010 article in ESPN the Magazine entitled, "Internal Affairs" by Seth Wickersham portrayed me as an "icon in the industry" who usually gets a call from those in similar situations because I "fought the system and won."[92] I certainly was a bit uncomfortable with those kind words and status and I really did not win anything. However, knowing that I can potentially inspire others in the industry to fight back and potentially serve as a cautionary example to other schools looking to scapegoat the lowest common denominator, it makes me realize that I did the right thing. I did not file suit to punish any one or to antagonize anyone, I did because it was simply the right thing to do and Marshall University left me no other alternative in spite of my best efforts.

One thing I tell those who call me for help, whether people in compliance who do not want their names revealed, or coaches like Jackie Sherrill, Ronnie Cottrell, and Ivy Williams, is that it is not easy and time is your enemy. However, if you feel you were wronged by the system—you must stand up for yourself. Sadly, this has become the only way for those with integrity and who desire for college sports to be what they are intended to be and to salvage their dignity and reputation. There seems to be one constant in lawsuits—it really never should have gotten to the point it got to, and that was certainly the scenario in my case.

Endnotes

1. Information on previous Marshall University NCAA Infractions cases can be found at https://web1.ncaa.org/LSDBi/exec/miSearch

2. The lengthy NCAA investigation, Infractions case M179, is discussed in several forums that are publically accessible to include the full NCAA Public Infractions Report at https://web1.ncaa.org/LSDBi/exec/miSearch.

3. According to www.sportsad.ohio.edu Ohio University boasts the first accredited sports administration program in the world. Still recognized as the leader in sports administration education, the program was started in 1966. The genesis of the Ohio University Sports Administration Program and O'Malley's influence can be traced back to New York. In the 1950s, O'Malley and Dr. Clifford Brownell, a professor at Columbia University, conversed on several occasions about the business of baseball. Always the pragmatic businessman, O'Malley lamented the lack of properly trained administrators for the Brooklyn Dodgers, the organization of which O'Malley had been majority owner and general partner since 1950. More specifically, the Dodgers were lacking in well-trained individuals for the team's business-related areas. Wouldn't it be something, O'Malley reflected, if a university could train students, in areas such as contract negotiation, facilities management, and marketing, which could contribute to more efficient and effective sports organizations like the Dodgers? Remembering these conversations, Brownell later recounted them to a young James Mason, a doctoral student whom Brownell was advising at Columbia. After receiving his doctorate, Dr. Mason took O'Malley's revolutionary idea and brought it to life, founding the world's first sports administration program at Ohio University in 1966. Almost

90% of the programs graduates work in key positions in all facets of the sports industry around the world. Famous alumni include Andy Dolich, most recently the CBO of the San Francisco 49ers, Jeremy Foley, AD at the University of Florida, Mitch Barnhart the AD at the University of Kentucky, Chad Estis, Senior VP for Sales and Marketing for the Dallas Cowboys, and Mike Hamrick, ironically the current athletic director at Marshall University.

4. Houska had a stellar record as head coach at Ohio University. Houska arrived at Ohio University in the fall of 1960 as a state champion from Parma High School outside of Cleveland. He immediately became the toughest man on the Bobcat wrestling team and won the conference title at 167 pounds in his first year of eligibility. The following season, Houska moved up to 177 pounds, won another Mid-American Conference title and after not giving up a single point in 23 straight matches, lost in the 1963 NCAA finals. As a senior in 1964, he won the MAC heavyweight title and then dropped down to 191 and won the NCAA title, capping his collegiate career with a 76-3 record. After graduating from Ohio University with a physical education degree, Houska was an alternate on the 1964 U.S. Olympic team and two years later won a gold medal at the Pan-American Games and finished fourth at the World Wrestling Championships in New Delhi, India. At the age of 25, he took over the Bobcat coaching helm from his mentor Fred Schleicher, to become just the third head coach in Ohio Wrestling history. He ended up coaching the Bobcats to 11 MAC titles, including seven straight from 1970 to 1976. Under Houska's guidance, the Bobcats produced 69 individual MAC-title winners, 11 MAC Wrestlers of the Year, 17 All-Americans and two national champions. Houska was named MAC Coach of the Year five times and was inducted into the Ohio University Athletics Hall of Fame in 1972, the Ohio Wrestling Hall of Fame in 1986, and the National Wrestling Hall of Fame in the Fall of 2010. http://www.ohiobobcats.com/sports/m-wrestl/recaps/021206aac.html.

5. Arslanian had a long time relationship with Weber State University as a player, assistant coach and later, head football coach from 1989-1997.

6. Belnap was and is a big name in Utah sports history. Most noteworthy was his tenure as head men's basketball coach at Utah State University in Logan, Utah from 1973-1979. His six season record was 106-58, still one of the better records in USU basketball history. During his tenure Belnap had Jim Harrick, former head men's coach at UCLA, Pepperdine, Rhode Island, and Georgia, and former Louisiana State University coach Dale Brown on his staff. Belnap worked in the banking industry for many years

before getting back into college sports as the Athletic Director at Weber State University from 1995-1997. Belnap was replaced by John Johnson in late 1997. Johnson remained in the position until 2004. Johnson is now the Senior Associate AD at Washington State University and has been in his current position since 2004. Belnap also briefly served as Interim AD at Weber State after Johnson left for WSU. (http://findarticles. com/p/articles/mi_qn4188/is_20040710/ai_n11474084/; http://www. wsucougars.com/genrel/johnson_john00.html).

7.   The scandal du jour at several schools during the late nineties concerned men's basketball players taking correspondence courses for credit from a university by the name of The Southeastern College of the Assemblies of God in Lakeland, Florida. This school was discovered to have offered the right correspondence courses that could enhance eligibility with very few checks and balances. SCAG inadvertently became a choice of many schools to use because of this. Coaches at several institutions took correspondence courses on behalf of athletes through SCAG, prompting an NCAA investigation of at least 40 athletic departments. Among those hit with sanctions were: Auburn, Baylor, Georgia Southern, New Mexico State, Texas Tech, Cal-Fullerton and Texas-El Paso. The summary of the violations for WSU can be found at https://web1.ncaa. org/LSDBi/exec/miSearch Specifically, Weber State was found by the NCAA to have had coaching staff members assisting on player with his enrollment in, and helped pay for, correspondence courses at SCAG. There were also findings of the coaching staff permitting two athletics representatives to have recruiting contacts with a prospective student-athlete. Head coach Ron Abegglen assisted a prospective student-athlete with tuition costs for correspondence courses and arranged a tutor at no cost; assistant coaches, most notably Mark Coffman, arranged for a proctor and assisted with obtaining and returning course materials at SCAG including Coffman mailing papers for a correspondence course on behalf of a student-athlete;. Other violations included Abegglen allowing prospective student-athlete to stay in his home for one or two days, arranging for two prospective student-athletes to have recruiting contact with an athletics representative, providing host money to prospective student-athlete, which was used to post bail for student-athlete, and employment of prospective student-athlete in summer camp. The final findings included improper academic eligibility certification improper certification of and awarding of financial aid to ineligible student-athletes, unethical conduct, and lack of institutional control.

8. Mason initially accepted the Georgia job in 1996 and had an initial press conference in Athens, GA announcing his hire. At the time part of Mason's divorce agreement was that he could not take his kids out of Kansas for visitations. He decided to return to Kansas where he coached until becoming the head coach at the University of Minnesota in 1997. He was fired by Minnesota after the 2006 season.

9. Grobe is now the head coach at Wake Forest University. He was hired in 2001 He has been extremely successful at Wake Forest guiding the Demon Deacons to an overall record of 62-60 and four bowl games to include the 2006 ACC title.

10. Much of the information from this chapter was gleaned from Lou Sahadi's book on Jim Donnan and the Marshall Thundering Herd entitled, "*Winning my Way: The Glory Years of Marshall Football*" published in 1994 by Tiger Press and Bob Pruett's own book "*Purpose and Passion: Bobby Pruett and the Marshall Years*" by Pruett and Bill Chastain published by Grace Associates in 2005. Also important to the information provided in this chapter was a Power Point presentation prepared by Lisle G Brown, Curator of Special Collections and Nat DeBruin, University Archivist at Marshall University for The Annual Meeting of the Society of American Archivists August 13-16, 2009 in Austin, Texas. Other articles used include "*Marshall's success forcing others to adapt.*" August 27, 2000 by John Harris of the Toledo Blade. Other sources included the Warner Brothers movie, "*We are Marshall,*" (2006) and the excellent documentary "*Ashes to Glory,*" (2000) developed by John Witek and Deborah Novak. http://www.huntingtonquarterly.com/articles/issue37/ashestoglory.html

11. Information on all three NCAA major infractions cases regarding Marshall University can be found at https://web1.ncaa.org/LSDBi/exec/miSearch.

12. Gilley was president of Marshall University for eight years from 1991-1999 He was replaced by Dan Angel officially at the end of 1999 after local Huntington lawyer A. Michael Perry served as interim president. Gilley was once the nation's youngest college president, at the age of 29 at Bluefield State University (WV). He became president at University of Tennessee in 1999 and presiding over the beginning of the academic fraud scandal there that was uncovered by Linda Bensel- Meyers. He left Tennessee in 2001 in his own scandal after it was revealed that he has an inappropriate relationship with a female subordinate. Over 400 emails some explicit were revealed to the Knoxville press between Gilley and Pamela Reed. Reed was later dismissed by UT amid allegations she

embellished her resume. Knoxville's Most Wanted: Tracking down Some of the City's Most Controversial Newsmakers of the Last 50 Years. Metro Pulse [Knoxville TN] November 16, 2006. http://www.metropulse.com/articles/2006/16_46/cover_story.shtml.

13. Sahadi & Donnan, 1994

14. http://sports.jrank.org/pages/3352/Moss-Randy-Chronology.html and Kirkpatrick, Curry. "Does this guy look like trouble?" *Sport* (October 1997): 58.

15. Information on the 1990 infractions case involving Marshall University men's basketball and former head coach Rick Huckabay can be found at https://web1.ncaa.org/LSDBi/exec/miSearch and the 1994 Maynard v. Charleston Gazette WV Supreme Court case which can be accessed at http://www.state.wv.us/wvsca/docs/spring94/21815.htm.

16. The MAC is one of the few conferences, the PAC 12 being another, which has its own infractions process where the conference can hand out penalties and sanctions for running afoul of NCAA and conference rules. If the conference determines the violation is secondary, any sanction or decision regarding the infraction must still be approved by the NCAA. If the conference determines a violation is major, it is passed on to the NCAA for adjudication. In some cases the NCAA may review conference secondary violations and review them further if they think they may indeed be potentially major infractions. http://www.pac-10.org/genrel/061107aaa.html

17. Fournier is currently the athletic director at Wayne State University (Michigan). He was appointed to that position in 2000. http://wsuathletics.com/roster.aspx?rp_id=1154.

18. Vingle, Mitch, July 13, 1999, Charleston (WV) Gazette. "*NCAA Rep Questions Herd Visit*"

19. Ricard was the football and men's basketball team doctor from 1981-2008. He was a former Cuban Olympic team physician and actually defected to America on a sports trip to Mexico. Woodrum, Joel (2008, July 5). Herd Family loses Dr. Ricard, Donte Newsome. *Herd Insider*. Retrieved on June 28, 2010 from http://marshall.scout.com/2/767141.html.

20. Academic clustering and the problems with it have been recently publicized by two very prominent scandals at Auburn University and the University of Michigan. In each case it was determined that a friendly professor was providing an massive amount of independent study courses to athletes

which aided in eligibility maintenance. Specifically in the 2007Auburn case, Professor Jim Gundlach alleged that Psychology Department chair Tom Petee had been supervising over 100 independent study courses predominately for Auburn athletes to maintain eligibility. See *Top Grades and No Class Time for Auburn Players* by New York Times investigative reporter Pete Thamel at http://www.nytimes.com/2006/07/14/sports/ncaafootball/14auburn.html. At Michigan a very similar ruse was uncovered in 2008 four-part series by the Ann Arbor News and detailed in the following articles under ACADEMICS AND ATHLETICS: A Four-Day Ann Arbor News Series on the University of Michigan at http://www.mlive.com/wolverines/academics/ authored by several reporters. The Michigan situation consisted of John Hagen, a professor of psychology at the University, supervising over 100 independent studies primarily for UM football players along with allegations that many UM athletes, predominantly in the sports of football and men's basketball, were steered into a General Studies degree program to maintain eligibility.

21. After several years as Associate head coach at Florida State University Berndt is now head softball coach at Monmouth University.

22. Gilley's articles and writings on intercollegiate athletics include, Gilley & Hickey (1987) *Administration of University Athletic Programs*. New Directions for Institutional Research. Volume 1987, Issue 56, pages 37–47, Winter 1987 *and Gilley, J. W.; Fulmer, K A.; and Reithlingshoefer, S. J. (1986). Searching for Academic Excellence. New York: Macmillan.*

23. Gilley's famous downfall at the University of Tennessee covering his stormy less than two-year tenure at Tennessee is chronicled in many articles which include allegations he had an affair with Pamela Reed, whom he'd installed as executive director of a new interdisciplinary research center at UT. http://www.bishop-accountability.org/news2006/11_12/2006_11_16_MetroPulse_KnoxvillesMost.htm

24. Frost, now Melissa Frost-Fisher is the current head women's softball coach at the University of Indianapolis and weathered the storm and threat to her career pretty well. She was named head coach in 2004 after compiling a 70-54 mark as the head coach at NCAA Division II Wheeling Jesuit College. http://athletics.uindy.edu/coaches.aspx?rc=119

25. Gale has been the lone holdover from the Donnan years. He has remained at Marshall since 1990 in various capacities on the football staff under three previous head coaches (Donnan, Pruett, and Snyder). He is currently the Director of Football Operations for current head coach

John "Doc" Holliday. http://herdzone.cstv.com/sports/m-footbl/mtt/gale_mark01.html.

26. Bond, Shoeneck & King is recognized as the gold standard of law firms in dealing with NCAA matters and defending institutions and individuals accused of NCAA violations. The firm, led by former NCAA investigators Mike Glazier and Stephen Morgan, has been involved in over 100 NCAA investigations in the past 16 years to include some of the most prominent and public cases over those years. http://www.bsk.com/groups/service.cfm?type=Collegiate%20Sports%20#404

27. Dell Robinson is now the Commissioner of the NCAA Division II Conference, the Great Lakes Intercollegiate Athletic Conference. He was named to the position in March 2009. The league currently boasts 12 full members, nine of which are located in Michigan, and three in Ohio. The league's Ohio institutions include Ashland University, the University of Findlay, and Tiffin University, which is in its first year of membership. The GLIAC's members in Michigan include: Ferris State University, Grand Valley State University, Hillsdale College, Lake Superior State University, Michigan Technological University, Northern Michigan University, Northwood University, Saginaw Valley State University, and Wayne State University. http://www.gliac.org/general_news/2008-09/GLIAC_Commissioner_Announcement_09.

28. The information of Randy Moss was primarily gleaned from http://sports.jrank.org/pages/3352/Moss-Randy-Chronology.html and Kirkpatrick, Curry. "Does this guy look like trouble?" *Sport* (October 1997): 58.

29. According to the *2001 NCAA Manual Bylaw 15, Financial Aid*, these were the limits that NCAA Employment Legislation allowed athletes to earn. Concessions were made for those in different categories such as those who were on scholarship or not. These were the rules in 1999 after sweeping changes to the rule in 1998. Employment legislation has been deregulated since 2002 and the earnings caps do not exist anymore, but rate of pay and other restrictions still exist. The new rule states: *Earnings from a student-athlete's on- or off-campus employment that occurs at any time is exempt and is not counted in determining a student-athlete's cost of attendance or in the institution's financial aid limitations, provided The student-athlete's compensation does not include any remuneration for value or utility that the student athlete may have for the employer because of the publicity, reputation, fame or personal following that he or she has obtained because of athletics ability; The student-athlete is compensated only for work actually performed; and the student-athlete is compensated at a rate commensurate with the going*

rate in that locality for similar services. Essentially, this means that a large portion of the infractions found against Marshall in 2001would not be considered violations today.

30. An NCAA investigator does not have to discuss details of an allegation prior to making a campus visit, but there is no rule that specifically forbids it. According to *NCAA Bylaw 32.3.7.1,* an NCAA investigator only has to disclose that an individual is requested to be interview to discuss their knowledge of or involvement in potential NCAA violations.

31. Osburn, Lisa, January 12, 2000, *Herd football player arrested, accused of beating Huntington detective's son.* The Huntington Herald-Dispatch. Smith was a backup player on Marshall's football team and was arrested in connection with an attack that Huntington police said was racially motivated. Police said five other Marshall players also taunted the victim, the son of a police detective, in the incident, which occurred eight days before the 2000 Motor City Bowl. Smith was indicted and received probation.

32. According to www.msuspartans.com, Smith is still Associate Athletic Director at Michigan State University and was appointed to that position in 2001. She was Crane's compliance assistant at the University of Louisville in the mid 90's prior to moving to Michigan State.

33. Pat Britz email to Ridpath and Hilliard dated February 2000.

34. Information on Reynolds was primarily gleaned from his interviews with the NCAA and a Huntington Quarterly article authored by Jack Houvarous (ironically Arica Houvarous' Uncle) in 1999. The article is entitled *"The Expanding Empire."* The subheading says, *Marshall Reynolds, the state's premier power broker, is making all the right moves and amassing a small empire along the way."* The well written article can be accessed at www.huntingtonquarterly.com/Issue33/powerbroker.html.

35. Sherrill served as the head football coach at Mississippi State University from 1991 through 2003. Sherrill sued Jones and fellow NCAA investigator Rich Johanningmeier, along with University of Mississippi booster Julie Gibert, in 2003. Sherrill maintains that Johanningmeier, lied to witnesses by telling them that their testimony would remain confidential, and that Johanningmeier, Jones and Gibert fabricated charges and then used the media to try the case in the public court. The case is still active in the Mississippi courts as he seeks $15 million in damages in his claim. I was officially retained as an expert witness for Coach Sherrill in 2011. Sherrill maintains that publication of the allegations made by Johanningmeier, Jones and Gibert were intended to

permanently damage Sherrill's personal and professional reputation and career. http://www.freewebs.com/sherrill-vs-ncaa/casechronicles.htm.

36.   Williams was a partner in the Huntington WV law firm of Huddleston Bolen, LLP at the time of the NCAA investigation. He is now a trial attorney and Office Managing Partner at Nelson Mullins Riley & Scarborough in Huntington WV.

37.   Pruett has long denied telling the players to sign false statements and partially, he is correct. He was not involved, to my knowledge, in telling the players to sign the 2001 statements, but he did direct the players to sign the statements in 2000 based on information provided to me and the testimony of Tynes and Goines. Chuck Landon, showing his colors as a Pruett apologist and a pathetic excuse for a journalist by not checking out all sources (for instance, he never once called me during the entire investigation and I would have gladly talked to him), joined in with a commentary in the summer of 2008 regarding cbs.com articles by Dennis Dodd about Pruett possibly providing false and misleading information to the NCAA during the Marshall case. In the article entitled, *"Huntington attorney has inside details of MU suit,"* in the Huntington Herald Dispatch on August 20, 2008, Landon used two individuals with questionable credibility in Marc Williams and Tom Yeager as his primary sources. Williams who is a longtime season ticket holder and benefactor to the Marshall athletic department stated in the article that Pruett was not present during the signing of the affidavits and that he was "too smart" to be involved in NCAA violations. Williams, neglected to mention the 2000 affidavits and the fact he himself was not even fully involved in the case until 2001, but he still knew about the 2000 statements and said nothing. Yeager said he remembered me being bitter and uncooperative during the hearing, which I wholeheartedly dispute. There is no doubt that I fought for my rights and I am able and even encouraged to do, but it was far from bitter and uncooperative. Statements like this are just another example of the unfairness of the process given that I had no mechanism to respond to such ridiculous statements until I went outside of the NCAA process. Yeager also bloviated that he "could not imagine" the Marshall case being reopened because of this possible new evidence. An embarrassingly absolute statement for a former chair of the Committee on Infractions to make given he was likely unaware of the new evidence and in direct contradiction of NCAA rules regarding the statute of limitations. It didn't surprise me because Yeager did not want to be exposed, along with the process, as a sham.

38. The editorial that ostensibly blamed me for the violations by stating, *"What is obvious is highly paid administrators did not do their jobs,"* was written in the Huntington Herald Dispatch on September 1, 2001and approved by its editorial board.

39. The prehearing conference is a required component of most NCAA infractions hearings that are to be heard by the Committee on Infractions. When all involved parties have responded to the alleged rules violations found by the NCAA staff, a hearing date is set with the Committee on Infractions. A prehearing conference with the school and other involved individuals is held four to six weeks before the hearing. During this conference call, the allegations are discussed before the NCAA sets forth their charges in an official case summary. It is then up to the institution as to what allegations they agree with or dispute. Those are the issues that are discussed at a COI hearing. Enforcement Process How does the process work? http://www.ncaa.org/wps/wcm/connect/public/NCAA/Key+Issues/Enforcement/The+Enforcement+Process.

40. Paul Ambrose, the son of Marshall University professor Ken Ambrose, was aboard Flight 77 when it crashed into the Pentagon on September 11, 2001.

41. Landon, Chuck (2001, September 12). Someone should pay for MU's problems. *Charleston(WV) Daily Mail.* It can be accessed at www.dailymail.com. Landon currently works as a columnist for the Huntington Herald Dispatch which is ironically owned by Marshall Reynolds.

42. Tim DiPero is a partner in the Charleston WV law firm of *DiTrapano, Barrett & DiPero.* He represented White at the Marshall NCAA hearing. Kelly, who represented Pruett, is now deceased, and was a prominent attorney in South Carolina and had defended numerous coaches in front of the NCAA. DiPero also served as Randy Moss' agent for several years until he was fired by Moss in May 2010. DiPero had a 15-plus year association with Moss and represented Moss during his early legal troubles while he was a student at DuPont High School in Rand, WV. Associated Press, June 1, 2010. *"Moss' agent says he's been let go."*

43. Chryst's tenure as the Commissioner of the MAC ended in 2009 after 10 years. He is currently in private law practice in Cleveland of Counsel in the Sports Law section of Walter & Haverfield, LLP.

44. Ambrose was the son of Marshall University professor Ken Ambrose. He was killed when Flight 77 crashed into the Pentagon on September 11, 2001.

45. Meyer was named head coach at Ohio State University in December 2011. He and Gonzalez coached together for several years after Bowling Green, including stints and Florida and Utah. Gonzalez is now the Offensive Coordinator at Illinois.

46. All NCAA Division I-A games were cancelled for two weeks following the September 11th terrorist attacks.

47. It is hard to say whether Hilliard was telling truth with his claims that "multiple members" of the NCAA enforcement staff and COI told him that it would be easier for Marshall if I was out of the picture given his own credibility problems. He stated as much during a phone call that I secretly recorded in November 2001. According to NCAA Bylaw 32.1.1 Confidentiality, the COI, and the enforcement staff, is forbidden from having ex-parte (outside discussions with those involved in the case or for that matter, not involved in the case) discussions with anyone regarding their decision making and Potuto specifically denies any impropriety regarding the disposition of the Marshall case or any case for that matter. There exists anecdotal evidence that discussions may have taken place regarding my status because of a week plus delay after the hearing before taking any adverse action against me, the personal relationship between Jones and Hilliard, the ongoing working relationship of Marsh and Hilliard simultaneously preparing the defense of the University of Alabama in its infractions case, and the September 28, 2001 letter from Yeager at least implied that there better be additional action on the part of the institution to potentially avoid a LOIC charge. It is hard to imagine that discussions did not take place concerning the status of Marshall University and as to why I was not terminated before or directly after the hearing.

48. This is one of the dirty little secrets of the NCAA enforcement and infractions process. It is often the institution that will assess the penalties against individuals spurred by direct or tacit encouragement by the NCAA. No appeal is available unless the NCAA specifically assesses the sanction, such as the famous Jerry Tarkanian case and other legal tussles (See Tarkanian v. NCAA) It is a good get out of jail free card for the NCAA and individuals usually acquiesce to institutional whims because he or she wants to keep their current job, or at least still work in the industry. In addition NCAA Bylaw 19.7 Restitution gives the NCAA additional authority to punish institutions should an accused individual prevail in the court system. This was a main reason that the University of Colorado did not support Jeremy Bloom in his civil case against the NCAA. See Bloom comments in Due Process and the NCAA: Hearing

before the Subcommittee on the Constitution on the Committee on the Judiciary House of Representatives, 108th Congress, 2nd Session, September 14, 2004, Serial No. 106. www.house.gov/judiciary.

49. The official mission statement of Judicial Affairs at Marshall University states: *"Marshall University supports the development of an intellectual community within an environment that fosters respect, integrity and individual growth among its members. The Code of Student Rights and Responsibilities - also referred to as the Code of Conduct — reflects these expectations and standards. The Code and student judicial system are founded on principles of fairness and due process, and a commitment to the educational development of students, and are designed to balance the interests of University community as a whole with the protection of students' individual liberties."* http://www.marshall.edu/judicial-affairs/

50. Angel, Dan (January 20, 2002). *"Marshall's goal in Athletics is to become as Pure as a bar of Ivory Soap."* The Herald Dispatch (Huntington, WV).

51. Fullerton is still in his position as Commissioner of the Big Sky Conference (Based in Ogden, Utah) and is in his 19th year at the helm.

52. O'Malley was a longtime assistant of Bob Marcum who brought O'Malley with him from the University of Massachusetts when he took over as athletic director at Marshall University in 2002. Marcum replaced West who was transferred to a university alumni relations job. Marcum, a Huntington native, served as AD for seven years before stepping down in early 2009. O'Malley is still at Marshall serving in the position of Associate Athletic Director/Chief of Staff under current AD Mike Hamrick. Baumgartner is currently the Senior Associate AD at the University of Georgia. http://herdzone.cstv.com/staffdir/mars-staffdir.html.

53. The public Marshall University Infractions Report can be found at https://web1.ncaa.org/LSDBi/exec/miSearch

54. While Reed was never officially interviewed by the NCAA, I was insistent that at least Hilliard and I interview him so we would have a record of his testimony. This interview, which praised my efforts in compliance, was ironically later used by Hilliard to show that there was a good employment monitoring system in place—after I was removed.

55. Moon was interviewed by Luann Humphrey via telephone in 2001 while he was the athletic director at the University of Wyoming. Moon emphatically denied having any involvement or knowledge of this employment scheme and speculated that it was people in Huntington

trying to get back at him. Whether the meeting happened or not is unknown, what is clear that one or more of the parties is lying. Moon is the current athletic director at the University of North Florida.

56.   One of the many ironic things about this whole sordid episode is Pruett did talk to me directly several times about employment issues for athletes. He stated that he did not want his athletes working during the academic year because their grades might suffer. In one specific case Pruett contacted me about offensive lineman Jimmy Cabellos who said he needed to work to support his child and young girlfriend. Cabellos was a starter and Pruett was understandably nervous about him working, playing football, going to school, and supporting his family. Through my efforts I was able to find free child care, available to all Marshall students, for Jimmy when eliminated the need for him to work. Former prop Eugene Mitchell was sent to Dave Reed to seek approval to work as a prop. He was sent to Reed's office by assistant football coach Mark Gale. Interestingly enough, Mitchell had been fired by Russell May at Chapman Printing prior to him contacting Reed about another job, because he continually showed up late. Of course I was never notified of Mitchell working there nor did I in any way approve it, but he somehow knew that he had to seek permission for outside employment.

57.   Calhoun, is the celebrated and very successful men's basketball coach at the University of Connecticut .

58.   Josh Moon of the Montgomery Advertiser wrote an excellent article on June, 15 2010 entitled *"NCAA Investigations not held to Judicial Standards"* eloquently summarizing the thoughts I have had over the years regarding the patently unfair aspects of this process and lack of transparency and accountability. This includes that even with the increased power of being able to subpoena witnesses comes increased responsibility because evidence must be built solid evidence and credible witnesses. At this point, many of the case are built on weak and circumstantial evidence. I also agree with Moon that many times investigators form early opinions, whether justified or not, and then slant the rest of the investigation to fit that narrative, rather than a proper, thorough investigation. This is exactly what happened to me in my case.

59.   In reality Marshall University has not completed the requirements of its own self imposed sanctions with regard to the disassociation of Reynolds. Reynolds sternly stated to my counsel Jon Matthews during his deposition in May 2008, that he had not nor will not "pay a red cent" to Marshall for that case. Yet Reynolds is back in good graces with the university as a fully

engaged booster with no strings attached even though he did not fulfill the requirements of the show cause sanction something to which the NCAA has taken no further action on. In a personal conversation with former Marshall Athletic Director, Bob Marcum in September 2010 in Athens, Ohio, Marcum stated he was able to get the financial penalty waived but I have not seen any official notification from the NCAA on this. In this same conversation Marcum also called Pruett a "pathological liar," and "someone who is incapable of telling the truth."

60. Bob Tscholl was an All-American wrestler under Houska during the 1973 season. He placed 5th in the 158 pound weight class.

61. Svare, B. (2004) Reforming Sports Before the Clock Runs Out. Borderlice Press

62. Although my Doctor of Education is officially from West Virginia University, my course of study was at the time a cooperative program with Marshall University with most course being delivered at the former MU/WVU Graduate College in South Charleston, WV. It does say on my degree that it was in "cooperation with Marshall University. Those in this program had the option of graduating in Morgantown on WVU's campus or in the Marshall ceremony. I chose the Marshall ceremony as many of my classmates were walking through it and we actually wore WVU Blue and Gold regalia to the ceremony and our degrees were conferred by the Dean of the College of Education at WVU, Bill Deaton. Angel endorsed the degrees and sat down behind the podium while Deaton handled the pleasantries. I made sure that Angel looked me in the eye after I was hooded with my colors signifying that was now a "Doctor."

63. Ketchum is currently a West Virginia Supreme Court justice. He was elected to bench in 2008 as a Democrat. Ketchum is also a 1964 graduate of Ohio University.

64. Although I did not win the grievance challenging my loss of the adjunct faculty position, the material gleaned from the process was invaluable as far as laying the groundwork for a retaliation claim. The United States Court of Appeals for the 4th Circuit took special note of this situation when ruling on Marshall's motions for dismissal of the case based on qualified immunity as a state agency (Nos. 04-1314; 04-1328 Decided May 11, 2006). In the opinion by Judge King-called scathing by the Charleston Gazette (Searls, Tom. May 12, 2006. *Sports lawsuit goes on; Ridpath says he was made scapegoat.* Charleston Gazette), King stated, that I alleged that *"the administrators retaliated against Ridpath for making protected statements they did not like. Such activity does not merely implicate*

the gray edges of the right (1ˢᵗ Amendment Free Speech Claims) *Ridpath asserts; its goes to its very core."* Consequently, I did not lose the grievance on the merits of my claims as they were never really addressed by the ALJ. Essentially I lost it because I did not file the grievance in time—10 actual, not business, days by West Virginia state standards, even though I argued unsuccessfully that I met the time period requirements. According to the decision by WV Administrative Law Judge Sue Keller, "Grievant failed to timely file this grievance, or to demonstrate a proper basis to excuse his failure to file in a timely manner." The full text of the grievance and decision Docket No. 03-HE-361can be found at http://www.state.wv.us/admin/grievanc/decision/dec2004/ridpath.htm.

65. Simpson is the current athletic director at the College of St. Elizabeth in Morristown, NJ. She was a women's basketball coach for several years at many institutions to include Bucknell, Cincinnati, Amarillo Junior College, Arizona State, Marshall, East Stroudsburg, and Central Washington. Simpson is also a charter member of the Women's Basketball Hall of Fame and was a member of the gold medal winning 1976 Olympic women's basketball team. Her teammates included Pat Head Summit and Anne Meyers-Drysdale. http://www.lehighvalleylive.com/sports/index.ssf/2009/08/juliene_simpson_east_stroudsbu.html

66. I served as an expert witness in 2005 for the Plaintiff's, Cottrell and Williams in this case. My testimony primarily revolved around the unfairness of the process and in consistency of the process. Ultimately I am not sure how much I helped out the two former Alabama assistant football coaches, but I felt an obligation to give it a shot. There were several iterations in this case including appeals going all the way to the Alabama Supreme Court but the initial case was *Cottrell & Williams v. NCAA et al.* While Williams was eventually dismissed from the case as was the NCAA, Cottrell did win a 30 million dollar verdict against recruiting analyst Tom Culpepper, who was revealed as a secret witness for the NCAA during the civil litigation. The verdict was later thrown out by Tuscaloosa judge Steve Wilson who presided over the trial. Cottrell did appeal and it appears his appeals are exhausted.

67. An excellent book that covers the dramatic effect of US Supreme Court decisions regarding the NCAA including my lawsuit against Marshall (*NCAA v Board of Regents-1984 and NCAA v. Tarkanian-1988*) and how those cases have impacted the business of college sports in the 21ˢᵗ Century is *The Supreme Court and the NCAA*, by Brian Porto, University of Michigan Press, 2012. Porto, a University of Vermont law professor, has long advocated more due process protections in NCAA investigations.

68. The full text of the congressional hearing and all written materials submitted by the witnesses and congressional staffers can be found at www.house.gov/judiciary/

69. Judge Steve Wilson overturned the 2005, 30 million dollar jury verdict for former Alabama assistant coach Ronnie Cottrell against recruiting analyst Tom Culpepper. The case began when the NCAA, which investigated the Alabama football program and later penalized it allegedly acted improperly in using Culpepper's secret testimony after promising Alabama officials otherwise. Culpepper's testimony helped the NCAA in connecting former Tide booster Logan Young to the recruitment of Memphis blue-chip prospect Albert Means. Culpepper's testimony was the decisive factor in additional NCAA charges against the football program in the recruitment of Stevenson blue-chipper Kenny Smith and booster Ray Keller. Cottrell and fellow assistant coach Ivy Williams were fired by Alabama largely based on circumstantial evidence of alleged improper connections to Logan Young and specifically in the case of Williams, involvement in the recruitment of Means and illegal payments to Means' high school coach Lynn Lang. Wilson later published a book in 2010 entitled, *"A Lynch Mob Mentality: Ronald W. Cottrell vs. NCAA, The Untold Story"* See *"Judges Book goes Behind Scenes in Cottrell Case,"* by Doug Segrest, The Birmingham News, September 19, 2010.

70. Messenger, Tony, December 20, 2004*"Another Possible Scapegoat emerges in the NCAA Blame Game."* Columbia (MO) Daily Tribune. This article details the reasons why Hilliard was disbarred by the Illinois Attorney Registration and Disciplinary Commission. Hilliard who admitted he had a serious gambling problem, stated in 2003 he used a $15.000 retainer check from former Missouri head men's basketball Quin Snyder to pay gambling debts rather than depositing it with his law firm, Ice Miller. Hilliard later tried to conceal the misdeed by forging emails from Snyder indicating the retainer had not been paid. Hilliard lost his law license for five months.

71. The 'Restricted Earnings Coach case' is one of the many prominent cases the NCAA has lost in court. It was an attempt, in a cost saving measure to limit the earnings of certain coaches on staffs to $16,000 per year along with an additional four thousand dollars earning ability through camps and clinics. The NCAA agreed to pay $54.5 million to entry-level coaches who won a class-action suit in 1999 charging the NCAA had no right to limit their salaries. http://articles.chicagotribune.com/1999-03-10/sports/9903100083_1_coaches-full-time-assistant-andy-greer

72. While Angel feigned ignorance during his 2008 deposition, there was a confidential meeting during the summer of 2001 in Chicago that included Angel, Pruett, then Conference USA commissioner Slive, and ESPN regional representative and Marshall alumnus, Dan Shoemaker. Marshall at the time was unbelievably considering a football only move to C-USA and putting all of the other sports in the Horizon League. Hilliard told me that the NCAA case summary (the document that details the NCAA's case against a university) was shared with Slive to get his take on it and to see if there were any problems that would inhibit Marshall's entry into the league. This was a blatant disregard for NCAA confidentiality and process. Slive should have never seen this document, plus he was a member of the NCAA Infractions Appeals Committee and could easily be prejudiced. Hilliard also led me to believe that Slive, a former NCAA investigator and litigator for Bond, Schoeneck & King, suggested that I be removed as a corrective action and Pruett and Angel shot it down and praised me for my diligent efforts in the investigation.

73. This email is no longer under protective order as it was part of several publically released depositions and documents during litigation of the civil case. The specific phrase used by NCAA investigator Luanne Humphrey in her response to Marshall Reynolds trying to clarify his role in the Marshall Infractions in 2004 and printed many times in the media was "someone tried like hell to throw us off track on this thing from the beginning, and the evidence overwhelming (sic) points to a cover-up. But unfortunately, we may never know who was the real culprit." Humphrey also stated in her deposition in 2008 that she "had concerns" that "Coach Pruett and/or other members of the football staff were involved in a cover-up at MU. A good compilation of the documents concerning this case can be found under "CBS Sports Reports on Suit Against MU, Bobby Pruett: MU Argues to Postpone Oct. 21, 2008 Trial in Federal Court by Tony Rutherford at http://www.huntingtonnews.net/marshall/080818-rutherford-marshallsuitagainstmu.html. Huntington (WV) News Net. This link also includes the protective order, some depositions, some affidavits, and links to many of the legal documents relating to the civil action that are public and not under seal.

74. Dennis Dodd of CBS Sports.com wrote several articles in 2008 concerning the civil action. The articles used and referred to include, "Court documents tie ex-Marshall coach Pruett to academic fraud," August 17, 2008; "Booster Disputes Possible NCAA Violations against Marshall," August 19, 2008; "Marshall, Former Compliance Director Settle Suit," February 2, 2009; "Marshall Scandal Leftovers," February 8, 2008.

75. Tynes retracted his statements that he attested to on a sworn affidavit in an interview with Huntington TV personality Keith Morehouse of WSAZ TV on August 20, 2008.

76. Kelly is the current head coach at Georgetown University and was appointed to the position in January 2006.

77. Kopp was the Provost and Chief Academic Officer at Ohio University from 2002-2004 before he became president at Marshall University on July 1, 2005.

78. WV MetroNews Talkline appearance with longtime WV news personality Hoppy Kercheval on March 12, 2009.

79. Pruett resigned on March 9, 2005, the day before the start of spring practice. Pruett only said it "was time" to leave and he wanted to spend more time with his grandkids. According to Marshall Reynolds, in an article in the Huntington (WV) Herald Dispatch by Scott Wartman entitled, *"Marshall Coach Bob Pruett Announces his Retirement,"* Pruett's reasons for resigning were due to differences with Dan Angel, mediocrity of the football team and the pressure of the lawsuit. Reynolds said he urged Pruett to stay and followed up in his deposition in the summer of 2008 saying that Pruett, "let a bunch of lightweights run him out of town."

80. Snyder is now the defensive coordinator at the University of South Florida. He resigned from Marshall on November 29, 2009. McGill, Chuck (November 29, 2009). *"Snyder Resigns as Herd Football Coach."* The Charleston (WV) Daily Mail.

81. A March 22, 2001 article entitled *Bruce Pearl's First Con, And The World That Created A Monster*, discusses Hilliard's other questionable forays into NCAA investigations. The reporter, Daniel Hibit was unable to find Hilliard despite numerous efforts. The article can be accessed at http://deadspin.com/5784437/bruce-pearls-first-con-and-the-world-that-created-a-monster

82. Shapiro In 100 hours of jailhouse interviews during Yahoo! Sports' 11-month investigation, described a sustained, eight-year run of rampant NCAA rule-breaking, some of it with the knowledge or direct participation of at least seven coaches from the Miami football and basketball programs. At a cost that Shapiro estimates in the millions of dollars, he said his benefits to athletes included but were not limited to cash, prostitutes, entertainment in his multimillion-dollar homes and yacht, paid trips to high-end restaurants and nightclubs, jewelry,

bounties for on-field play (including bounties for injuring opposing players), travel and, on one occasion, an abortion. http://sports.yahoo.com/investigations/news?slug=cr-renegade_miami_booster_details_illicit_benefits_081611

83. One of the great books written on the NCAA enforcement and infractions process written before the 1991 recommendations for reform is Don Yaeger's' 1991 book "Undue Process: The NCAA's Injustice for All" published by Sagamore Publishing. In this book it is easy to see that the process has improved by adopting many of the Lee Commission's recommendations in the early 1990's. Some of the improvements include allowing people to be represented by counsel, tape recording interviews, and installing an appeals process. While the improvements were laudable, several recommendations were not adopted to include an independent trier of fact, the right to cross examine witness and make those witnesses known, and public hearings.

84. The full written statement can be found at Due Process and the NCAA: Hearing before the Subcommittee on the Constitution on the Committee on the Judiciary House of Representatives, 108th Congress, 2nd Session, September 14, 2004, Serial No. 106. www.house.gov/judiciary.

85. Although the NCAA can say that they directly did not sanction me and it was Marshall that made me a corrective action, the COI still accepted Marshall University's self-imposed sanctions as their own. Yet, even though these self-imposed sanctions were adopted by the NCAA, I still had no appeal route through the NCAA process. This is one of the main patently unfair issues to individuals involved in the process and does not even come close to American jurisprudence and due process protections.

86. Oriard, Michael (2009). *"Bowled Over: Big Time College Football from the 60's to the BCS Era."* University of North Carolina Press, p. 128-129.

87. Ibid, pp. 182-190.

88. The full Drake Group plan can be found at www.thedrakegroup.org

89. The Drake Group has been a catalyst for the recent push by congress to examine the business of college sports. In 2006 Congressman Bill Thomas of Nebraska sent a sharply worded letter to Dr. Myles Brand, then President of the NCAA asking him to explain the non-profit status of the NCAA given the excess commercialism and diverted educational money to the enterprise. More information on the efforts of the Drake

Group and others, including the letter from Thomas and the responses by Brand and The Drake Group can be found at www.thedrakegroup.org.

90. The NCAA membership fought implementation of the Campus Security Act as part of the Student Athlete Right to Know Act in 1990. This mandated that all colleges and universities must publish the graduation rates of its athletes using a six year time frame, on an annual basis using existing federal measurements. The NCAA, led by then President Dick Schultz, felt that college athletes could not be effectively evaluated because of special concerns like transferring and taking longer to graduate than other like students. Ridpath, B. (2002). *"Factors that Influence the Academic Progress and Graduation of NCAA Division I Student Athletes."* Published Doctoral Dissertation. UMI Dissertation Services, Ann Arbor, MI.

91. Oriard has an extensive discussion refuting most of the oft cited benefits of intercollegiate athletic success in Bowled Over, p. 244-248. He specifically cites a study done for the Knight Commission by Cornell economist Robert Frank in 2004. Frank's conclusions refuted the many repeated myths of athletic success such as increased applications, higher quality of students, increased fund raising for academic programs, and increased marketing exposure stating that at best the evidence for all of these benefits were "meager and inconclusive." Frank, R. (May 2004). *"Challenging the Myth: A Review of the Links among College Athletic Success, Student Quality, and Donations."* Another study commissioned by the NCAA in August 2003and written by noted scholars Robert E. Litan, and Jonathan and Peter Orzsag entitled *"The Empirical Effects of Collegiate Athletic: An Interim Report,"* also challenges many of same accepted myths and cautions universities on overspending to achieve benefits that may not actually materialize despite the rhetoric.

92. *ESPN the Magazine* article by Seth Wickersham entitled 'Internal Affairs" August 2010 Issue.

Index